A DREAM OF HITCHCOCK

A DREAM OF HITCHCOCK

MURRAY POMERANCE

Some material in chapter 5 appeared in a different form as "Angling *To Catch a Thief*," *Film International* 15, no. 1 (2017).

Cover image from *To Catch a Thief* (Alfred Hitchcock, Paramount, 1955), digital frame enlargement.

Published by State University of New York Press, Albany

© 2019 State University of New York

All rights reserved

No part of this book may be used or reproduced in any manner whatsoever without written permission. No part of this book may be stored in a retrieval system or transmitted in any form or by any means including electronic, electrostatic, magnetic tape, mechanical, photocopying, recording, or otherwise without the prior permission in writing of the publisher.

For information, contact State University of New York Press, Albany, NY
www.sunypress.edu

Library of Congress Cataloging-in-Publication Data

Names: Pomerance, Murray, 1946- author.
Title: A dream of Hitchcock / Murray Pomerance.
Description: Albany : State University of New York Press, 2018. | Includes bibliographical references and index.
Identifiers: LCCN 2017059914| ISBN 9781438472072 (hardcover : alk. paper) | ISBN 9781438472089 (pbk. : alk. paper) | ISBN 9781438472096 (e-book)
Subjects: LCSH: Hitchcock, Alfred, 1899-1980—Criticism and interpretation. | Dreams in motion pictures.
Classification: LCC PN1998.3.H58 P655 2018 | DDC 791.4302/33092—dc23
LC record available at https://lccn.loc.gov/2017059914

10 9 8 7 6 5 4 3 2 1

TO NELLIE

I like life and prefer sleep, not because of its emptiness, but because of its dreams.

—Gide

Being has not even "forgotten" its past, for forgetting would still be a form of connection. The past has slipped away from it like a dream.

—Sartre

CONTENTS

Acknowledgments, ix

Introduction: On the Island, 1

1. All in the Game: *Strangers on a Train*, 14
2. Don't Look Now: *Rear Window*, 58
3. His Own Sense of Life: *Saboteur*, 94
4. Rebecca's Shadow, 134
5. Catching *To Catch a Thief*, 166
6. *Family Plot:* The Spirit Is Never at Home, 192

Notes, 227

References, 235

Index, 247

ACKNOWLEDGMENTS

I owe a debt of gratitude to all those who have kindly helped me with this book in ways they may not recognize themselves: Alexis Bouton (Toronto), Laurent Brion (Toronto), Marilyn Campbell (Princeton), Michael Chazan (Toronto), Tom Conley (Cambridge), the late Leslie Fiedler (Buffalo), Larry Frascella (Irvington), Michael Hammond (Lymington), Jason Jacobs (Brisbane), Mark Kermode (London), Bill Krohn (Long Beach), Daniel Lindvall (Högdalen), Norman Lloyd (Los Angeles), Leslie Mitchner (Princeton), R. Barton Palmer (Atlanta), the late Victor Perkins (Coventry), Andy Rector (Newhall), William Rothman (Miami), Dan Sacco (Toronto), John Sakeris (Santa Barbara), Matthew Solomon (Ann Arbor), George Toles (Winnipeg), Dan Varndell (Southampton), and Linda Ruth Williams (Brockenhurst).

I have derived untold assistance from the staff of the Margaret Herrick Library, Beverly Hills, especially Barbara Hall, Louise Hilton, Linda Harris Mehr, Jenny Romero, Matt Severson, and Faye Thompson, as well as from Ned Comstock at the Cinema-Television Library, Doheny Library, University of Southern California, and Brett Service at the Warner Bros. Archives, USC.

The staff at SUNY Press form a long-lived collegial family, to whom I would like to express humble and very sincere thanks: especially James Peltz, Rafael Chaiken, Ryan Morris, and Aimee Harrison. To Eric Schramm, my long-time copyeditor and a true lover of cinema, undying thanks for helping in so many ways to make these sentences flow.

Nellie Perret and Ariel Pomerance helped research this work and inspired me all the way through.

—Murray Pomerance
Toronto, August 2018

INTRODUCTION

ON THE ISLAND

The presence of music, Alfred Hitchcock wrote in a 1965 contribution to the *Encyclopedia Britannica*, "is perfectly in accordance with the aim of the motion picture, namely to unfold an action or to tell a story, and thereby stir the emotions" (in Gottlieb 222). Elemental for him was the link between musical form and the stir of emotion, between the felt and the recognizing response to an aesthetic moment. Hitchcock's films have always struck me as musical, essentially. Not, surely, in that they are full of tunes or that their challenging musical scores provide a central avenue toward understanding, but that as organized works, as forms, the films follow some fundamentally musical principles of construction. They involve not only statements but also recapitulations and inversions; the anticipation and the reprise are crucial to the structure. The films contain, inevitably, a full-fledged harmonic logic, and a harmony for the eye that plays on color, spatial definition, and the riddles of perception. In their scenes, episodes, and moments, and as entireties, they have phrasing, preparation, and cadence. And of course, like the greatest music, Hitchcock's films are unforgettable.

This book, a discussion of six Hitchcock films, is a sequel to my earlier book, *An Eye for Hitchcock*, in which I explored *North by Northwest*, *Spellbound*, *Torn Curtain*, *Marnie*, *I Confess*, and *Vertigo*. That volume, the reader should be assured, need not be read as a preface to this one, though it might bring the pleasure of illumination—or the illumination of pleasure—to anyone interested in Alfred Hitchcock or in the appreciation of cinema altogether. In *An Eye*, I explored some of Hitchcock's repeating variations of verticality: physical, social, economic, mythical, philosophical. Here, I am interested in the recurring motif of the dream—dreamscapes, dream processes, the dream effect, the otherworldly, the unknown and unknowable, the feelingfulness of experience, the nightmare of history. I certainly do not mean to offer here a theory of dreams or dreaming; or a watertight compendium of dream moments—for instance, *Marnie* contains some of the most startling evocation of dream experience to be found in cinema, but it gets no discussion here; or even to set forth an argument that Hitchcock wanted to tell us something about the dream process. Perhaps he did. But we can find our lessons at any rate, and my readings of the six films included here—*Strangers on a Train, Rear Window, Saboteur, Rebecca, To Catch a Thief,* and *Family Plot*—mean only to dance through the filmic structures in a respectfully musical way, echoing my curiosity and, I would hope, the structures Hitchcock has given us.

Six and only six films: which is to say, no claim will be found here that I uncover the deeper meaning of Hitchcock the personality, or a blueprint to his vast oeuvre. The films are too rich, too much overflowing with ambiguity, for one thing, and I am too wrapped up in my commitment to responsiveness, for another. The act of watching a film is part of our living experience, vital, fleeting, deeply provocative. At its very best—and Hitchcock doesn't fail to stand at the apogee of cinema—films are troubling and wonderful for being vital and provoking in that way. Yet, while numerous scholarly volumes and critical appreciations have worked over Hitchcock's films, there has been a sad superfluity of dependence on what I would term canonical readings: simplistic repetitions of the surface structure of his plots, in effect the publicity materials according to which the films can easily be typed, classified, sold to a public hungry for escape. These chapters aim toward close readings, and also toward refreshment, often themselves moving forward with a kind of dream twist. In working my close readings, I follow an important and well-established scholarly path that began in Michel de Montaigne, worked its way through Henry James and Walter Benjamin and Norman O. Brown, and became the tight-focus technique of V. F. Perkins, Stanley Cavell, Bill Krohn, William Rothman, and many other scholars inside and outside cinema studies whose attentions have been caught and nurtured by the sorts of riddles that perplex Hitchcock as well. The eye and mind move in rather than standing back, look beneath the surface, derive sense from the architecture of the film as a complex—in Hitchcock's case riddling—assemblage of articulate moments. Within some delimited space, one allows for meditation upon what one sees (instead of just following the superficial story), for trying to live in the world of the film, to know the beings one meets in their own terms, and to take them as seriously as Hitchcock did. As in dreams, there may be passages on these pages that seem to wander in strange, circuitous paths, but that is because beneath the surface of his films Hitchcock himself wandered in strange, circuitous paths to illuminate questions about life as he knew it. I wish at the very least to hint at how that can be seen in the films. These essays are written for any engaged and eager reader, and do not presume familiarity with any particular lingo or analytical approach. Perhaps light will be thrown not only on these six films but on films altogether, how we can more patiently and more dreamily watch and become absorbed in them.

THE HITCHCOCKIAN MODE

Born and raised in a post-Victorian ebbtide, Alfred Hitchcock had benefit of (that is, was subjected to) a classical education, certainly as regarded literary texts and the English language. He will never permit himself to be cheerily ungrammatical, in the way that nowadays we find so often in speech and film: markedly abbreviated, fliply casual, brutally curt, ambiguously elliptical, careless about syntax and vocabulary. His shots are sentences, fully spelled out and very frequently interspersed craftily with interior modifying clauses, virtually in the Latinate manner. When one looks at a Hitchcockian shot (see Pomerance, "Shots"), especially noting the amount of visual information he includes and the elegant and balanced way in which he uses his camera to include it, one finds a great richness of expression, sometimes what could be described as forestial density. It is typical that the material in the Hitchcockian shot refers back, often to more than one previous moment, and also anticipates what is to come, since Hitchcock is a master of not only expressivity but also preparation, and is conscious of the passage of time. We live in a world of such violent spontaneity now that time is contracted; and preparation, as a form in itself, has gone by the wayside. Artful modification seems a useless discardable excrescence in the face of information, the only thing many people think language is devised to hold and transfer. For Hitchcock the idea of a snap shot (say, less than one second's duration onscreen) is anathema except for the purpose of causing alarm, alarm, one must note, carefully arranged in a context: the finale of *Spellbound* with its flash of red; the shower scene in *Psycho*. In order more generally to contain surprising, disturbing, aggravating, or stimulating movement in his frame, Hitchcock conceived very elaborate camera movements (often movements difficult for his team to execute). Always for him the grammar of articulation is a paramount concern.

Hitchcock's work has invited and entertained commentaries both deeply moving and shockingly facile, from fans, critics, and serious scholars. Many have certainly thought it effective to take a glib approach, as even the brilliant François Truffaut—typically very perceptive about this body of work—does near the end of *Hitchcock* (1985), when he comments that the director films his murders like love scenes and his love scenes like murders. It's a fabulous tag line, ringing in the ears with the charming tinkle of a cocktail glass in a toast. But we must struggle some, I think, to arrive at what could be meant by Truffaut's words. Perhaps that there is always something of the subterranean erotic even in Hitchcock's summative violence: in *Frenzy* we see this explicitly; and in *Torn Curtain* there is a marvelously suggestive murder, ending in a kind of corporeal embrace. But surely Hitchcock knows love, and when he shows it—when he films an authentic "love scene" (Melanie Daniels bringing Lydia Brenner tea in *The Birds;* Fred and Emily Hill reunited back home after the daunting experience of their sea voyage in *Rich and Strange;* the dining car lunch in *North by Northwest*)—he is not fooling with violence, nor, interestingly, is he fooling with sex. (There is comparatively little sex in Hitchcock. The most revealing scene, early in *Psycho*, is staged backward as a joke, and in *Family Plot,* as we will see, sex is talk.) The more one penetrates Truffaut's summative comment about love scenes and murders, the less it helps one to see. Yet a simpler truth is evident: Hitchcock is interested in both murder and love, not as forms of one another and not necessarily in some convenient formulaic relationship. Should we not beware, at least a little, of vastly popular and too easily accepted bromides about Alfred Hitchcock's work?

Can we, for another instance, seriously maintain that he was obsessed by blondes simply because we can adduce some particular case studies—blonde women who were already, Hitchcock notwithstanding, established as major screen figures of their time and thus available to him, as to other filmmakers, for lead roles (in part exactly because they were blonde standouts)? And he has plenty of non-blonde female characters who are treated with the greatest sensitivity and the most telling eye: Teresa Wright in *Shadow of a Doubt,* Joan Fontaine in *Rebecca* and *Suspicion,* Barbara Harris in *Family Plot,* Karin Dor in *Topaz,* Shirley MacLaine in *The Trouble with Harry,* Ruth Roman in *Strangers on a Train,* to name some. Hitchcock loved to tell interviewers how exciting the buried (sexual) passions of apparently "icy" blondes could be, but he certainly loved to drum up publicity—this little revelation could not fail to help—and knew how to favor misconceptions already entrenched with his public.

Followers of popular culture, and of Hitchcock's reception and acceptance there, jump to label him the "Master of Suspense," an epithet he willingly abided, since it did nothing but help promote his work. But when Hitchcock himself spoke of "suspense" he did not mean by it what most people interpret: the chilling, gripping, terrifying, exciting, charging, shocking, debilitatingly sharp uplift of attention and expectation that comes with rainy dark streets, shadowy strangers, grimacing faces, shrieks of mortality—"suspense" as fear or shock. Speaking with Truffaut and numerous others, he was particular to distinguish suspense from surprise, and to make clear that for him *suspense* involved situations where the audience is given access to some information that a crucially important character does not have. The issue is, when will the character learn what we already know? And the turn to illumination for a character may be slow and deliberate, even casual and fragmentary. There is a *kind of* suspense at play in this book, quite differently. It involves levitation, a removal from earthly grounding, a flotation above the practical, the everyday, and the rationally explicable. When we suspend judgment we pass into the zone of wonder, speculation, curiosity, doubt, and perhaps emotional involvement of a deep and perduring kind. Neither Hitchcock's films nor the discussions a reader will encounter here work according to formula. One must spend the time—the time of one's life—in moving through the composition, in wondering and struggling to remember.

DREAMS

This pathway is philosophical in aiming at illumination, not economic in aiming at profit, and is also, therefore, the dream. Hitchcock as philosopher? But surely any serious consideration of his scenarism, his vision, the motion and intensity of his camera, his characters, his sense of place—any serious consideration could find him nothing other. Of philosophy, we learn from reading a "decent-looking elderly man" named Edwards, quoted by Boswell: "Philosophy, like religion, is too generally supposed to be hard and severe, at least so grave as to exclude all gaiety" (955; 957); and Hitchcock is philosophical in exactly a gay and enchanting way, eschewing the hard for hardness's sake and the severe for severity's, never putting aside the thought of harmony while at the same time being riddled by mortality. He is thus fully alive. As to the dream, why should we not follow the line of James M. Barrie's observation (Barrie, the author of *Mary Rose*, the film Hitchcock did not live to make), quoted pungently by Bill Krohn in his *Hitchcock at Work*: "To be born is to be wrecked upon an island" (277). What, on an island, but a dream life? And can we not claim—or at least carefully suppose—that in his filmmaking Hitchcock was living out a life of the mind?

The idea of the dream, as invoked here, offers a way of traveling to the "unearthly," notably irrational quality in Hitchcock's work. One film, *Rebecca*, revolves around the problem of memory, nostalgia, and history, moving us backward as a way of progressing; almost everyone in the film, almost all the time, is obsessed with what happened *before*. Another, *To Catch a Thief*, circles around uncertainty, since at its heart is a vital question to which no moment seems to afford an answer. A third, *Saboteur*, expresses the pungent aspiration for an American utopia. A fourth, *Rear Window*, queries the expanse of intellect as bounded by the limits of imagination. A fifth, *Strangers on a Train*, celebrates a delirious madness. A sixth, *Family Plot*, invokes and reinvokes intuition and its peculiar logic. Memory, uncertainty, aspiration, intuition, imagination, madness—all of these are dreams. I think it signally important to warn that Hitchcock uses various means of invocation, not merely spoken dialogue. Often the quality of an image—its lighting, its positioning, its framing, its juxtaposition with other images—bespeaks the oneiric, and often we must be prepared to leave behind simple, rational calculation—following the "map"—in order to grasp what he means to give. Thus, in thinking about Hitchcock, one really mustn't overattend to the storyline alone. Every creature needs its form, and in these films the storyline functions nicely enough as a skeleton, but it is not the thing itself. And further, attention to plot tends to privilege spoken dialogue, and Hitchcock works as a pictorial artist, picturing not speaking his narrative world. A picture is both a theory and a recounting, and it is certainly an idea. And pictorial riddles—philosophical riddles in pictorial form—are surely as pressing to Hitchcock's concerns as unfolding tales.

My own method for thinking through Hitchcockian work has for its mantra a simple, yet challenging, directive, that the film should inform the theorization; not the other way around. Too often, it seems to me, critical appreciation is attached to the toolkit of theory, entirely independent of a film as a work of art. The critic is pleased to import his toolkit to the viewing experience, which is to say, the toolkit preexists the film. For me, the best approach is to empty the mind as much as possible and let the work flow and operate, before working to think it through: indeed, *thinking it through* is only one (perhaps too tactical) method of approach. One must see and see again; and live with what traces emerge in memory, so that recollection and musing overtake opinion. The film preexists consideration. Canonical dicta are more often than not restricting distractions, indeed, a typical approach of Hitchcock's is to openly assert, and then dismiss, the predictable canonical reception of his work: in *Rear Window*, for example, he opens and sharply closes a conversation between Jeff and Stella about Peeping Tomism, its moral implications, and its offense to propriety; the film is *not* about a Peeping Tom. One should let the Hitchcockian images resonate. One should give the eye room and time—the outer eye and the inner eye—to observe the continuities and linkages that are graphed onscreen. I watch Hitchcock's films directly, and what theory I use finds its way into my approach only afterward, often very long afterward. If, by contrast, one took only the canonical approach, one would be tied to the conventional reading of Hitchcock's plots, a reading that almost invariably skips over, elides, neglects, or forgets something vital and fascinating that is as much on the screen as everything else. Six examples, from the films I write about here, of what is often forgotten: that at a moment in *Strangers on a Train* Bruno escorts a blind man across a street; that in *Rebecca* the camera focuses persistently on an absence; that in *Rear Window* we watch a man in agony; that in *Saboteur* we are in California in wartime; that in *To Catch a Thief* Cary Grant's sweater is difficult to look at; and that in *Family Plot* there are many kinds of family, many kinds of plot.

The typical Hitchcock film is set in a real social space, that is, a world and set of locations that actually existed at the time of filmmaking, and that actually signaled particular class and cultural references. He is obsessive in his detailed depiction of social reality, and worked intensively with his designers, his research team, and his camera team to represent objects and spaces tellingly. At a flashing moment in *The Wrong Man* (1956), Henry Fonda walks up to the door of an insurance company, the name of which is etched in the glass: Associated Life of New York (Since 1897). This happens so perfunctorily in the film that viewers might be shocked to learn that the research team came up with dozens of potential names for this "company," each of which could represent an insurance firm in New York City in the mid-1950s. Or, reflect that the tennis match in *Strangers* takes place not in a constructed set but at the Forest Hills (New York) stadium, which was at the time *the* prestigious home of professional tennis in the United States (as Wimbledon was, and is, in the UK). The game we see played there has all the attributes of a real championship contest. Or, in *The Man Who Knew Too Much* (1956), the Albert Hall concert scene takes place, in actuality, in the Royal Albert Hall, London, which seats more than three thousand people: watching this part of the film, we are attending a real concert. In *To Catch a Thief*, we visit the real flower market in Nice. In *Family Plot* we enter the sanctum of Grace Cathedral. In *Saboteur* we climb the Statue of Liberty, all the way to the topmost top, with studio sets built after carefully detailed research on the proportions and design of the real place. Further, the characters who interplay in these settings are drawn from the real precincts of everyday life, too. They know what real people in their positions would know. They have come out of a real past, which is to say, if not an actual past then one that actual people could have experienced. In Hitchcock's "drawing" style, the lines, spaces, distances, surfaces, textures, and points of focus all make sense as parts of a social world that could be actual, whether or not it happens to be. If we look at screwball comedy, for example, but leave out his own contribution, *Mr. and Mrs. Smith* (1941), we find something radically different: a dramaturgical space that is entirely fabular, entirely caught up in the surface of design.

HITCHCOCK'S ARCHITECTURE

Any serious consideration of Hitchcock's films must take architectonic design as the heart, must understand that more than recounting tales this artist was interested in designing a show: of event, of condition, of happenstance, of monument. From the start he builds his pictures, less with flamboyance than with old-fashioned, long inherited construction skills. He builds an architecture, and according to the soundest principles that have guided English builders for centuries. Here is the guidance of Sir Joshua Reynolds in 1778: "The regular progress of cultivated life is from Necessaries to Accommodations, from Accommodations to Ornaments" (qtd. in Brackett 125). The appurtenances of cultivated life are built up, then, in three tiers. Nothing can supersede the foundational character of "Necessaries"—support for the covering, framing for enclosure. Next may come "Accommodations" to the human need for organic existence, nourishment, access to water, sanitation of some kind, warmth. And only when these are all in place does one seek "Ornament," the beauty and relish that make life worth living or, as in the case of Hitchcock—whose work is nothing if not densely ornamental in this respect—that signal, about people and their actions, the conditional motivation that opens the gates of understanding. Reynolds's structural positioning of ornament allows us to see how it is not decoration. Decoration covers, distracts; but ornament graces and reveals. In watching Hitchcock one must never attribute to him a decorative intent. He is constantly filling out the pictorial space with informative design, indeed all the design in Hitchcock tells us something important, about either the character and her intent or the scene in which that intent can have realistic meaning. For example, in one of the essays here I make very brief mention of Barbara Bel Geddes's character Midge in *Vertigo*, at the moment we meet her. She happens to be wearing a lovely banana yellow cashmere two-set, which if it glows prettily against her blonde hair more crucially states her social class and sense of decorum, her professional composure at work in her private space, her desire for physical comfort. To listen to the dialogue in this scene or watch the action without noting details like this one is to miss a great deal of what Hitchcock intends to show. At the conclusion of *The 39 Steps*, we attend a variety performance in company with a large audience: but this takes place at London's Palladium, not any random theater. There is a rich history of vaudeville and musical performance underneath the scene, and a class story as well, since the Palladium was top-of-the-line for variety showmanship in England at the time. In *North by Northwest*, Roger sneaks into Eve's berth on the Twentieth Century Limited en route to Chicago: this isn't just a sleeping compartment, it's a high-style sleeping compartment of the most expensive kind, on the most expensive train in America; Eve is being kept by Vandamm as his girl, but in the most sumptuous luxury possible. This tells us about her, but even more about him. Luxury always offers telltale data about social structure: in *To Catch a Thief* and *Rebecca* we visit the wealthy of the Côte d'Azur; in *Saboteur* the *haut monde* of Fifth Avenue; in *Family Plot* the palaces of Pasadena; in *Strangers on a Train*, a palace of Maryland; and in *Rear Window* we vicariously dine at 21.

Hitchcock's ornamentalism is a case in point of a broader and deeper endeavor in his work, one with significant philosophical implications. Following an approach originated and publicized by Alexander von Humboldt and then the Comte de Buffon late in the eighteenth century, he works in scene after scene to lay before the viewer what, in writing of Frederick Church's *Heart of the Andes* (1859), Jennifer Raab calls a "catalogue of ... wonders, all part of one great cosmos" (51). Humboldt's travels had taught him the exceptional value of being "awake to the charms of nature" (127), especially the delight and utility of carefully noting the vast array of telling details which, in synthesis, could lead to a grasp of natural reality. What this scholar—in the 1850s, as Stephen Jay Gould observes, "Humboldt may well have been the world's most famous and influential intellectual" ("Art" 93)—undertook with geology and vegetation (he "collected sixty thousand plant specimens, drew countless maps of great accuracy" [95])—Hitchcock undertakes in the social depictions of his films. What Humboldt undertook writing as a naturalist—"A few bushy euphorbiums, the cacalia kleinia, and Indian figs (cactus), which are become wild in the Canary Islands, as well as the south of Europe and the whole continent of Africa, are the only plants we see on these arid rocks" (Humboldt 123)—Hitchcock undertakes as a portraitist, meticulous always as to the way bodies hold and configure themselves, how they disport through dress, how they are positioned vis-à-vis one another in action, how personalities design living spaces and cultivate their environments in order both to affiliate and to distinguish themselves. Raab mentions sensory invocations (in Darwin's work), which "make a case, at the level of language, for the 'beauty and infinite complexity'" of the natural world (54); consider in light such as this, Hitchcock's variegated portrayal in *Rear Window* of an urban-centered, highly sophisticated, variate, delicate, evocative social world. Or the way that by using locations with intense specificity, not only as to their selection but as to the angle and lens through which he shows them, Hitchcock creates a topology of powerful subtlety and nuance in *Family Plot*.

The metaphysical conundrum Raab poses in relation to Church's painting and to the "struggle to define the function and significance of detail during the mid-nineteenth century" applies as well, and with even more charge, I think, to Hitchcock:

> Were details, like "Nature," proof of God, and science "the progressive disclosure of His soul," as James Jackson Jarves stated in *The Art-Idea* (1864)? Or were the minutiae of the physical world fundamentally different from the divine, governed by different laws and shaped by different forces ... ? (61)

In *Rebecca*, is the rococo design of life at Manderley a divine intervention on some level, or is it mere mechanism, mere contrivance of power and puissance? But to put this question more baldly is to see Hitchcock's real insight. Is the organization of our life fully, but only, an effect of socially formed power and cultural pressure, a resultant of the forces of social or psychosexual development adumbrated by such powerful thinkers as Marx and Durkheim, Freud and Sombart? Or, the ideas of all these thinkers (and more) being taken with full seriousness, might there be, still, another order of being to be considered, a world residue accessible only through vague traces of the past and of intuition?

And this is why it has seemed to me not only important but also wholly involving (a dearer virtue) to think, here, through the possibilities of Hitchcock's dream world, by which I mean to point not only to fantasy in his work, and to improbability, but also to doubt and disconcertion, hope and memory, intuition and belief, all the details of our real and cinematic worlds that don't simply answer queries into practical reality. The oneiric comes to the center of waking life.

Always, the pieces of the Hitchcockian puzzle must be seen to fit. "Coherence is the prerequisite of meaning," writes V. F. Perkins. "It is the means by which the film-maker creates significance. The *spectator* employs a continuous coherence-test in order to recognize meaning at all levels. It is the means by which he *makes sense* of the images, the means by which he adjusts both his visual and his mental focus" (116). Assenting to this, I would take a further step: the visual images being entirely primary, a good deal of the viewer's "adjustment" concerns artfully resisting the pressures of language—which vie for placement in our interpretation—and learning again how simply and fully to see. To see and hear what the screen offers without translating it all as story, in a purely verbal language of thought—as though on its own, without definition and categorization, a sound is not a thought; a picture is not a thought; an experience is not a thought. Our attention must be relentless. Hitchcock is a strictly classical artist. Every cadence is prepared. And the work is pared and pared again, until nothing is left but the vital essence.

A warning. In our age of mega-popularity, Hitchcock has become mega-popular and mega-famous, a virtual meme unto himself. Everyone has something to say about him (much of it gleaned from publicity releases he caused to be made about himself). It is notable, and salutary, that Gould recognizes about Church's *Heart of the Andes* how, as rumors spread of the painting's immense monetary value, "public interest . . . veered from the sublime to the merely quantitative" (91). A kind of quantitative appreciation has fallen to Hitchcock's work, too, in the rapturous consideration of his mischievous plots and repetitive themes, his films' relationship to prevailing cultural issues of powerlessness or identity or control, and his position, always methodically calculated by adjudicators and detractors alike, in the pantheon of directorial greats. All these appreciations sum to magnitude, but not necessarily to depth. Some who have studied Hitchcock again and again have found the sublime. The sublime, itself a kind of dream, may be our grail. Not merely bloodiness, or mere darkness, or fear, or villainy need code Hitchcock for us if we can see the poetic light in his shadows.

On our voyage into Hitchcock, we must not lose the Hitchcockian sublime, the grace and intimation that riddle his films and bring us, as we watch and wonder, close to our own most confounding selves where, as Deleuze saw, we "speak in our own name only" (xiii), speak while wrecked on an island. It is from my own island, as yet not fully explored, that these pages emerge to be sent across the waters to you.

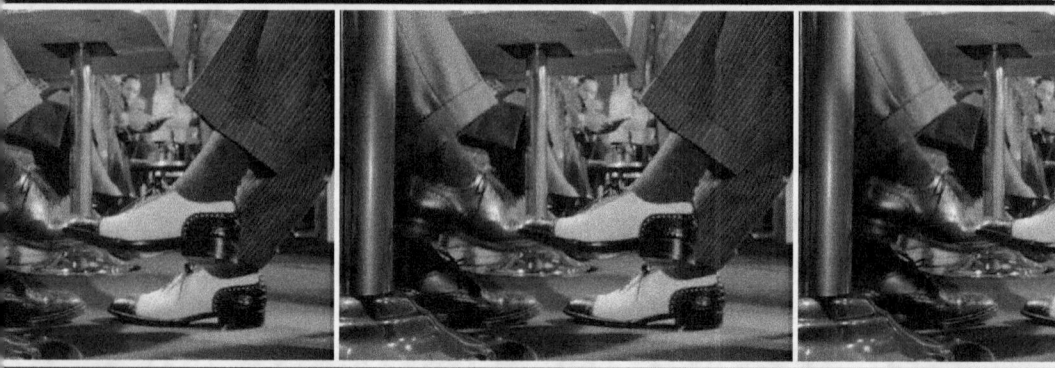

CHAPTER ONE

ALL IN THE GAME

Strangers on a Train

> Many a tear has to fall
> But it's all in the game.
> —Carl Sigman and Charles Gates Dawes

In December 1860, the corpse of a police inspector was discovered, bathed in blood, in a compartment of the train in which he had traveled with his killer. Wolfgang Schivelbusch quotes from a wry report in *Le Figaro* of the twentieth of that month: "In every well-arranged train we find a carriage reserved for smokers and another one for ladies who desire to travel by themselves. Why not provide a carriage with the legend: *compartment reserved for assassins*. But we know those gentlemen well: they are perhaps too shy to want to attract attention" (81). Trains were designed increasingly for comfort and luxury then, and train travel could evidently be dangerous.

TRAINS FOR STRANGERS, STRANGERS FOR TRAINS

Fans of the film will easily recall, and the uninitiated no doubt find it curious to learn, that *Strangers on a Train* (1951) begins with a sidewalk-level

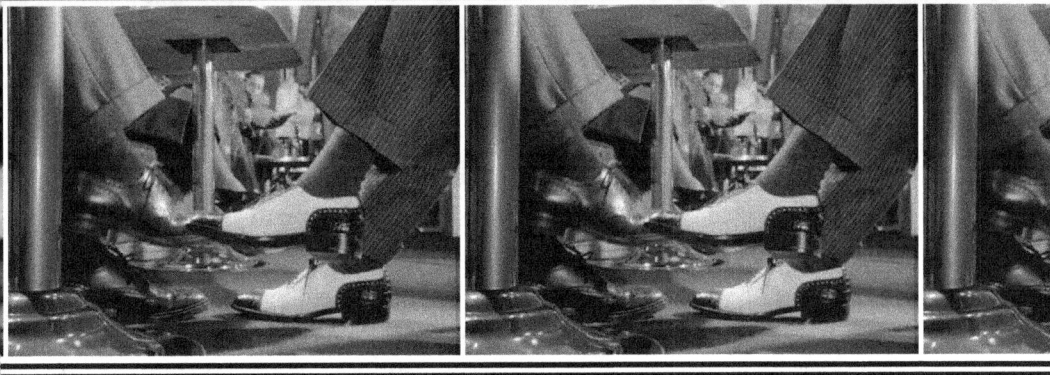

view of a railway station, a sort of dog's-eye vision of the world—to be specific, Union Station in Washington, DC—thus a perspective offering a complex display of feet in motion. Feet as characters. As taxis roll up and their doors are opened we see shoes emerge, contrasting styles, and legs pivoting and twisting, garbed in gabardine and wool. Then, as we dog along, purposeful strides. Marching, marching, brogues and Oxfords, and, look!, there!, tweeds and a trail of tennis equipment. One has the sensation of being leashed, obedient but confused as the feet of many masters lead off in many directions at once, perhaps to cover the globe. Soon the train tracks ahead are leading off and splitting, crossing over one another: the trains, too, are multidirectional. The effect of this brief overture is to attune us, in only a breath, to the somewhat contradictory ideas of fixity and flux, knowledge and the search, and also to the experience of being led, since we are both bound to the strict attention of a particularly systematic observation and on the move, heading into the future, and just in the manner that our guide would wish. The breath of attunement is a dream breath, a mixing and revolution of antinomies and also a gliding under Hitchcock's hand: we are being led inexorably onto the train, and then carried ahead by a force impossible to see. In the specific case of trains, that force is the train system itself, the thrusting power of the steam engine, the calculated and architected regularity of the rails, the design of the spring-loaded carriage, the arrangement of schedules, stations, clocks, and itineraries as in one single-minded universe. In the case of a Hitchcock film, the force is Hitchcock's directorial intent.

We can experience or imagine concreteness in this scene, even the promise of permanence: the intentionality of the architecture of the station (a curving driveway for the taxis; an enormous echoing foyer) and its overarching splendor (Greek columns, a vaulted sun-drenched ceiling), as well as the groundedness, the stability, of the nearby pavement, and the sense in which this place, though it is traversed inexorably, never yields its definitive presence and locus. While the camera is showing society and social variation, with the bodies in motion and the edifice built expressly to house them moving, our point of view puts us down near the ground, where gravity pulls everything with equal force. Thus, the principal characters of the film are first and foremost physical structures themselves, bodies as mechanical structures, if erect and motile nevertheless balanced by way of their extensive legs upon the building's unyielding pediment. We are cued to think that if we will momentarily be watching a drama in which the characters are particular social types, nevertheless there exists a foundational understructure, a system, that girds and establishes everything in view; and the grave solidity of that understructure helps accent the differences in character, the alignment, intentionality, and style that people arrange for themselves as best they can. As to that accentuation: apparent difference will become important. Because we discern clear contrasts among the stepping feet, we can be attuned for the upcoming appearance of a deeper telltale difference, built upon the common base of human experience. Social class is going to show itself. It always must, especially in Hitchcock. And perhaps another, more deeply provoking difference as well.

    Hitchcock's choice of setting offers a display of, and venue for, incessant, if only vaguely patterned, progress. The railway is built to accommodate the purposive shuttling of strangers. Watching the many feet in motion, one may reflect on how those of one person are strange by comparison with those of another, do not quite perfectly coincide in vector or style. So many people share this place and the activity it houses, without exactly being alike. Hundreds of strangers per minute trudge through, and in legion other stations like this the same thing happens at the same time. This is a microcosmic view, then, of a very broad social fabric. And that fabric is tight-woven, its strands are worked to fit. In physical and social proportion the train is designed to fit the station,[1] that gathering spot for the variably busy, who have no prior experience of one another except as types who populate locations like this. If Hitchcock's theme appears to be transportation—mechanical, promising, rhythmic—more deeply, as we will see, it is unfamiliarity. The strangeness of modern life. Every day we see people with more and more frequency and ease interrelating with, or sharing experience with, strangers they have never met before; do not expect to meet again; and do not, in more than the most cursory sense, sincerely meet now. Strangeness is linked to urbanization, in that the growth of the city seduces the commitments of former rural laborers who now immigrate from every town and village to be part of the burgeoning explosion of trade and commerce, yet not as familiars.

Before the mid-1960s (when the American airline industry's popularity ballooned),[2] the sophisticated way to get from one place to another, inside continental North America, was the train. The luxurious parlor car in which Guy Haines's and Bruno Antony's shoes kiss at the beginning of *Strangers*, with its etched glass panels, recessed lighting, plush seating, and waiter service, was a typical feature of high-end railroad travel in the days before cost-cutting to avoid bankruptcy spread through the business and the train experience became notably less decorative. Here, a voyager could easily retreat into sedate tranquility while gliding through space. As the train passed over the track points, a pleasing rattling, rhythmic, throbbing beckoning brought the traveler out of the tedium of reality. In a car not unlike this one, with my father, in December 1958, I met—traveling northbound from New York City, comfy in his lounger, and hiding behind his unfolded *New York Times*—a very sweet, profoundly freckled, and grandfatherly Leo G. Carroll.[3]

In his book *The Railway Journey*, Schivelbusch makes clear how in the original design of rail systems urban stations were expressly placed so that passengers could be delivered from their journey directly to the center of town, passing without obstruction into the principal thoroughfares where multitudes mingled to breathe life into the economy. The train delivered people straight into the urban heart. But movement went in two ways. In *Strangers*, our walkers are leaving the city behind, moving into the countryside (and, historically speaking, toward the past, because America of the nineteenth century was principally rural) in an atmosphere of circulation and strangeness. The railway, writes Tom Gunning, "embodies the complex realignment of practices which modern circulation entails" (15). And the circulation of strangers permits a curious freedom. In the circulating crowd, observed Walter Benjamin, "an individual is, so to speak, unknown to all others and thus does not have to blush in front of anyone" (*Baudelaire* 40). If their paths cross on journeys, as they head toward or from the urban mass, strangers experience little beyond the general criss-crossing that is part of city life, with bodies navigating here and there and collisions major and minor being avoided—or not quite. The city is a paradigm of "strange" movement, and the presence of such edifices as Union Station facilitated, developed, exacerbated, and dramatized the strangeness, the "unknownness," and the shamelessness of people. On an outbound journey, in particular, interaction between the unintroduced might well stand out more, seem more touching, bring consequences less quotidian and more alarming, since the city, as an incorporating and homogenizing vortex, was being dropped behind into an unseen wake. The future could seem expansive, airy, full of possibility.

The glyph of crossing tracks or pathways, of intersections, offers far more than passing interest in its various centralities to the film. At crossings, collision is avoided only through signaling systems, or etiquettes, shared among friends or members of a solidary community——but potentially arcane and obscure between strangers. In molecular collision is heat, but also promise. Discussing the figure of the stranger as an outside agent in economic transactions (and with what could easily seem prescience about what we are about to see in this film), Georg Simmel pointed to the fact that "in trade, which alone makes possible unlimited combinations, intelligence always finds expansions and new territories" (403). In discovery is the unfolding of potential. But what is important structurally in *Strangers* is collision *inside a system already built upon the propensity for it*. Small-scale collisions of personalities—this film tells the story of one such collision—make up a cauldron of commerce in which seethe and bubble economic transactions geared from outside the community. In modernity, transactions occur in the absence of community altogether, since the proliferation of strangers and their variably dense interrelations in urban space work especially to exclude or reduce the salience of historical familiarities, the recognition of types, and occupational commitments, and to foster always-new prospects for Simmel's "unlimited combinations." It is Guy Haines whom Bruno Antony is going to bump into on the train this morning, as we shall see, but should Bruno happen to be obstructed he would bump into someone else, and there would follow a chain of events other—yet not dramatically less distinctive—than the one in which we will find ourselves bound. Toes are pointing all over the place.

"Criss-cross": I cross beside you while you cross beside me. I cross into your life while you cross into mine. It is possible that in respective movement, two bodies and personalities could come near enough to barely touch. And the barest touch may be enough to trigger a mortal relation. Is this type of mortal relation intimate? Even sexual? To this query I shall return, yet not, perhaps, along a direct route. The pleasure is in the journey.[4]

"OOPS": AN EQUIVOCAL GESTURE

A sketch of the film's main events:

Guy Haines (Farley Granger), tall, dark, and handsome, a glamorous and by now much-famed tennis pro, has been married to Miriam (Laura Elliott), a *lumpen* shopgirl from the small town in which he was born (Metcalf).[5] But in his genial and devoted way he is in love with the daughter of a prominent US senator. This is Anne Morton (Ruth Roman), dignified, groomed, cultivated, canny, and quite as well placed as any young woman might be in quietly catty Washington society. She has a younger sister, Barbara (Patricia Hitchcock), a whipper-snapper with optical problems, who continually demonstrates loyalty, sweet-natured innocence, and the pain of suffering a crush on her sister's boy. Guy has been accepted into the family, with the old senator (Leo G. Carroll) a loyal, if somewhat taciturn, fan and mentor. One day on a train Guy accidentally meets Bruno Antony (Robert Walker), only son of a reclusive financial magnate (Jonathan Hale). Dapper, even too dapper, Bruno loathes his father and feels encumbered with a dotty artistic mother (Marion Lorne). With his giant black Great Dane he lives in the suburban Antony mansion, stuffed behind vast lawns and high trees and emerging only, it seems, to give play to his sadistic streak in prodding, manipulating, and otherwise toying with the lives of other people.

Bruno invites (seduces?) Guy into his compartment; they lunch and drink; they chat as young men will do. Soon enough (too soon?) Bruno makes it evident he would like to be rid of his father, and knows, through intuition and addiction to the gossip columns, that Guy would like at least as much to be rid of his noxious wife. He proposes they trade murders. "Trade murders!" Guy is aghast and titillated in a breath. *"Criss-cross!"* There could be no discernable motive in either case, urges Bruno. They would be committing a perfect crime. As the clockwork of the plot unwinds we may sense a condition of which John Locke warns: "The dueling disposition threads its way through the *ordinary speech* of men, with strands of it here in this challenge and there in that retort" (48). Guy pays a visit to Miriam, finding her even more obnoxious and demanding than ever and unwilling to grant him a divorce. On his own initiative Bruno makes his way to Metcalf, locates her, follows her to an amusement park on the edge of town, and on the black lake there, upon a small island that young lovers pay to visit, coolly strangles her to death. He informs Guy. "Now it's your turn." The lothario is stunned and terrified, since he never meant to actually agree to any such thing as murder; not *real* murder; not *really*. Will he proceed to slay Bruno's father? And whether he does or does not, what might be the outcome of the relationship between these two men?

Actually, Guy does make bold to enter the Antony mansion, but only in order to warn the father about his insane son. Bruno is a step ahead of him, however, lying in wait in the father's bed. The gig is up. He lets Guy know that he intends to plant Guy's cigarette lighter, left behind on the train, near the scene of the killing at the fairground. In a spectacular finale—we might say a multi-spectacular finale, since as it unwinds spectacles build upon spectacles—we find Guy racing desperately through a championship tennis match at Forest Hills in order that he may elude the police and try to catch Bruno in Metcalf before the lighter is planted. Bruno is in his own race, because outside the town railway station he has dropped the lighter through a sewer grating. While he speeds against time to fish it out, Guy speeds against time to end his match (for a discussion of Hitchcock's masterly use of the camera in the criss-cross between these scenes see my "Sports Film"). Bruno is finally trapped at the park's carousel, where with gay and chilling bravura (and moral closure) the agony ends.

That climactic tennis game: we are skillfully shown the boundedness of the court as setting; the tightly organized movement of competitors according to a rule structure that defines the game; intensity of "antagonism"; rhythmic progression through a set of predetermined and yet plastic "moves"; and at the same time—through a delicate shifting in the camera's determination of perspective and point of framing—vital body parts gesturing energetically, broad long shots displaying the territory and the crowd, and through these the elaborate social construction of tennis as we know it. Guy's enemy Bruno is meanwhile shown in his own desperate—if comparably mundane—contest against time, gravity, accident, and social pressure as, trying to implicate Guy in a crime he did not commit, he fishes for his precious treasure. The tennis match sequence—lovers of tennis will admire it—reflects Guy's identity as tennis star established early on, to provide a palpable hint that gaming competition is a central, not a marginal, feature of the expression here. We see in the sequence what we found hinted at strongly before, that Guy is a fierce and muscular competitor. Bruno's physical slackness has been a camouflage, because he is a fierce competitor, too. Game competition involves bounded space, specified rules, and moral discipline, all extensions of the courtly geste.

But the prime collision in this film, the molecular smash that sets the fission off, involves a gesture of the most splendid equivocality, a characters' gesture and the filmmaker's as well. The tip of one man's shoe glances against the tip of another's. Point to point. Since even here in the train's club car we have retained our puppy's point of view, near the carpeting, we are confronted with the trousered legs decorously crossed on both sides of the screen and, again on both sides, the upper leg stretching out for comfort— already a criss-cross, an extension and merger of the frame boundaries. The actual touch indicates the closing of the interpersonal gap, that threshold where—as Leslie Fiedler commented in an unpublished talk given at the University of Michigan during my undergraduate days—"the self stops and the world begins." If we do not wonder at the instant, we must surely come in retrospect to ask: Is the contact accidental? (Convention leads observers in the West to read motive from the face; and here the faces are invisible.) Surely it must be a touch produced by ecological stress, two bodies crammed into an inadequate space. But not at all: the club car is notably capacious, even luxurious; and the gestural tone of both bodies is relaxed and easy. Neither man is fidgeting to adjust to tight quarters. Is it by intent or happenstance, then, that one of them has seated himself directly across from the other? These two are hardly the only available seats in this car. Could this moment evidence one man's desire for proximity, or have we seen a mere thoughtless, reflex motion that under other circumstances might have led to nothing?

Etiquette is instantaneously summoned forth on both sides, mutual apology as though each player recognizes how easily he could be misinterpreted as an audacious claimer to more space than is his due (in this public venue designed for sharing). The apologetic tone seems to betoken a natural (and beyond the confines of this picture, generally diffused) cultural Achilles heel, the undisclosed fact that every man knows himself to be prone at any instant to being taken as a threat by any other. Apology lives on the tip of the tongue. Thus the very immediacy of the excuse, not to say its stark abbreviation. It is a sign both taken for granted and only superficially communicative. The delicacy and casual grace make plain that each of these men—at this moment they constitute mere stand-ins for any masculine identities at all—lives on a knife edge of alerted fear and anxiety, warily (but subtly) conscious of his surround, lest—deepest possible horror for one and the next!—in the turmoil of mass living he might inadvertently provoke, and in provoking mobilize the aggression of, a neighbor. The touch without atonement may be an attack.

LOVE ON THE RUN

We have the distinct sense of a hypermasculine force stored—secretly—within each of these two protagonistic bodies: secretly, because as male types Guy and Bruno are civil, even unexceptionally so. This hidden force can presumably be triggered and freed on physical contact.[6] What is the dynamic play through which it acts?

Clearly—claims a certain speculation about *Strangers on a Train*, based on the idea of a sensual connection between the good-looking Guy (played by the acknowledged homosexual Farley "Fa" Granger, who, not long before, had been expressly homosexual as Phillip in Hitchcock's *Rope* [1948]) and the good-looking Bruno (creatures invented originally by the homosexual Patricia Highsmith for her source novel)—this force is, and can be nothing other than, homoeroticism. Certainly, the homoerotic is at play in this film. Bruno, in particular, is designed to be seen as exaggeratedly fey. Alexander Doty surveys the major observers of male-male attraction here, including Robert Yanal, Robert Corber, Donald Spoto, and Michael Walker, who sees Guy as a "repressed homosexual" (486ff.) Patrick McGilligan notes screenwriter Whitfield Cook making Bruno a "dandy, a mama's boy who speaks French, and who professes ignorance of women" (442). And in Guy, Susan White detects a man "pushing away the current of homosexual attraction to Bruno that moves like a riptide under the film" (192). The "homosexual reading," as I would dub the approach that foregrounds sexual identity as explanatory of this film, is easily pinioned to deep-seated American cultural fears in the postwar period. Corber specifically notes, for example, how "it would be difficult to exaggerate the significance of the ensuing investigation undertaken by the Senate Appropriations Committee into same-sex behavior," especially "the discovery that there were 'deviates' who could 'pass' as heterosexuals" (114). Perhaps in Bruno it is especially easy to read the sexual monster. When they are lunching, his inching across the little compartment table in Guy's direction; his gracile smile and effeminate pout; his momma's-boy attire, with the flagrant lobster tie; later on his sitting in the stands at a tennis match, gawking at the youthful male figures in motion; his smarmily worming into the social relations of Anne Morton's French friends; his resentment against young (heterocentrist) boys in the amusement park; the aggression in his murder of (the threatening and oh-so-buxom) Miriam; and at the moment of his own death the vaguely post-orgasmic sigh, in which he expresses pleasure at the thought of Guy being executed for murder. All these placements, gestures, alignments, and apparent attitudes probably sum to his hunting the beautiful, straight (because as yet uninitiated), unresisting Guy: hunting, craving, tasting at a distance, preparing to devour. But can we seriously propose that the dynamism of *Strangers* springs from homoeroticism in a significant way? Is male-to-male friction and touch what this story leads us, finally, to see and think about?

Reading the film as a pickup story is a tactic employed frequently both by those who wish to unpack *Strangers* and by those who would probe into homoerotic or homosexual strains in American cinema more generally. Even the performers themselves had it somewhat in mind. Vito Russo attests that Walker had the idea of playing Bruno as a homosexual (qtd. in Doty 486). Seekers after homosexual tonalities take the film's murder and chase as mere set-ups that operate to deflect attention from what is fundamentally a pickup, leading, perhaps, to a conversion. Innocent Guy tasted and then swallowed by the ravenous stalker. Seen this way, the protruding shoes at the initiatory moment are nothing less than symbolic phalli, and the resolving contact of the toe tips is a kind of (perhaps not so) metaphorical frottage.

Can we detect notable limits in the pickup theme? Guy's insinuation into the Morton family circle is one of them: Bruno is excluded from that, to some degree because of the senator's paranoid circumspection and to some degree because, as Hitchcock showed, the class background from which Bruno emerged was above the machine of Washington society. Another block is Bruno's distinct lack of psychological balance, which Walker lends exquisitely sharp markings: this is not simply a homophobic derision, on the filmmaker's part (as generally on the part of sanctimonious Americans), of Bruno's queerness but a straightforward suggestion that there are indiscernible and unpredictable forces at play with this young man. As we shall see, a dominating third problem for the pickup reading is the train setting—it is emphasized, not backgrounded, and it invokes strangeness, movement, the peculiar disillusionment that Schivelbusch named "panoramic perception" (64) much more than intimacy and consummation. I will here forebear to mention the tennis match—that is, the metaphor of aggrandizing competition—more than in passing, but the deep structure invoked there is combat to the death, not bonding or love (notwithstanding that the former often invoke or include the latter). Indeed, competitiveness and achievement orientation both suggest a platform much larger than sexual orientation or inclination, much larger than the limited sensualities of the everyday. Even without a homosexual undertone in this cold-war scene, the touch of Bruno upon Guy and Guy upon Bruno constitutes a danger, less a danger that provokes a thrill than a danger that predicts a future. Again, in the world of men, danger is everywhere, and not simply because men's secret pleasure is so vulnerable to being released on contact with other men. In a culture controlled by men, each man's private controls become very significant, and vulnerable.

There are good reasons, all based in the diegesis itself, for doubting the centrality of the clear homoeroticism in *Strangers*. While one may or may not wholeheartedly agree with Douglas McFarland's wry observation that "there is virtually no chemistry generated, homoerotic or otherwise, between the two male protagonists" (293),[7] or wonder, with Robin Wood, "Which, in fact, *are* Hitchcock's gay characters? It seems to me a matter far harder to determine than has often precipitously been claimed.... the claims largely rest upon heterosexist myths about homosexuals" (345), Guy's complex, conflicted, and self-directed involvements must be given full weight of consideration. And as to his "masculinity"—so to name it, in our present age of popular gender inspections—it is easy to forget that male sentimentality was rife in America of the 1940s and 1950s, a relation in itself and not a mere cover for something hotter and more unspeakable.

The heroic male's sentimental high regard, even love, for his comrades, his ability to touch them with affection, his deep care for their lives often mitigated by attention to mechanical action of one kind or another: all these "battalion effects," as we might think them, were present in American culture and on the American screen before *Strangers* was made: for an exceptionally telling example see Robert Montgomery and John Wayne in John Ford's *They Were Expendable* (1945). This male sentimentality need not be understood as masked sexual desire.

And even the eroticism that seems unmistakably here can serve other purposes beyond signaling one or more characters' identity. One such purpose is catching the viewer's hunger for the salacious and thereby distracting attention from a more explosive problematization, set out in excruciating detail, as we will see. Were Bruno's principal intent only a bald pickup; were his sexual thrill resident in the very strangeness of this possible partner; were all the heterosexual elaborations of the plot—Guy's early marriage; his brutal wife; his lovely girlfriend—nothing more than bearding, so much of what is elaborated onscreen—the very extended tennis match, to point to only one possibility—would be rendered nonsensical, fruitlessly decorative, or cheaply admonitory, and this from a filmmaker who had already demonstrated the detailed moral necessity of each element in his constructions (for elaboration on which, see Krohn; and Rothman, *Must We Kill*). A more complicating, and therefore finally more enlightening critical strategy is to consider Bruno's motive as not hunger but resentment, in which dark endeavor he operates as an unwitting instrument of the tennis star's moral education. And further, perhaps there is a way in which Bruno, full of action and gesture, lacks motive entirely, at least the sort of motive that would make sense to a man like Guy.

Here is a telling case of a superficially erotic moment that has numerous subterranean, and very unerotic, implications: Guy and Anne are visiting the echoing (and salutary) halls of the National Gallery. We see them strolling aimlessly among marble columns when suddenly a whisper of his name calls Guy off. Anne watches from a distance as her beau meets a young man with a gold tie pin that reads, "Bruno." You're making me come out into the open, Bruno whines quietly, as though to say, "You're putting public light on our secret relationship." The double entendre lends the scene a frisson, but this isn't sexual secrecy covered up by public encounter; it's murder covered by the mask of sex-being-covered-by-public-encounter. "Public light" on a "private relationship" is precisely and fully what *is* threatened, but the "private relationship" isn't criss-cross bed play, it's criss-cross killing. One might even imagine Bruno going so far as to imagine that a part of what will make his murder plan "perfect" is the homoerotic impulse that will be attributed as motive for his relationship with Guy, an impulse he may or may not feel but which he can recognize as wholly useful in any case. These two will be read as lovers, not conspirators in a double killing. He is counting on the public's failure at understanding (Susan Sontag will much later note in *On Photography* that understanding begins "from not accepting the world as it looks" [23]). Accepting the way things look blocks true understanding, and is thus a perfect cover. How deeply will observers probe if they can be satisfied with the titillating, unannounceable thought of two passionate men together? We, too, are in that audience wandering the gallery. The "male-love plot" is Hitchcock's contrivance of an easy way out, a bromide that, tickling our hidden organ of repressed pleasure, saves us from seeing and weighing authentic moral trouble instead, not that one man is aroused by an object deemed socially inappropriate but that he is willing to entrap someone into a capital crime, merely on a whim. Anne, like us, is saved from this blackest of thoughts, by making that tickling sub-rosa interpretation.

Very like Guy Haines, graceful but hesitant, sensitive but (if charmingly) stilted, numerous young males in America of the 1950s were as yet unaccustomed to the choreographic demands of heterosexual love—some of them even after marriage. They spent their days in frustrating competition with other men, whose world of domination, brutality, self-aggrandizement, and challenge became theirs, too, by dint of socialization. Male prerogative was everywhere. Guy, a pretty boy, is as cognizant of that prerogative as of his own good looks, yet he knows beauty is not exactly his accomplishment and that, because he was not one of those, like Bruno, born to success, accomplishment is his basic task in life. If he is not naïve and has become somewhat accustomed to being sought after for men's pleasure—Adonis's fate—still he has not given himself over, perhaps hasn't even thought of it, focused narcissistically, as he is, on his glowing aura and the glowing career it presages if only he plays it right. The aura is his tennis ball, as it were. Playing the thing is the whole game.

Guy's pathetic marriage to the lowly Miriam and his relentless quest for the ethereal Anne are two sides of a single coin: having detected his position in the class hierarchy, with true chagrin he has confessed to himself that his wife, charged and appealing as she may have been at the start, offers no real opportunities for advancement, particularly in the public domain where his star image resides and his future lies in wait: he confesses at one point that he hopes for a career in politics (in emulation, that is, of the senator, his "true father"). Buxom Miriam is, and is from, *below*. If when he bedded her Guy was *from below*, too, he has by now discovered a more Olympian clime and has been planning a change of scene. Anne Morton gives off all the right—read, elevated—sparkle; moves with High Bureaucrats; carries herself like a proud filly at a horse farm retreat in bluegrass country. Miriam afforded Guy a sexual education. Anne holds out the promise of social mobility. Young Barbara has a much richer imagination of sexual, romantic, and adventurous pleasures than either Guy or her sister, but we aren't following Barbara (since in the gallery of portraits that this motion picture constitutes, she is only our cicerone).

As to the problematic Bruno: Robert Walker's performance emits flashes of cunning and malice—what could be read, in the wake of Freudian thought, as sexual inversion or, with a more intensely moral focus, as evil inclination. His deep desire is to produce a stain, to make the spotless Guy literally less immaculate, less holier-than-thou. Guy is so prim and holy, after all, that no mark of experience has besmirched his alabaster skin. Bruno will make a mess upon this clean canvas. But he will start, let us not forget—the "pickup" interpretation of this film always does forget—on a moving train. Hitchcock understands that the railway setting permits him to show a system in which an encounter just so equivocal as this one could occur, dark with potential yet as normal as sunshine.

CONFIDENCES

Pretexts are followed by texts, and the touching feet of Guy and Bruno are only a pretext. As the touch produces apology and excuse, the apology and excuse may produce something further. During their chat (when two strangers acknowledge each other's presence, a nugatory little chat must arise to defuse the situation), Guy is given opportunity to discover in Bruno a mirror reflection—an ominous mirror reflection—of his own fame. As a talented athletic nobody, hot to climb the ladder of success, he never estimated the full panoply of troubles fame could bring: one's marriage and its devastations opened for all to view in the newspaper (in today's world it could be Fox News or the BBC); the intricate byways of one's personal life now captioning glamorous (perhaps indecent) photographs. Bruno, a media fan, has "made" Guy.[8] Guy is therefore no longer fully—or only—himself; he is a cipher in a broad national directory, readable to unknowns. More than just picking him out, Bruno has been building and treasuring a file on this celebrity, can openly cite general knowledge about Miriam and the difficulties of Guy's divorce-in-process. If, as Simmel had it, a stranger "often receives the most surprising openness—confidences which sometimes have the character of a confessional and which would be carefully withheld from a more closely related person" (404), it is also true that beyond receiving openness Bruno can directly and successfully solicit it. Guy is on show, therefore open to question.

The venue changes, as the shadowy interrogator casually suggests they move into his compartment for lunch. A display of wealth and generosity, as well as a set-up for confidentiality and a well-lubricated "third degree." The jabber becomes more personal, more interactional and interrogative, and Guy, a "new" celebrity, behaves somewhat strangely—almost from the start, and in a general way: he makes himself amenable, curious, open if shy, and alluring as a social type: he *goes along*. If great potency lies in his personal allure, in his expensive cigarette lighter and (attractive) clothing, in the light flooding his face, in the opened innocent eyes and polite articulateness of his speech, Guy is distinctly, while civil, not just a civilian. The Hitchcockian architecture here sharply reflects early developing media culture, a particular inflection of modernity that turns up the heat between the molecules of individualities in rapid motion, thus aggravating their propensity for momentous collision (Marshall McLuhan suggested the communal aspects of expanded media, following from the work of Harold Innis and Walter Benjamin). With Bruno's newspaper here—the haven of Guy's public identity—we have a keen reminder of Benjamin's observation that the newspaper reader thinks, with a characteristic impatience, that he has the right to see his interests expressed ("Newspaper" 741), thinks it sensible to take personal interest in the alien material he discovers on the page. A kind of false community is constructed, where people who have neither grown up in one another's presence nor even made acquaintance take it as a matter of convention to be fascinated by details that do not directly concern them.

Sensing a need for climax—I mimic Hitchcock's mimicking of sex—Bruno draws his interlocutor along. He makes plain his knowledge of Guy's miserable marriage, then reveals that he has a miserable affiliation, too, being son to a man he thinks monstrous. A later scene, where he schmoozes with his mother as she paints a figuration derived from the (currently in vogue) abstract expressionism of Abraham Rattner—abrupt slashes of color criss-crossing a gaping monstrous eye—has Bruno in stitches: "Oh yes! That's father!" (Is Mrs. Antony "artistically" messing up her canvas, showing us the origin of her son's desire to mess up Guy, or is she painting with careful deliberation? Their audiences at first wondered how serious the abstract expressionists were.) You have troubles, I have troubles, implies Bruno: but for him the statement of this equivalence, the simple sharing of woes, cannot suffice. The hungry spirit has come upon a joint "solution" to what is never actually framed as a joint problem, except by way of the implication that because they share traps, hatreds, and agonies the two are parties to a relationship. And what we must notice about Guy in this scene, since Bruno is clearly excessive (if not outright crazy), is his affability. If he does not accompany Bruno's thoughts he would at least seem to, which, in a situation like this, full of nuance and manner, overloaded with seemliness and face (the retreat to the private compartment prevents other passengers from penetrating the dyad), amounts to the same thing.

Beyond that it would ruin the movie (and we cannot have that), why does Guy not just stand up and walk away?

MEETING "CUTE"

The encounter between Guy and Bruno is a striking case of "meeting cute." Two characters "bump into" each other inadvertently, as though influenced by fatal forces. For Hitchcock, a filmmaker whose presence, as Rothman stresses, is always felt, the fatality indexes both the controlling artist's manipulation of his story (from without, and from above) and the implicit interior presence of guiding principles and predispositions. In the modern world, surely in the city, almost anyone could "bump into" almost anyone else, and indeed the railway terminus is a notable locus of such molecular collisions. In 1945, Vincente Minnelli had given serious play to the station's role in forming "accidental" relationships in *The Clock*, also starring—and in a far more sympathetic role—Robert Walker. Walker, Hitchcock would have seen (he was an inveterate watcher of films), wore on his face a perfect combination of attractive, graceful concentration and bland anonymity: a man who stepping out of a crowd attracts instant interest but becomes invisible when he steps back.

The twist for Hitchcock, an issue that fascinated him repeatedly in his work, is a certain adaptation city dwellers make, perhaps out of some inherited guilt of losing the communalism of agrarian life. In the urban thriller, the stranger, a powerfully shocking intruder, is omnipresent; everyone has come from somewhere on the outside and the shock of encounter is routinized through superficial etiquette. But at the same time, cognizant of this superficiality, players in the game make amends of a sort by initiating and proceeding through conversations that seem personal. This urban gregariousness is false personability, a mask of a social bond. There is a mannerism to traveling in the lounge car of the train, with parties aware they may sit in abject silence next to one another but also, on the spur of a garrulous moment, become chummy: "make friends." What Hitchcock saw was not the simple maneuver of amicability but the structural tension between, on one hand, a vastly populous and unintelligible strangeness and, on the other, temporary amity under pressure. This tension would later underpin the strange relationships Jeff Jefferies has with his neighbors in *Rear Window*; the strange circumstance of the dying Louis Bernard coming up to find Ben McKenna in *The Man Who Knew Too Much* "out of five thousand people, in a great marketplace"; and Norman Bates's affable behavior at the motel desk when people come to do business with him. The world as "friendly place."

In order to accomplish his mad "criss-cross" plot, Bruno must secure from Guy not only warmth and the exchange of obscure secrets but, in an apparently normal, casual, unreflected moment, assent. Guy's opening reaction, after all, is affronted withdrawal. He is an emotional person, one whose purposes are served by expression instead of action. But while he hates Miriam, and can easily say he'd like to see her dead, he doesn't mean that he wishes to see her corpse, that he would entertain the actual thought of murder: their explosive argument—utterly silent for us—in the soundproofed listening room of the music store gives evidence. There is a signal difference between talking about murder and doing it: another Hitchcockian motif, all the way forward from *The Lodger* (1927). Guy therefore has no trouble "reading" his strange mate's intention when he avers he'd like to kill his father. Talk talk talk. We all get very angry sometimes, we all say things. But can Bruno actually be planning *action*? Unthinkable in civilized society. Impossible in a friendly place.

Not only do we witness the diabolical gleam in Bruno's eye; we see Guy witnessing it.

Highsmith wrote her train scene from within Guy's consciousness, so we could have no doubt of what he thinks as Bruno (there, Charles Bruno) engages him in conversation. The shift from the lounge into Bruno's compartment, for example: "What did it matter after all? And wasn't he utterly sick of himself?" (thinks the depressed Guy) (12), an attitude our filmic Guy doesn't share, blooming with health and optimism, if meditative. On paper Bruno's cabinette is a rat's nest of suitcases: "The room amused him and gave him a welcome sense of seclusion" (12); but in Hitchcock the in-flooding window light sharpens contrasts in a rather tidy space, keeps Guy's attention on the edge. "Actually," writes Highsmith, "he was thinking of Anne" (15), but Granger's Guy is focused on the incalculable Bruno, even while sparing information about Anne. And at heart, Highsmith's Guy—being the narrator's pet—is an innocent: when Bruno complains about his father, Guy "echoe[s] involuntarily, 'Of course' " (16), the extroverted sympathy pasted up as a natural element of his personality and disposition. As unhinged as the novel's Bruno may seem to Guy, obliquely, he is the possessor of a certain wisdom, applicable to the Miriam about whom Guy has been telling him: " 'Women like that draw men,' Bruno mumbled, 'like garbage draws flies,' " the shock of which "detache[s]" Guy "from himself" (24). Bruno's unyielding conversation begins to nauseate Guy, who "want[s] to get out and take a walk, but the train kept on and on in a straight line, like something that would never stop" (29): here Bruno is metonymized by the train itself, and for that matter by the train system. There is a distinct and ineradicable continuity to him. He doesn't stop until he reaches the terminal. And in Highsmith the dialogue between the men becomes abrupt and to the point, revealing no hidden motivations in Guy—

> "Shall I tell you one of my ideas for murdering my father?"
> "No," Guy said. He put his hand over the glass Bruno was about to refill.
> "Which do you want, the busted light socket in the bathroom or the carbon monoxide garage?"
> "Do it and stop talking about it!" (29–30)

—at least no motivations of the sort Hitchcock will soon reveal. Hitchcock's Guy isn't a man to encourage Bruno, after all; out of anger or impatience at his own revulsion ("I'm sick of this" [31]). And in the book, the moment of the proposal itself is a culminating one, in terms of Guy's withdrawal (at least in his own consciousness):

> Bruno slammed his palms together. "Hey! Cheeses, what an idea! We murder for each other, see? I kill your wife and you kill my father! We meet on the train, see, and nobody knows we know each other! Perfect alibis! Catch?"
> The wall before his eyes pulsed rhythmically, as if it were about to spring apart. *Murder.* The word sickened him, terrified him. He wanted to break away from Bruno, get out of the room, but a nightmarish heaviness held him. (30; emphasis original)

Hitchcock's Guy will not experience a nightmarish heaviness. And he will encourage Bruno in a way that at first is not, perhaps, explicit.

In the film, Guy does not admit that the murder plot is making him sick; that he is terrified. We are led to surmise that a man who looks as he does, dapper, clean, polished, young, and with a sweet smile, might feel terror at the thought of being pushed to kill; yet the cinematic Bruno, dark but svelte, gracile, even somewhat twinkly, hardly more than a player with words, is no pusher. He is tickling his new friend's brain cells, not drawing out and pronouncing a criminal strategy.

And the telltale moment—the moment that I would call the pivot of this film—comes as Guy is finally on point of leaving Bruno's airless cell. Bruno has been acting as though they have struck a deal for mutually relieving murders, whilst we have no reason to believe Guy thinks so at all. But with a pleasant smile, moving through the door into the saving corridor outside, Guy says: "Sure, Bruno. Sure."

Here shines Hitchcock's ongoing delight in the structural balance of ambiguity. Ambiguity, not lust. In an ambiguous structure or moment, two often contradictory interpretations are counterpoised, as on a scale, and with exquisitely calculated equality. Their implications are directed to opposite poles of experience with a similar force and to the same degree. In this way, as Hitchcock so fruitfully understood, an expression can be made vulnerable to glittering misinterpretation, and the door opened to comedic situations wherein characters spectacularly fail to grasp one another's purpose until a culminating moment when swiftly, surprisingly, the veil of implication is lifted and a hard, redeeming glare of factuality illuminates the world. In *Mr. and Mrs. Smith* (1941) Hitchcock had shown himself a master of ambiguity in comedic marital situations (the staple of screwball films; and a dynamic center of Stanley Cavell's "comedies of remarriage" [see *Pursuits*]). Here in *Strangers* we see an invocation of complex ambiguity, performed *en passant*, abbreviated, with the voice low; an ambiguity with which we can all be presumed to have long familiarity, and with which we can be thought to have found easy relation: when you *don't* want to do something ugly, you say you *do*, and you back away. The clear implication, as people take it—the implication, not the statement—is that nobody in his right mind would agree to a plan like this, and the assent means only, "Yes, I heard you. I acknowledge your presence and I say goodbye"—yet none of this in a way that could bring trouble upon the head for speaking. "I say 'No' in such a way that you cannot possibly take me—here and now—to be doing so, thus you can have no rude or violent comeback."

This is the second time in a short period for Guy to say "Yes" when he means "No." On the invitation to dine in private, he first searched the public dining car and, finding it full, agreed to the invitation: but his gazing around was a statement in itself, a declension. "I would rather not join you," fully modulated to an agreeable "Yes."

Guy is a producer of nothing less than ambiguous speech. "Sure," and yet this so effortless "yes" to a murder contract, after so effortless a conversation in such effortless circumstances—and after several drinks!—surely does not oblige one to action. In other words, our Guy Haines has no difficulty making promises that he has no intention to keep.

GOING ALONG

We may sense an undertone of still something else infusing Guy's words: that in this circumstance he is the superior man, talking down to someone whose ideas do not merit clear response. "Sure, Bruno. Sure." Subtly, dismissively—Bruno will not catch this—he condescends to this pathetic soul, in order to demonstrate unimpeachably a garrulous face (in modernity, garrulousness is prized). Yet at the same time, because of the perfect ambiguity in his utterance, Guy could be heard as saying, quite bluntly and boldly, "Yes! Kill for you? Sure! I'm eager! I'm your man!" "Sure, Bruno," that is, "I assent to what you suggest, I cheerlead, *I go along*."

"I go along," but also "The last thing I would do on earth is go along." Sarcasm and sincerity in a perfect sandwich.

Is the fear that leads Guy to so ambivalent an expression only emotional? He's a timid little lamb and Bruno's a big, bad, conniving wolf? Or might Guy's interest and investment of the moment be tactical: that something might be gained from not appearing negative in Bruno's calculating, all-encompassing eyes?

To grasp Guy at this apotheosis more fully, one must see him in fuller context, in the modern urban world jittery with social mobility, status realignment, class climbing, changing one's life. The train epitomizes the public transportation system but also movement more generally, which implies the encounter with hungry strangers, people whose histories are hidden and whose intentions may or may not harmonize with one's own. Bruno is a somewhat familiar type for Guy: one of the super-rich whose positions in society he admires and whose admiration he would cultivate—but with whom he can claim no intimacy. Guy is a celebrity, touted in the media of note, bearer of a public face that covers his private life. And maintaining a successfully publishable public face, keeping up appearances is important for his career hopes. Indeed, we may note the overwhelming value in the modern urban world of striking an appealing appearance, regardless of the not-so-appealing back structure in which one strikes it. Above all things, Guy wants to "pass," so that he can fit into the Morton family's sphere (in which everyone may be "passing"). This means being able to attend Washington soirées without awkwardness or embarrassment; being able to escort Anne in public; being able to drink sherry with her much-esteemed and powerful father. Once Miriam's death is revealed and the Mortons become somewhat embroiled in Guy's position, since now he is being surveilled by the police (in particular a bloke named Hennessy who has enchanted Barbara with ghoulish tales), we get a clear picture from the senator about the lethal power of adverse publicity to affect the public view of a man in his position. Adverse publicity directed at Guy, if Guy is hooked into the family, will rub off on all of them.

Guy Haines is perhaps hard to read as a social climber because in the modern urban audience from the middle of the twentieth century onward (watching this film on its release, and still now), almost everyone has become a social climber, too. Hence the appeal of a high-society film, even a dark one, to viewers who do not inhabit high society. Guy is more than eager to leave unsophisticated, too plain-spoken Metcalf behind, which is why there is resonance in the fact that the finale of the film, in which he must return there to save his own life, is freighted with such pain for him. He wants entirely forgotten the boy who fell for Miriam, acting out of an unkenning nature rather than perspicacity. He wants his smiling, entirely beneficent face to appear on the society page, unbesmirched by telltale connections to off-the-wall sorts like Bruno.

Yet he cannot deny that Bruno breathes the rarefied air he craves. He wants to taste Bruno's life as much as he can, vicariously through the facial expressions and strange personal confessions—anything that might give him a taint of the perfume he hopes ultimately to wear. "Sure, Bruno. Sure."

And lastly, the issue of masculine pride, and the offence one might commit by denigrating it in another man: Guy must not, under any circumstances, say or do anything to make the other, his physical equal, openly observe that he considers himself ensconced on a higher platform, an entertainer of higher thoughts. Or, on the other side, allow Bruno to suspect he thinks himself unable to participate in playful combat sport ("I kill for you; you kill for me") at a matching level. Thus Hitchcock's invocation (departing entirely from the novel, where Guy is an architect) of Haines as a tennis star, a fellow who routinely puts his body on the line against a competitive male's in an exhibition of prowess and endurance, tactical sharpness and cunning. Guy cannot seem a lesser jock than Bruno, and so he must play the game. But in this case it's only posing and mockery (much as, we might well imagine, in some of his tennis matches, Guy being by far the better player, his strenuous feints and slams are somewhat posed and easy for him to handle). "Sure, Bruno. Sure" means "I can take you on." To read Guy's "assent" as simple assent, then, or any of his gestures as simple signs of attraction and felt equality is, structurally speaking, an error. He has sociably signed a death warrant but as what he would consider only a "death warrant," and as a matter of what he would think valor and competition.

A BOYS' GAME

Bruno's "slam-dunk," the murder of Miriam, is played as something of a film-within-the film, a simple and positive entertainment, which, as an audience of one, Bruno himself watches build toward its climax in rapt, even dreamy titillation. There is surely oneiricism in its weaving and its darkness. Even Bruno's passing gestures of affiliation with other characters, of standing inside the tale beside them, are echoing or vague, hesitant or resonant in a queer, super-realistic way.

He has trained to Metcalf, as though on a pleasure jaunt, and has looked Miriam up in a phone directory at the station. We see him near her house in the evening, as she emerges with two jabbering adolescent boys. The three of them hop on a city bus, as does he, and ride to the outskirts of town where an amusement park is in full swing—Douglas Gomery points out how "late in the nineteenth century, amusement parks were built at the end of trolley lines in major cities in the United States to encourage riders to journey through the entire system" (8). Tailing Miriam and her boys, Bruno has the delight of dreaming out the relationship between them: the boys are what only a few years later Americans would come to call "teenagers." What sorts of pleasure might be produced by them, for each other's engagement? As with watching films generally, the observer takes pleasure in imagining—dreaming—the characters' interiors, and we take pleasure in imagining Bruno's interior as he projects the interiors of the three young people. For him, they are on show. At the park, they stop for refreshment, Miriam acquiring a glowing white vanilla ice-cream cone, the sweet creamy ball of which she mouths suggestively, one boy at either side, like twinned janissaries. (Later in the film we will see these boy-types again, somewhat more mature, on opposite sides of a tennis court where a different white ball is put into play between them.) Miriam is teasing her dates: teasing each by inviting the other; teasing both by switching her gaze playfully back and forth. Meanwhile, thinks Bruno (mirroring the viewer), can either of them offer her the thrill she truly wants tonight?

Now, a boy of a different magnitude. A tiny balloon-wielder, dressed as a cowboy, passes Bruno. He pulls out his cap pistol: "Bang! Bang!" "In movies," we are reminded by George Toles, "the most compelling use of objects is to allow characters' thoughts, and their accompanying feelings, to become visible. In a Hitchcock film, the viewers' thoughts, aligned with a character's, may tilt" (116). Bruno gazes down quite seriously at this little mannequin, as though put to the challenge. Takes his lit cigarette. Pops the balloon. This clue to Bruno's character resonates with the lunch "game" in the railway compartment. Guy, another child of sorts (a player, an innocent) in costume, was playing by the rules of a game, thus both exposing and limiting himself; but for Bruno games did not—do not—exist: not as a separate dimension of real experience. There is only one unified reality for him, and what we might choose to call the "game" is just another facet of the expansive everyday. With Guy we would understand games to constitute "serious" make-believe, serious unseriousness, serious rehearsability, to be seriously set off from the non-gaming "serious reality" through some agency of guying and transformation (for a much more replete development of thought about which, see Goffman, *Frame Analysis* chap. 3). Bruno does not see things this way, however.

He uses his cigarette weapon with a force equal to the little boy's exertion with his "weapon"; is engaged to the same degree yet without a "toy"—which is to say, artfully oblivious to the separation between the pretend cowboy, the child's put-on, and the unplayful world. Bruno and the boy are both energetically deployed in the moment, but they don't understand it the same way. If players are always absorbed by their play, take it seriously as the dominating dimension, Bruno is a more inventive player than this kid can have imagined: dangerously so.

More inventive, and more ultimate. The play transpositions typically treated as momentary and plastic are converted by Bruno, through his destruction of the balloon, into the eternal and definitive. I find it hard to see how, as Steven Sanders puts it, "Bruno knows how to game the system" (127). For the little cowboy, the balloon was a prop, while the "bullets" in his "gun" were imaginary and intended to produce only a "wounded reaction" from his new playmate. Bruno stepped outside the play territory to attack, not the "play image" of himself as "whole" (by correctly "getting wounded") but his play partner's non-play substructure. "When you play with me, everything's up for grabs" is his message. Everything, including existence itself (the balloon no longer exists). The kid's chagrin makes it plain he doesn't get it. And very like this little boy, Guy didn't quite get it either.

The theme of big boys and little boys has been twice enunciated at the amusement park, first through the more mature Bruno's observation of the ice-cream purchase with the flanking teenagers; and second in Bruno's confrontation with the little "cowboy." To give this some background: in the Highsmith, Miriam is accompanied to the park by a pair of adult men, who use a car, not a bus, so that they can stop along the way and pick up another girl, thus making a pair of pairs, a conventional "double-date," rather than the off-balance flirtation structure—a game within the game—we find here in the Hitchcock. Highsmith's Miriam gets a frozen custard, and for his own delight Bruno picks up a balloon. As a young boy passes by, he considers whether he ought to gift the balloon to the kid and makes an executive decision to keep it for himself. No gunplay, no explosion (of innocence, or any other trust). There is a visit, as in the film, to the Test of Strength kiosk, but in the book Bruno merely watches men trying to impress Miriam with their strength, entertaining—but immediately abandoning—the thought that it could be pleasant to kill her with the sledge hammer. In the film he allows her to catch sight of him in a distinctive way. He watches her boyfriends, who are both impotent to make the weight ascend all the way to the top, and shows off that he has the muscle required. In short, Bruno is the "big man," the grown-up, that these teenagers haven't become yet. Now for a ride on the carousel, where Bruno hops a horse not far from Miriam's and she giddily observes him doing so; she can stretch her game of seduction now, try out tactics for luring an older man. In all this, Laura Elliott's Miriam is pudgy and saccharine, a sexual candy. Bruno will have a sample taste of her delight, and find her morbidly unappealing.

Hitchcock's nocturnal sky is pitch black, the black in which dreams float. The sparkling illuminations of his amusement park are piquant and beckoning, markers of dream civilization in the dream wilderness. Jabbering chatter, squeals of delight are everywhere; lights flash against the darkness; the merry-go-round's harmonium blares "And the Band Played On," a melody that repeats and repeats ad infinitum, like lapping waves. There is a dark lake with boats for rent, a tunnel of love, a private island, cinematic apotheosis of Arnold Böcklin's "Isle of the Dead" (1886) that inspired Rachmaninoff. Miriam eggs her boys on. Bruno follows in a tidy little craft named "Pluto." The lake waters are like pitch.

In a boat of our own, we follow the follower. . . .

AMUSEMENTS

A high-contrast sequence with vivid blacks and shimmering highlights. Echoing distant music, as if far away or in memory. Movement without direct sound. The lake a spreading silence. Indiscriminate voices echo across it and fall off. The park sounds, a tinkling cacophony, drop away. The Tunnel of Love is an ersatz mountain emerging from the water. As the kids' boat goes in, we watch them proceed toward the game of sexual conquest by way of flickering silhouette shadows on the wall, a perfectly Platonic vision. From the lake on the far side of this rock, near the ride's exit, a hideous scream tears the silence. We easily imagine to ourselves that Bruno has done his deed inside the tube, a spermatozoon of evil conjoined with an ovum of innocence (indeed, Highsmith's Bruno is under the impression from Guy that Miriam is pregnant). But then the kids' boat emerges and we find that it was a scream of pleasure, not agony. How interesting to reflect, if briefly, before the boats head on their way to the Island of Lethe, that joy and pain may signal themselves indistinguishably, that in the heights of vocality we reach some ultimate ambiguity.

The tunnel-of-love sequence is ostensibly immaterial to the plot, which requires only that Miriam's boat and Bruno's move from the dock to the lethal island, and that Bruno's returns. What is served by the tunnel is a conjunction between Bruno's violent impulse and Miriam's sexual one, a suggestion—tangible only in the setting and the characters' reactions to it—that she is comfortable with and hungry for sex while he not only isn't (at least with her) but actually finds her hunger repulsive, threatening. Fodder for the homoeroticism thesis, to be sure, but only if Bruno has a sexual appetite of some kind, if he enjoys genital pleasure but directs himself away from women. Here such a hypothetical appetite is directed away from Miriam and girls like her, which is to say, frank girls, healthy girls, girls who (to anticipate a much later popular cultural mantra) want to have fun. Highsmith's Bruno is a young man who finds Miriam objectionable on the face of it, Miriam but perhaps not other, more passive women. Hitchcock's Bruno has been watching her with a relaxed and canny sense of comprehension and purpose. He isn't here for pleasure, he's here for business. Young and vibrant, younger than he is, less settled into herself, Miriam must be slain so that his father can die, according to the rules of the idiosyncratic, solipsistic game of life that he is playing.

Hitchcock's use of the tunnel also points to a more decorous interest on his part (an interest in decorum, not decoration). Rides like this one were popular in the early part of the twentieth century, and went into decline as the 1960s came near. They had served a proper social end, that young people could have some temporally and spatially limited sexual interaction as part of normative courtship and in days when public displays were not tolerated (see Pomerance, *America* 200). The Tunnel of Love, with its enchanting boats of limited size, by design encouraged cuddling and necking without leading de facto to socially problematic behavior. The amusement park more generally constituted an ultimate space of moral sanctity. As Gregory Waller notes of Lexington, Kentucky's "Joyland," a "commitment to propriety and order" was emphasized, in a promise stipulating, "You may be as jovial and jolly as your nature will permit, that is what you come for, but order will be maintained at all times" (228). When we stand back and evaluate Miriam and her friends' experience in the Tunnel of Love, we find that this stipulation has been carefully followed. Yet at the same time, there is no mistaking that it is a sexually vibrant Miriam Bruno kills a few moments later, a girl stimulated by her two boyfriends, a girl generally susceptible to stimulation. The ebullition of feeling, too, was part of amusement park culture. Writing of Reginald Marsh's paintings of Coney Island, for example, John Kasson finds young women who "fairly explode out of their clothes in their sexual ripeness and availability" (94; qtd. in Nye 129).

It is a notably ripe Miriam who will die. In an earlier scene, at the music store where she works, we discovered her reptilian cunning and careless disregard for Guy. But here Hitchcock offers us opportunity to forget all that, just as the amusement park more broadly offered Americans opportunity to put aside their everyday worries and observations in the name of "good, clean fun." If the Tunnel of Love piques our curiosity about Miriam as a sexual being, we may notice emphatically that Guy is uninterested in, even bored with, this side of her. When he seeks the company of the Mortons, when he woos Anne, it is not for her (equally ripe) sexual promise but for higher rewards she signals more tantalizingly.

On the remote island, in yawning nocturnal shadows, Bruno strangles Miriam, playing his part in a game few others would recognize as such. *Criss-cross.* "Is your name Miriam?" (What a thrill for us to hear Walker ask, since his Bruno uses a voice we have never yet heard, soft, melodious, pure.) Guy's pilfered cigarette lighter flicks, a flame comes up double in the two bulbous eyeglass lenses marking her face. His thumbs press on her pharynx. We see a yielding, almost transcendent relaxation of her facial expression. Her eyeglasses tumble down into the grass, with Hitchcock—as has been much celebrated—dropping the camera to watch the death throes as reflections in the lenses. Gravitation again. (This is cinematic death, an affair of lenses and for the lens; not actual death, an affair for the body: a moviemaker's game.) A giant pair of glasses was prepared for making this shot (reminiscent, perhaps, of the giant pistol and partial hand that he used in the finale of *Spellbound* [1945]). Production notes for the film recount how both Elliott and Walker stumbled through the scene, since the eyeglasses she wore had been doctored to narrow her eyes as we saw them through the lenses, thus throwing off her normal vision; and Walker needed eyeglasses in everyday life, but here could have none.

Why, in order to frame this vision of murder, does Hitchcock invent, of all things, an age spectrum? Youthful, innocent, barely post-adolescent Guy (in the novel he is older, more sanguine, more matter of fact); sacrilegious, but still effete Bruno, morally older if psychotic (in the novel he is more dependent, continually thinking about his mother); the horny teenagers in Metcalf; the presumptuous little boy with the balloon and the six-shooter; coming a little later the aging and canny Senator Morton, who pulls strings in Washington, and knows what public relations imagery can do to wound. At different ages, people make various approaches to action, imagination, rehearsal, gaming, and simulation. The invocation of characters around Bruno who are more serious than he is, or distinctively less serious, allows us to think evaluatively of his behavioral motive. Is he being real in this murder plan, or just playing at being real? Is Miriam a living game piece for him, as the little boy with his cap pistol is a living game piece, as the ice-cream cone and merry-go-round horses were game pieces? It becomes vital to know how serious or playful things are when we encounter strangers who may not share our vision of the world—and so many of the encounters in the film are between strangers. Not only Guy and Bruno, but Bruno and the little boy; Bruno and the teens he watches; Bruno and Miriam; later on, Bruno and Anne, and her sister, and her father. Are we all strangers in the way Bruno is a stranger, at least until a point in life when we accept the social contract and know how and where to fit in? Guy is trying to renegotiate his social contract—until Miriam's death an apparently hopeless cause. To play at reality, as the little "cowpoke" is playing, is to work through the limits of one's experience in learning social fit, since navigating the potentially treacherous straits between seriousness and play is a skill not typically mastered by children.

Why, indeed, the fairground and the island, although Highsmith had them as well? She had much else that Hitchcock discarded; and there is much that he brought in—since he never regarded his source material as anything but a skeleton upon which to construct the story he wanted to build for his own reasons. The fairground to bring in the merry-go-round, its charming but also noxious tune, and the giddy peri-urban space in which crowds of strangers mingled (for happiness, or not?) in the nightworld—Wheeler Winston Dixon refers to a "domain of perdition poorly lit and eerily inescapable" (43)—where the daytime economy dissolves into darkness. The fairground to provide the dark lake and the Island of Lost Souls, too. If the Tunnel of Love replicates the erotic, a sense of penetration, a cavern of pleasure, it throbs in its inwardness with potential and friction. The self and the other; the self and the shadow on the wall; the present moment and the moment as desired or craved. But the island—the island is beyond eroticism, a place of finalities. Beyond this place, no adventure happens, no space opens. We are to imagine, I believe, crowds of teenagers absorbed in necking, petting, perhaps intercourse beneath these indistinct bushes. Final accomplishments, in a zone of mortal contact. The silence creates distance from civilization (the American frontier, at a far remove from forces of law and order). Bruno escapes by stepping softly into his boat and throwing it into reverse; silently, efficiently, darkly backing it out, turning, and heading across the water, an Angel of Death now reconfigured into his everyday identity as a typical-looking man with an empty face, a face no one feels the need to remember.

MRS. CUNNINGHAM

Anne Morton's august father is throwing a soirée—which is to say, a political negotiation dressed up like a night club—and the single-minded Bruno has wormed his way in. "The characteristic Hitchcockian moral tone," notes Robin Wood, "is felt in all its disturbing complexity" (99). Here the dignified and bejeweled of Washington society gather in a fog of empty conversation, soothed and spiced by food and liquor they needn't pay for, facing each other with rigid rictuses of sweetness and propriety. A central dramaturgical point of the scene is to present the always-scouting Barbara with a concrete display of Bruno's aggression, so that she will be chilled enough to confide to her sister and in this way bring the questionable relationship between Guy and his "friend" into focus for more serious investigation. But before this display can be grounded—Hitchcock always grounds his dramatic moments in an architecture—the viewer must note how "high society" functions when it is cloistered to itself "backstage," there being no better place to get away from public scrutiny and hide with others of one's class, in Washington at least, than a senator's private residence, at night, in an invited crowd.

Aside from Anne and Barbara, the women are all married, chained by gold and diamonds to the men who banter about law and order (easily, as though neither applied to them). Indeed, the women at this soirée are notably facile. They have each hooked an aging husband guaranteed to ensure a lucrative lifestyle, and possess no obligation other than "wifeliness," whatever that can be construed to be as, moment by moment, they show teeth and pretend loyalty. These are "successful" women of their time, the ones at the top of the Washington totem pole, each having captured her prince in the way that Anne has been planning to capture Guy (to his manifest delight and relief). A critical view of their sort was provided openly by Cousin Charlie (Joseph Cotten) in *Shadow of a Doubt* (1943), a man who killed off widows seriatim because they had vitiated their husbands' lives and leached their fortunes; his inheritor has come to the party tonight, and will show himself soon. But to give them credit, let us take a second look at the glittering wives on display here. What do they reflect—that Hitchcock can show them reflecting—about America of the time?

That America, Hitchcock's soon-to-be-adopted home (he took the oath of citizenship in 1955, during production of *The Man Who Knew Too Much* [1956]), was certainly a culture of distinctive class separation and social cloistering, where, as David Halberstam notes, "People took care of their own" (245). The classes hung together. If one didn't bump into "others," in a mobile world where strangers collided, one bonded with those who resembled the figure in the mirror. Regarding the cloister, Halberstam quotes John Keats, who points out how at the newly created Levittown the house next door was "inhabited by people whose age, income, number of children, problems, habits, conversations, dress, possessions, perhaps even blood types are almost precisely like yours.... [These houses] actually drive mad myriads of housewives shut up in them" (139); and goes on to adduce Ron Rosenberg's observation that Don Siegel's *Invasion of the Body Snatchers* (1956) seemed a metaphor for American middle-class life: people "could be taken over by alien vegetable pods—*and no one would know the difference*" (140; emphasis original).

In this environment of more or less hermetic isolation, identity was shaped and controlled, in all social classes, through the agencies of advertising and public imagery. And in advertising and public imagery, there loomed what we now sharply discern—but what was then less dramatically felt—as a gender gap. Nowadays it is commonplace, regardless of one's personal opinions on the matter, to express understanding of the systematic arrangements that keep women largely confined and repressed in a male-dominated world. Indeed, since the pattern of male domination is no longer considered either new or shocking, the lethargy with which women's structural inequality has been successfully addressed does seem deplorable. In the 1950s, however, many a woman typically married in order to preserve her aspirations for status in society, and once married took on the status attributes of her husband. Max Lerner observes this general—and generally unbalanced—pursuit of happiness:

> For the woman it is likely to lie in a home, children, and social status, for in the woman's case—far more than in the man's—marriage is the determiner of status. For the male the impulse to marriage is not—as Freud suggested, with his eye on the European social structure—to emulate the image of the father's family authority. For the American male it is rather the desire to be part of a family which is a going social unit, with a wife who is a good homemaker, a good mother, a good hostess, and wears clothes well; and on her part, with a husband who has a good job, is respected in the community, is a good father, and has a circle of friends with whom the couple can "spend the evening." (593–94)

The wife wants—Lerner writes—"an adventurous and exciting life, but another voice tells her that she lives in a culture where few women can make a go of it on their own, and where therefore she must find the marriageable male who will invest her with security and status. As for the city girl, especially in the minority ethnic groups, she too is encased in a protective armor of what is 'expected' of her" (600). Nineteen fifty-one America was a world in which "what women become is ... largely what they are expected to become by the standards of a culture in which the male is held to be the prized quarry and the female the lucky or luckless hunter" (609).

It was not for a dozen years after the release of *Strangers on a Train* that Betty Friedan picked up in *The Feminine Mystique* the strains of a critical melody Simone de Beauvoir had sung out in France in the late 1940s, herself reflecting on American popular thought of the 1930s (as we can hear echoed by Cavell). If more or less repressed in American popular thought by the 1950s, this melody was evocative and plangent: "It is only in marriage that the mother is glorified—in other words, as long as she is subordinate to her husband" (de Beauvoir 569). "According to the common wisdom of the time," writes Elaine Tyler May, looking back, " 'normal' heterosexual behavior culminating in marriage represented 'maturity' and 'responsibility'; therefore, those who were 'deviant' were, by definition, irresponsible, immature, and weak. It followed that men who were slaves to their passions could easily be duped by seductive women who worked for the communists. Even worse were the 'perverts,' who had no masculine backbone" (91). The *grandes dames* of Washington's high society at mid-century, wrapped in glitter and silk, coiffed like queens, with their noses climbing above one another's in the perfumed air, were, like "aristocratic" women everywhere, merely posing as royalty. In reality they were trapped in the convention of subordination, albeit swimming in lucre. For a moment's fascination and reverie, any suitably dignified-looking man, young or old, might seem pleasurably dominant, might give them license for playing out the gracile passivity their ubiquitous social depreciation demanded. The husbands received what Halberstam calls "an extra receipt for their money in the form of visible prestige marking" (127).

Enter Mrs. Cunningham. Seated on a divan in rapt (but empty) conversation with the wife of a judge—who stands clasping her leash not far away, jawing professionally with another jawing professional—this hefty and marvelously shiny matron is a fountainhead of curiosity, attentiveness, perspicacity: a character lifted, indeed, from the world of Henry James (at least as she would love to believe). It is important to her to collect facts and opinions, but she lacks the intelligence to arrange them into shapes. In short, for all her twinkle, she is dull. We find her discussing—if that is the word—various means of committing murder, in this way positioning herself as a total abstraction against the somewhat more practical background of Bruno's plot, and Bruno, abstraction of abstractions, has insinuated himself into the sphere of her notice. He's got a much better method than any she has considered, and offers to make a little demonstration. "Do you mind?" reaching out for her alabaster neck with his long fingers. "Oh," giggling conspiratorially, "No . . .!" A broad grin of titillation and adventure, as though finally, finally, a window has been opened into her stuffy cell and she can smell fresh air. He is upon her, and she is smiling the gratitude of the newly educated.

But soon, very soon, the fingers have closed into a lock and a look of vague absence has begun to shade the lovely lady's glow. A miniscule whimper creeps out. Across the room, Barbara is witness to this miracle, and as he performs it the out-of-control Bruno—some muscular spasm has overtaken him—is staring back at her. The light shines in the thick lenses of her eyeglasses (this girl who has a crush on Guy is a duplicate of his wife, especially now as she watches killing through lenses like the ones that showed us Miriam's death!). The light glitters with promise, and doubly, twin flames from a cigarette lighter held up to a face back on an island long, long ago. Back to Mrs. Cunningham, now, pitiably, very close to death, with the crowd, gathered around for the side show, shuffling to break in and terminate the music. (All this continuity and sudden discontinuity of artful performance will be replicated to much greater effect in *The Man Who Knew Too Much*). Bruno, in a faint, is carried off to a back room where Guy confronts him under the watchful, now suspicious eyes of the senator. The thug is escorted out, but he has made his point, and with an elaborate drama: direct evidence of physical strength and overwhelming passion, a little show revealing details of an earlier little show; but also a staging to catch the eye of a Morton, if not Guy's girl then her overly observant younger sister. "He was staring *at me!*" The family is now deftly implicated, and Guy's hopes to be adopted by them put at risk. All this by way of action carried out upon an extreme innocent of sorts: innocent broadly because, unable to fathom murder in the real world, she gaily submitted to what she took to be a parlor game, when her very life was at stake; yet innocent only to a degree, because our dear Mrs. Cunningham has of course been debating the best way to commit murder, not a very proper subject of conversation for a genteel lady at a soirée like this. Or is it?

Because only moments before, as we eavesdropped on the judge's conversation, we learned of his hard-line, even brutal, approach to capital punishment; his entirely sociable willingness to order institutionalized murder in the name of principles, perhaps the greatest abstraction of all.

Mrs. Cunningham, at any rate, has almost been a sacrifice, and is lucky to have escaped with her life, although she is too far gone to know that. And Bruno's malevolence has picked up a new undertone: that the loss of his perception of boundaries is occasioned by something interior and intractable. It wasn't exactly through his will that the little "demonstration" with Mrs. Cunningham subtly and indecipherably became real, the "game" a non-game, or that his two-man "contest" with Guy became real, too. The film is rich with demonstrations of Bruno's boundary trouble, a manifestation, too, of *our* boundary trouble, our incapacity to keep step with boundaries: from the pressing, too inquisitive interrogation of Guy's personal life on the train to Bruno's redefinition of a little boy's playfulness with a balloon and his own performance at the Test of Strength (where he smashes down so hard with the hammer that the weight, flying up into the jet-black sky, almost sails off its runners). He is a creature without proportion, posed against Guy, a creature trapped in proportion: championship tennis, after all, is a continuing chain of swift and determinate proportion challenges: where exactly will the ball be inside the rectangle, how to strike back to place it just where one wants it to fall? Indeed, Bruno's distinctive alienation is articulated in a much-celebrated shot—some think of it as a purely Hitchcockian shot, but all of Hitchcock's shots are purely Hitchcockian—where at a practice game the tennis audience swings its head right, left, right, left, right, left at a volley, with one single body sitting stationary and unconcerned in the middle: Bruno, for whom the proportion of rule-bound action is no matter.

The entirely well-proportioned Mrs. Cunningham was played by Norma Varden (1898–1989), a former virtuoso pianist turned character actor, whose screen career was long and auspicious. She specialized in playing sympathetic ninnies, such as the wife of a pickpocketed tourist early on in *Casablanca* (1942), and had roles small and not so small, often uncredited, in more than a hundred and fifty films and television programs, including *The Secret Garden* (1949), *National Velvet* (1944), *Random Harvest* (1942), *The Major and the Minor* (1942), *Gentlemen Prefer Blondes* (1953), *Three Coins in the Fountain* (1954), *Witness for the Prosecution* (1957), *The Sound of Music* (1965), and *Doctor Doolittle* (1967). Her work in *Strangers*, which was to her an extreme delight—"You're *still* my favourite director, even though I haven't worked for you since 'Strangers on a Train,'" she wrote Hitchcock in 1964—nicely evidences a broader Hitchcockian concern to employ, even for the tiniest of moments, the very most accomplished of performers (see Pomerance, "Two Bits"), whose solid work would swiftly gain the necessary weight.

OUT OF BOUNDS

Bruno's failure to tolerate, or to recognize, the boundaries other people carefully observe raises the fundamental question of perception and acuity, normal perception and normal acuity that discerns borderlines, diligently respects them, keeps this on this side of the line and that on that. We gamble our social order on other people's propensity to see the delicate tissues of division: social boundaries of propriety and class, boundaries of common etiquette, boundaries of privacy, boundaries of placement and setting. Indeed,

Bruno's dream-based insanity, in raising normative rational calculation to view, finally questions our proprieties, undercuts our clearcut distinctions. Organized life is shown to be a waking nightmare, by comparison with the fabular, slippery phantasmagorium Bruno inhabits. On the train he positions himself, perhaps, a little too close to Guy, closer than "normal" people would. "At intimate distance," writes Edward T. Hall,

> the presence of the other person is unmistakable and may at times be overwhelming because of the greatly stepped-up sensory inputs. Sight (often distorted), olfaction, heat from the other person's body, sound, smell, and feel of the breath all combine to signal unmistakable involvement with another body. (116)

Bruno intrudes both his body and his purpose into the most private spaces of Guy's life. Nor does he seem to require what so many depend on, boundaries for establishing recognition, and perhaps this is inherited: in her painting, that he has no trouble deciphering, his mother has overlapping and interpenetrating swirls, a marked absence of the boundary that divides form from form, space from space. Guy, by contrast, lives on the boundary line: juggling his marriage to Miriam against his exciting love affair with Anne, struggling from small-town insignificance to high-society fame like a tennis ball grazing the top edge of a net. And Guy is serious as he plays tennis, where one must see, be concerned about, and navigate around the lines; Bruno doesn't take lines seriously at all. That a tennis match with Bruno would be excruciating torture is an idea subtly invoked by Hitchcock but also an idea absent from the source novel: the tennis trope implicates Bruno's lack and Guy's obsession in a tight bond.

If for Bruno Antony life is *the* game, the only game and an unbounded game, Guy Haines has been given every opportunity to notice this unbounding consciousness. And about Guy we must know something more: he is an exceptionally competitive type. If for his new "friend" the world is a kind of amorphous mess, for him it is a ladder of success, on which definitively different forms and shapes are locked in a struggle for dominance. Bruno has even drawn attention to Guy's competitive athleticism, as noted in the newspaper—Guy, the *high-ranked* amateur who will be *playing at Forest Hills*. We have reason to be prepared for the viciously exertive, uncompromising competitor he will become on the court there. Bruno's train compartment can be understood by Guy as another game board, rich with points to be achieved and penalties to be avoided. So, on goes the game face, Guy's serious no-nonsense face (the one we will see later on the tennis court, perspiring, devilishly focused), as he says, "Sure, Bruno. Sure," in the stunning, straightforward manner of a man easily returning a serve. Whatever you can say, Bruno, I can say back—and better. If you can play, I can play. But again: *with no recognition that the wounded Bruno does not think of himself as a player.*

Indeed, he is willing to flaunt the social niceties that ordinary civilians undertake routinely, the proprieties of organized life. There is a stunning moment immediately after he murders Miriam. Having walked back through the amusement park and exited through the gate, he comes to the road where the bus dropped him off. As he is about to cross he sees at his side a blind man standing with his white stick. Graciously—as would seem to any passerby—he takes the man's arm and guides him across the road, gently, gently: this is one of the rules of good behavior children all learn in school, and here is Bruno, the "normal, well-behaved citizen," using a show of helpfulness to give him cover in his flight.

It is mortifying to Guy to learn that Miriam has indeed been slain, slain *for real*. And the cake of mortification is iced when Bruno admits to the killing (in the deep shadows of a wrought iron gate across the road from the Morton residence: another dream setting, with Underworld shadows streaking across faces). Not only must he acknowledge that Bruno wasn't merely making talk, Guy must grasp how Bruno may have seriously interpreted his unserious "assent": not as a bounded, hyperbolic, make-believe iteration, a pleasantry, a wisp of small talk, but as a commitment. For Guy, every moment must be taken as a game moment or a non-game moment, and his definition of his own obligations and structuring of his own comportment follow that division. He cannot fathom how the world could be otherwise; how, for Bruno, there might *not* be a difference between the idea of killing Miriam and killing her in fact. Guy's deep-seated competitiveness (belief in the idea that he can climb), his ability to so neatly model the modern urban predispositions toward rapid movement and social mobility, accounts for his volleying with Bruno in the train compartment. But here he has entered a championship match with daunting stakes.

Daunting because in working to ascend into the Morton family, Guy must learn new protocols, and failure might be catastrophic. The "tennis match" with Bruno, which is the essence of the film's plot (only miniaturized in the actual tennis match sequence), is, in effect, Guy's confrontation with his own confrontational personality. Bruno shows him what competition is all about, but without recognizing himself doing this: since for Bruno it's all a delicious entanglement, a smearing, that urges him forward from felt moment to felt moment (as in a Tunnel of Love, or as in riding a train) with no absolutely predictable outcome.

A DREAM LIFE

Might Hitchcock's Bruno Antony be living a dream life?

In dream consciousness, dream space, dream experience—the oneiric, the remembered, the imagined, the disconfigured—situations are to be penetrated, not mapped. Spaces with all their dream plasticity are for dwelling and meditating, and traversing them is magical, not navigational. Experience and touch conjoin, so that the personality of the dream-other is to be tickled and petted, even caressed, but not decoded. The past and the present merge, as with Bruno's easy sporting of the necktie gifted by his mother (suggesting her continuing presence around him, and his continuing presence within her), or his easy gathering up of Guy's cigarette lighter as token and jewel. The amusement park sequence is pungently set as a waking dream, the high contrast between gaudy lights and chilling darkness flaunted in every shot. Bruno's movement forward there seems somnambulistic (as is our experience in train rides, where we sense movement and placement together): through the gate, to the shooting stand with the ice-cream, to the little boy, to the Test of Strength, to the dark lake. The silent, gliding, nongravitational movement of his motorcraft across the waters after Miriam, giggling with her friends. The echoing, trembling Tunnel. The mysterious island. The silent return to the motor craft, its silently reversing from the island, the silent sweep across the lake, the quiet exit of the man in his nappy fedora.

Guy, glorious and promising, is Bruno's dream hero. Guy and Miriam are his nightmare couple, Guy and Anne his pure fantasy (as much as Guy's). Bruno's life with his parents is, and was, nothing but *cauchemar*. In the tennis volley scene, what can it be that solitary Bruno dreams as he stares forward into dream space, munching his popcorn? What past horror conjoined to what hope for the future now embeds itself in his dream of the moment? One easily imagines a very small Bruno with a pistol and a balloon; and an irritated cigarette-toting father. Even the Antony mansion is a dreamworld, its vast lawns seen by night as Guy approaches to warn Bruno's father about his malevolent son; the shadowy neo-Gothic interior; that wholly morphed Great Dane, dark as Cerberus, not exactly unfriendly yet also menacing, and padding along, thanks to Hitchcock's, cinematographer Robert Burks's, and optical printer Hans Koenekamp's concoction, in slight slow-motion as we see his huge maw nearing Guy's delicate hand.

The recursive culminating tennis match at Forest Hills (that Guy must play swiftly, if he is to race away and bring himself to Metcalf before Bruno has had opportunity to place the cigarette lighter that could pin him to the crime): no less an authority than Rudyard Kipling—he of *The Jungle Book*—is called upon to authenticate the deep structure of its involvement in the film. As we make entrance to the stadium, a high banner flags our attention. "And treat those two imposters just the same," we read; but the entire quotation, from the poem "If," reads like this: "If you can meet with Triumph and Disaster / And treat those two impostors just the same / If you can bear to hear the truth you've spoken / Twisted by knaves to make a trap for fools . . . ." The text bears upon Guy's experience of Bruno, his life as warped and strained by Bruno's action, but the presence in the film of these words strapped in the air at the stadium indicates Hitchcock referring to a game that is acknowledged as such, to "two impostors" pretending themselves in battle when in truth they are only playing at it, not fighting for real. The game "battle" will have an ending, a boundary. There will be an exit into daylight (as with the moviegoing audience, who will find their way into the street). The Hitchcockian position is thus, finally, Guy's position, at least in terms of recognizing when by one's actions one intends to signal a deed instead of doing one.

SPINNING OUT

And at last, the optically elaborate finale. Guy has followed Bruno to the amusement park. It is again night, with the lights asparkle and the merry-go-round broadcasting "And the Band Played On" as if it is the only song in the universe, and a very profound song, too. (In this place, a capitalist microcosm, every night is the same, every gesture a routine, every transaction aimed at profit—as with film projection in the theater. And, too, as in Rilke, "here is no place / that does not see you.") Close behind Guy are his police minders, whom he elided at the tennis court; and nearby them is Capt. Turley of the local constabulary (Howard St. John), with a sidekick. Bruno has lined up for the Tunnel of Love ride, and we see him in half-shadow. As he moves into a bubble of light the boat manager (Murray Alper) notices, appears to remember: the tell-tale necktie, perhaps, or the penetrating obscurity of the gaze under that fedora. He turns to inform the cops. But Bruno flees, and standing adjacent the merry-go-round Guy calls out his name and races after. They are on the spinning device as it whirls—"His brain was so loaded it nearly exploded / The poor girl would shake with alarm"— and a uniformed cop, thinking Guy the culprit he's been after, takes a few shots, one of which plugs the carousel operator who is poised in the center at the gears.—

   An indiscriminate figure, the operator of a whirling universe, poised in the center of its mechanism or its spirit. Gears of the universe. Operator at the center. A stray bullet taking him out. Is this the death of God?

   —As the operator falls he yanks off the brake and the machine speeds up. It has now been transmogrified into a diabolical instrument, spinning at high velocity with tiny boys and girls clinging to their horses for life. Bruno and Guy are fist-fighting. A mother on the sidelines screams, "My boy! My boy!" at which Hitchcock cuts to her little tyke, getting the kick of his life on his steed. This particular kid gets into the brawl, too, slamming Guy with a fist from behind as Bruno hits from the front. (Anybody, that is, might think Guy the villain.) A swift cut-in of Bruno's point of view, as the outside world blurs past in a culminating rendition of panoramic perception, a colossal *coup d'oeil*. Bruno is a man for whom the grounding perspective of order—call it divine order or natural order, it remains order—has (long) been lost, for whom the universe is always a blur. Guy and Bruno are on the floor, a horse's "hooves" slamming down on Guy's head. Bruno knocks the little boy away (oblivious that there are "teams" here, and the little fellow is on his team), but Guy saves him from flying off and tucks him into a pair of seats. Now Bruno is kicking at Guy: with Guy clinging desperately to a metal pole he aims his foot at Guy's hand (a precursor of Leonard's move to step on Roger's hand in the finale of *North by Northwest*).

Who will bring tranquility to this chaos?

The answer is a tiny old laborer (Harry Hines), one of the untold masses who keep the machines of our society lubricated and on the go. He has stepped up courageously and, throwing himself to the ground, begun to crawl beneath the spinning structure to reach its center, where he can stand up and pull the brakes. He succeeds (Hitchcock shot this without effects, and later, to Truffaut in interview, sincerely regretted putting the man's life in jeopardy: "If he'd raised his head by an inch, he'd have been killed. I'd never do anything like that again" [197]). But because the carousel grinds so abruptly and furiously to a stop, it is wrenched off its gears, crashes spectacularly, and, in a silent, smoky, cacophonous wreck (filmed with masterful rear projection), collapses in a heap. Bruno is trapped beneath the rubble. Turley, Guy, and the boat manager stand together, three characters out of Shakespeare:

> POLICEMAN (indicating Guy): Capt. Turley, he says this isn't the man we want. It's the one he was fighting with.
> TURLEY: What do you mean...? Not Haines?! But you said he was! You pointed him out!
> BOAT MANAGER: No, I didn't sir. I've never seen this man before in my life. I meant the other one.
> TURLEY: What's this all about, Haines?
> GUY: He has my cigarette lighter. He wanted to plant it... there on the island... to pin the whole thing on me. Let me talk to him. Let me show you. Where is he?
> VOICE *(off)*: Over here.

* * *

> POLICEMAN: He's in a very bad way, Mr. Turley.
> GUY: Can't you get that stuff off of him?
> POLICEMAN: No, I don't think they can until the crane comes.

* * *

BRUNO: Hello, Guy. Who is this?

GUY: This is Mr. Turley, the chief of police.

BRUNO *(working to produce a smile)*: Ohhhh, they ... they got you at last, huh, Guy?

GUY: Bruno, can you talk a little? Can you tell the chief you have my lighter?

BRUNO: I haven't got it. It's on the island where you left it.

GUY: Bruno, don't keep it up, not at a time like this.

BRUNO: I'm ... I'm sorry, Guy. I ... I want to help you, but I don't know what I could do.

GUY: Captain Turley, look—can't I go through his pockets?

TURLEY: No, Haines, of course you can't. Besides, he says he hasn't got it.

VOICE *(off)*: I think he's dying.

GUY: He's finished. *(Bruno's hand opens.)*

Bruno's hand opens, not Bruno opens his hand. Shall we think that this charming villain, in a final moment of lone reconciliation, makes acknowledgment, finally, that he understands it was all (only) a game, and renounces the self who was playing: does he adopt a new footing? Or does he continue to his very end as the Bruno we have come (too well) to know, the man for whom games do not exist as such, are not, as it were, parenthetical? What Hitchcock shows us is very exact: the instant of expiration and the hand slowly opening, as though not Bruno but some force beyond him has pried the fist apart, has made a final peace. Is God not vanquished at all, then, and has He opened the dead man's hand to reveal the lighter, shining with truth? Some beneficent force has certainly returned to the Center. Guy, at least, is redeemed.

STRANGERS ON TRAINS

Bruno is only one of the strangers met by train in this film, one hieroglyph emerging from a coherent underlying language that pertains to railway transit, modern experience, and unfamiliarity. While her killer was busy on the island strangling Miriam, we found ourselves riding in another lounge car with the never-less-than-charming Guy, now wrapped in conversation with a mathematics professor on his way home from a guest lecture (John Brown). Here is a chummy, entirely proper chat with a gentleman who makes not the slightest attempt to penetrate the mask of Guy's social life, or to permit penetration of his own. Call this modern friendship, the accommodation people happily make for one another when they are trapped in motion through an impersonal system structured to benefit the multitudes. Superficial, pleasant expressions of (insincere) mutual interest, language with no private reference and therefore no direct contact with the inward, dreamy mysteries of an individual's experience. Soon afterward, this man will be brought to police headquarters as the sole witness to Guy's claim that he could not have been at the amusement park that night; but having drunk far too much and been (as Barbara puts it) "blotto" through the whole encounter the professor is without memory and entirely useless. More evidence of the modern situation: that a conversation, clear and charming as it may seem, can have no solid existence in fact. The impression of civil relations is no guarantee. "Civility" has become inherently uncivil, unsupportive, apolitical.

The importance of this professorial tête-à-tête cannot be overstressed, because although for Hitchcock's design of a mechanism that could implicate Guy—through its absolute failure to indemnify him—it was necessary to show an encounter with such a character as Prof. Collins, nothing was to be gained from setting the encounter on a train. A bus stop would have worked, and been cheaper to film. The point for Hitchcock was not only the hopeless witness but the train as his environment. Once again a moment where Guy can be in a public space, heading forward to a destination he cannot see, and strike up a conversation with a man he hasn't previously met and will probably (he assumes) never see again: a "civil" gab. Once again the pressure of strangeness, the challenge of unfamiliarity that sparks, rather than silence, a peculiar form of talk, as in Kenneth Burke's nightmare vision:

> Always the Eternal Enigma is there, right on the edges of our metropolitan bickerings, stretching outward to interstellar infinity and inward to the depths of the mind. And in this staggering disproportion between man and no-man, there is no place for purely human boasts of grandeur, or for forgetting that men build their cultures by huddling together, nervously loquacious, at the edge of an abyss. (272)

In light of this generalized "huddling," we can see that Bruno Antony is a figure of opposition, not bonding. The modern world is at best a source of laughter for him (his reaction to his mother's painting) and at worst a jungle of monstrosities: a tiny child shooting one in the face, a married woman going off with teenaged boys, a society matron giddily offering her neck to a strange young man, an athletic hero with an insatiable hunger for the heights of fame, a blind man one can utilize as a shield. Is it a wonder, then, that he has pulled himself away to live in a reverie? That in his final moments he seeks refuge among children on a merry-go-round, and among carnival folk, those who carry forward into contemporary life the entertainments, chills, and delights of the long-lost middle ages?

Hitchcock's finales tend to be punch lines in the most dramatic sense. While he appended a brief scene for the British release, in which Guy "learns his lesson" and finally rejects yet a third stranger's attempt to meet him on a train, the American ending is more powerfully, more chillingly revealing. We are in the Morton sitting room as Anne takes the telephone call from Guy that brings her the relieving news. Barbara, typically, is by her side, eager to be woven in. As the screen fades, we see Anne's pleased smile as she reports, "He says he looks silly in tennis clothes." Guy was in a blazer and whites at the amusement park, because in dashing off from Forest Hills, with the conspiratorial assistance of Anne and Barbara, he couldn't do a full change of clothing. But his final comment, conveyed through the high-toned voice of the girl from above his station, seals for her his propriety and self-possession, whilst we, perhaps slightly more critical, may be given ample cause to wonder. He did look happy in his blazer, after all: handsome, well-fitted, somewhat posh. Why should he fret? Because as a costume it was all wrong for the place and time; just as, when first we encountered him, Guy was wholly right, striding toward his train in perfectly dapper tweeds. He is a person whose principal concern is calculated appearance, not trust; the self as projection, not sensibility. Anne is such a person, too, which is why she's tickled, not alarmed, by his comment. Because he's committed to seemliness just as much as she is, they are, already, a perfect match.

CHAPTER TWO

DON'T LOOK NOW

Rear Window

> We are bored when we don't know
> what we are waiting for.
> —Walter Benjamin, *The Arcades Project*

PEEPERS

In 1953, when Alfred Hitchcock was mulling over his *Rear Window* project with screenwriter John Michael Hayes, thinking about fashioning "a real index of individual behavior" (qtd. in McGilligan 480) in urban life by considering the phenomenon of neighbors watching one another, all the while maintaining emotional and cultural ties to the United Kingdom (Dover sole air-freighted regularly from London), a shocking and influential architectural revolution was underway in his homeland. For the British, vestiges of rationing had been stubbornly persisting. That the war victory (Churchill's triumph) failed markedly to deliver the utopia of which many had dreamed (Churchill's failure) had led to the election of Clement Attlee's Labour government, which soon proved notably less than utopian. After several contentious years, while it succeeded in nationalizing a number of industries (like coal) and instituted the National Health Service (in 1949),

Labour finally succumbed to Churchill's conservatives again, whose project it now was to revamp the nation's infrastructure and promote a shining future. A queen was crowned (2 June 1953), symbol of continuity and loyal allegiance, and also youthful and charming. Urban and suburban development—rebuilding after wartime destruction—remained high priorities, notably in the much-bombed city of Coventry. And in this context of bold optimism and vituperative cleansing, the New Brutalists, charging forward in the wake of Le Corbusier and championed by Durham graduates Alison and Peter Smithson, were projecting an unconventional way of life, one that left the terrace residence behind and argued for what in the United States would have been called apartment blocks, "vertical living."

David Kynaston quotes architectural historian Mark Girouard's assessment of Alison Smithson, "opinionated, outrageous, convinced of her own and her husband's importance" (279). While the Smithsons realized "the importance of the street and the community to their architectural projects" (a dying Labour ideal), what they wanted to build were "streets in the sky" (279). Here were just a few of the Smithson tenets, avowed in an essay on "Urban Reidentification" that Kynaston excerpts:

> Decks would be places, not corridors or balconies: thoroughfares where there are "shops," post boxes, telephone kiosks.
> Where a deck is purely residential the individual house and yard-garden will provide an equivalent life pattern to a true street or square; nothing is lost and elevation is gained.

Elevation is gained!: we can see the angels ascending. One of the Smithsons' conclusions, reflecting upon the traditional low-income terrace housing it was these magicians' brave intention to make disappear, provides a

59

stimulating foundation for Hitchcock's film: "You might argue that the back garden and front pocket handkerchief are necessary to look out on. *But what fills the windows of your day rooms is the houses opposite and the backs behind.* Do you really think this is a sustaining prospect?" (279; my emphasis). Everyone wants a vista, in short; but what sort of a vista did many civilians really have?

City dwellers were powerfully disenchanted with the prospect of suburban living. Kynaston quotes William Howell: "We wouldn't want to go and live there because everything from the bright lights to the art galleries, the continental restaurants, in short 'life,' the thing one goes to the city for . . . didn't seem to be happening out in the suburbs," and, he goes on, the Smithsons "fully shared these sentiments, but with of course the 'streets-in-the-sky' twist that made them an unlikely, ultimately unwelcome ally . . . in the cause of urban 'community'" (343). In New York City, as dense an urban environment as can be found, at least in the West, the cramped abutment of buildings was merciless, and therefore the proximity of residents to strangers around them was exacerbated. What typically results in apartment living—I write as someone intimately familiar with it, from earliest childhood on—is a systematic withdrawal from pleasing gardens and reposeful stoops, a pulling of vision and consciousness inward to a private and restricted domain optimistically imagined—yet only imagined—as spacious. Vision-in replaced vision-out, a development of early modern urban arrangements (discussed by Walter Benjamin and commented upon by Tom Gunning) whereby through certain particular devices and applications, images of the outside world were infolded as part of a décor valorized as personally expressive, protective, and nourishing. The feeling for the immediate surround, Gunning suggests,

> responds to an essential division on which the experience of the bourgeois society is founded, the creation of the interior as a radical separation from the exterior, as a home in which the bourgeois can dwell and dream undisturbed by the noise, activity, and threats of the street, the space of the masses and of production, a private individual divorced from the community. A cocoon of consumption, the *intérieur* becomes "not just the universe of the private individual; it is also his *étui*" (*Arcades Project* 20). ("Exterior" 106)

To say that the *extérieure* became a part of home decoration, however fragmentary—Gunning quotes Theodor Adorno's observation that the window mirror "allows the exterior to enter the room 'only [as] the semblance of things'" (107)—is not to claim that apartment dwellers felt the liberty or obligation to take in all of what was out there, to concentrate on their neighbors' lives and circumstances, for instance, as they did on their own. The "good fences" that "make good neighbors," in Robert Frost's phrase, were now both optical and principled. The idea of respectful privacy took precedence over curiosity, minding one's own business over spying, but the world's landscape could be mimicked as design. In an early scene in *Rear Window*, this theme is massaged into us, briefly but pungently, by Stella (Thelma Ritter), a trained nurse on a moral crusade against Peeping Tomism (which originated, ironically as may seem, in Coventry).

Privacy reigned, then, at least as a matter of principle. An ethic of civil etiquette prohibited the overly curious from "peeping" into the lives of neighbors, since in the back-to-back apartment complex, everyone was equally vulnerable to such spying: peepers could be peeped at. Privacy might be nothing but a blind hope or a low fiction, an idea, like a raft in the sea, to which those clung who had no reasonable expectation, at apartment-rental rates, of maintaining a discrete individualized existence. Popular dramatizations of the early 1950s, such as CBS's *The Goldbergs* (1949–1957), *The Amos 'n Andy Show* (1951–1953), or *I Remember Mama* (1948–1957), or Paramount Television's *The Honeymooners* (1955–1956), openly staged and drew attention to—yet framed as light entertainment, not moral precept—neighbors' awareness of, and opinion about, each other's lives in apartment complexes. To borrow from Adorno, as information if not as visions fragments of the outside world could be drawn into the *intérieur* to serve as décor, and such fragments could be constituted by nothing less than other people's actual daily lives if they were dramatic enough. People are interesting to people. Or, as Bob Merrill put it, perhaps with the deep lessons of *Rear Window* in mind, "People who need people / Are the luckiest people in the world." Benjamin acutely asks, "Why does the glance into an unknown window always find a family at a meal, or else a solitary man, seated at a table under a hanging lamp, occupied with some obscure niggling thing?" (218). What facets of action and personality that could be seen of other people nourished observers as much as they entertained, and ultimately gave basis for self-measurement in the modern hunt for success at any price. Any other person's life would in some respects resemble one's own, but the similarities and small differences were vital to politely espy and seriously think about. Benjamin continues that there is something age-old to be recognized in the dwelling, which is to say someone else's dwelling, "the image of that abode of the human being in the maternal womb" (220). In *Rear Window*, this is certainly the state of affairs for our protagonist, L. B. "Jeff" Jefferies (James Stewart), a man intimately and eagerly attached to the world outside his window, but who, because of his odd medical condition, has been quarantined inside the cell of his own isolation.

Worthy of note is a Hitchcockian innovation in this film, as regards the depiction of apartment dwellers' perduring observation of others. In the television programs I have mentioned, and in various *film noir* treatments of the same issue—Boris Ingster's *Stranger on the Third Floor* (1940) is one good example—the watcher's obsessive observation and detection are played out in direct interactional terms. Typically, neighbors make appearances and are treated by protagonists, openly in the story, as if their deepest secrets have already, somehow, become shared knowledge. On *I Love Lucy* (1951–1957), for example, the Mertzes (Vivian Vance, William Frawley), in their rhythmic visitations to the Ricardos' apartment, are normatively subject to their friends' predetermined knowledge of their privacies and vice versa: the open fiction is that Ethel and Fred have "no secrets from" Lucy (Lucille Ball) and Ricky (Desi Arnaz) (mostly, of course, from Lucy, since Ricky's psychological absence is the root of his humor), nor do Lucy and Ricky keep background secrets from them. With *The Mystery of the 13th Guest* (1943), William Beaudine, later a noted television director, introduced direct observation in some sequences, but with an unknown personality observing a group of people surreptitiously, and also knowingly, through a peephole device. But while he will cause this peephole technology to reappear in *Psycho* (1960), Hitchcock makes the bold step in *Rear Window* of creating a much wider panorama for spying, and in such a way as to both make fun of his observer, whose intention and personality are fully displayed for us, and chillingly raise the prospect that what goes on in the neighboring lives, to the likes of which one is typically not exposed, may be far less than a happy, storybook drama and certainly exceeds conventional speculation.

To return briefly to the Smithsons' comment: in suggesting that "the back garden and front pocket handkerchief are necessary to look out on," they plainly avow a dream that, at least in the early 1950s, could quite generally have been taken for granted. Not, in Benjaminian terms, that the outside world had its intrinsic value *as a materiel to be incorporated ritually inside the bourgeois interior*, but that the world was so alluring, indeed so charged as an aesthetic field, that any normal person might crave optical access to it, might seek any way of escaping the boring confines of the everyday. We all want windows. Here is the foundation for the dramatic alienation of windowless rooms, their configuration as laboratories (*The Fly* [1958]), sites of arcane (usually evil) manipulation (*Dr. Jekyll and Mr. Hyde* [1920, 1931]), boudoirs for the deeply repressed (*Gaslight* [1944]), horrifying sancta for the victimized (*Panic Room* [2002]). If the outside space commanded attention aesthetically, beyond that the need of the civilian to see the larger world trumped even a fundamental need for living space. But the Smithsons went further as they frowned, "What fills the windows of your day rooms is the houses opposite and the backs behind. Do you really think this is a sustaining prospect?" The "houses opposite and the backs behind"—New York apartment dwellers not infrequently referred to their buildings or apartments as "houses"—vulnerable as they were to peeking, gave opportunity for but a diminished, abbreviated, even snatched pleasure (snapshots). Unmet others in their daily motions would not be subjects of eighteenth- and nineteenth-century-style portraiture, deliberate, carefully considered, and patient. Nor was the vista of their windows a landscape (notwithstanding that in his early twentieth-century paintings of New York's downtown John Sloan had shifted our way of looking at apartment complexes). Configuring his drama in *Rear Window*, therefore, Hitchcock was hearing echoes of the Smithsons but taking an important step beyond: making the rear-window view seem enchanting, gripping, or humorously charming, and, as far as the structure of this filmic exposition went, never for a moment less than ideal.

Ideal, but comforting? Could we say that, with Jeff, looking out we are salved? Notwithstanding that the view through the apartment window was notably less bucolic than a landscape, even if the movement of one's fellow citizens was dramatically engaging there were good sociological reasons for thinking it might also cause alarm: this in a very general sense, regardless of the personalities in play and their individualized worlds of action. Who, after all, could really presume to know, and take for granted, the truths of other people's lives? Given that "it is through the medium of the senses that we perceive our fellow-men," as Georg Simmel wrote in 1908, and that "the sound of the voice and its meaning, perhaps, present the clearest illustration" of our obtaining sense-impressions, it seems true that "the glance in the eye of the other serves not only for me to know the other but also enables him to know me" and that "the expression of the face [is] the first object of vision between man and man" (*Sociology* 356; 357; 358; 359). There is, Simmel teaches, an intimate relation between this "expression of the face" and the "sound of the voice," which results in a radical difference between the sociological attitude of the blind and that of the deaf:

> In general, what we see of a man will be interpreted by what we hear from him, while the opposite is more unusual. Therefore the one who sees, without hearing, is much more perplexed, puzzled, and worried, than the one who hears without seeing. This principle is of great importance in understanding the sociology of the modern city. (360)

We never forget in watching *Rear Window* from Jeff's apartment that he is so far from the people he gazes upon that he cannot hear them; and when he uses his telephoto lens to "bring them closer," enhance his view, get more visual detail, as it were, the tactic does nothing to help him hear. "Perplexed, puzzled, and worried," indeed.

Hitchcock has made an urban thriller, then, a tale of emotional distress in the heart of, and derived from the structure of, an urban core, with a protagonist caught in extended anxiety—Benjamin thinks of the "eternally wakeful, eternally agitated being" (*Arcades* 879)—because unable to hear from the people he sees he cannot really make them out. His rather too calm policeman chum, Tom Doyle (Wendell Corey), blindly listening to his accounts at a distance, quite unable to see what whining Jeff is seeing, remains staid and unalarmed partly because he has professional training and partly because his eyes have not stimulated his curiosity as Jeff's have his. Between the extremes presented by the two men is brave Lisa Carol

Fremont (Grace Kelly), at first as blind as Doyle (because, even at Jeff's side she has not learned yet to look, or even to desire to look) but soon galvanized by her lover and opening her eyes, so that she is as caught up with the vision as Jeff is—though less functionally deaf. Unlike him, Lisa has developed a rich imagination for human interaction, and can use her intuitions to "hear" by way of memory and experience.[1] Her involvement galvanizes us into an active participation, a worrisome engagement with the events at hand.

As to these observers, looking out and dreaming (anticipating) the actions of their strange neighbors, are they not, also, dreaming futures? Let us remember Benjamin on Michelet, "Every epoch quotes the next one" (893).

TROUBLE IN SYNECDOCHE

As *Rear Window* begins, a broad Venetian blind is raised (like a theatrical curtain) to reveal a courtyard backing a cluster of Greenwich Village apartment buildings. With the persistent gaze of the fully curious we track around the inner facades of these structures, picking up a wandering black cat (who will soon dream his way to Nice and appear in *To Catch a Thief*) and, successively, a gaggle of socially and psychologically varied apartment dwellers in the process of living their routinized lives. We find that we are situated inside one particular apartment, from which, with notable ease, we can look out at all the others. The panning, curious camera picks out snazzy black-and-white photographs framed on a wall here (including one taken from the middle of a race track as a dislodged tire comes pummeling toward the photographer) and a pile of cover-shot negative reversals from the at-the-time universally famous *Life* magazine showing the head and shoulders of a striking young woman, before it discovers the dozing body of our hero, his pale pajamas decorously draped over and around a massive leg fracture. The leg is in a pronounced—even over-pronounced—groin-to-toe cast, hoisted onto the footrest of a wheelchair. This is the injured man's apartment, then, and we are tightly enough bound to him, *already*, from even before the moment of our recognition, to be waiting at his side as he sleeps; so tightly bound, indeed, as to pay no heed to our tight binding. He is the photographer who made the shots hanging on the wall. That looming tire was—a fraction of a second after his shutter closed—the cause of this present condition; in his residence he has causation literally frozen and mounted as part of present experience. (Did he earn his credentials as a combat photographer during the war?) Not only figuratively but in truth he risked life and limb—this very limb—to get the shot. A girl very like the girl on the magazine cover will appear soon, and will take on a signal significance.

All this elaboration by camera sums to a virtuosic cadenza, placed, amazingly but also modestly, at the beginning of the work where it might attract but little attention. The accomplishment here is what the French call a *plan séquence*, a single uninterrupted expositional shot that in some way meanders or crawls across a complex territory and reveals, in its movement, numerous significant features of the narrative landscape. Such shots must be carefully planned and rehearsed, as they involve multiple settings of focus, multiple lighting arrangements, the intensively choreographed movement of many performers on various cues, and a grip crew (the people who touch and move the camera) adept at bringing the photographic device through considerable movement of some kind, fluidly and flawlessly. Also, given the length and complexity of the "sequence shot," any tiny error requires retaking the entire thing (a problem Hitchcock had encountered bravely, and mastered, with *Rope* [1948]). "The shot," notes Christopher Beach about *Rear Window*, "involved numerous focus changes, and it required a good deal of planning and many rehearsals. It took ten takes and half a day of shooting to execute the shot to [cinematographer Robert] Burks's satisfaction" (126). At the very end of the film, this hero of ours will find himself back in this very same wheelchair, now with two broken legs and two casts. His girl will be at his side: chum, lover, helpmeet, muse. And the Venetian blind will slowly come down.

What the "leg-cast" brackets of *Rear Window* isolate and highlight is the exposition between them, a tale such as could center and excite any astute observer self-trained at carefully noting action and movement: Jeff the habitual photographer, the audience as habitual moviegoers. He is recuperating through a "busman's holiday," availing himself—as does Hitchcock—of a mobile perch (his wheelchair is a dolly) in order that the fruits of continuing surveillance can be captured. Being laid up, being withdrawn from the action and in no position to gallivant around the world on assignment, Jeff itches to be back in his routine (we hear him grumble during a phone conversation with an editor who has had to replace him on a job). The itch has become physical, too—a back scratcher inserted down the inside of the full-leg cast merely teases, doesn't really help him get at whatever noxious irritation is driving him crazy. His tactic of staring out the window at the facing apartments—an act that is framed as the narrative crux of the film—is really nothing but an outcome of his professional handicap, his forced (relative) immobility, his torturous hunger to watch the human condition again, and the resultant fact that his neighbors' privacy, revealed to his attentions, is the only available fodder for his hungry eyes. More about Jeff and recuperation, soon.

Many scholars have noted, with some humor, that our protagonist is something like a filmgoer, in the sense that the dramas played out all around are visible to him only through window frames, thus composed (and as though staged) within the confines of tiny rectangular "movie screens."[2] Indeed, a number of astute psychoanalytic critiques, based in the principle of scopophilia, have addressed the centrality of Jeff's incessant looking, his controlling gaze: its origins in an existential darkness of sorts and its symptomatic empowerment. Here the gazer is so hungry optically that he appears, in light of this theory, to shape or structure the seen world to conform to his deepest desires: as Anaïs Nin wrote in *Seduction of the Minotaur*, "We don't see things as they are; we see them as we are." Richard Allen goes so far as to intimate that Jeff has "his own darkest impulses toward Lisa" and is thus aligned "imaginatively, with the figure of Lars Thorwald" (169). Scopophilic theory doesn't seek to provide a reasonable alternative to the problematic nature of casting a gaze, to suggest what moviegoers might do in lieu of gazing at the screen. If, indeed, they see only themselves gazing, the film as an entity in its own right quickly disappears. In this way scopophilic theory does away with cinema altogether, at least with the idea of the pro-optic event being dramatic or bearing interest or, for that matter, having any character at all outside of our imputation. (There is only projection, the nature of the image cast out being a mere personal trivium in light of the fact of the casting itself.) Yet at the same time Jeff, the dreamer who is framing, imagining, conceiving, throwing out his visions of this apartment-complex world, inhabits a material condition as well as a psyche. He is bored, he is wearied, he is anxious, and he is fed up with being all of these, so his rear windowing is jerry-rigged as a creative and very helpful solution for him.[3]

Jeff's camera is almost always nearby, as much his utensil as are Prospero's books for him. We saw the framed photographs he made with a large-format device, but in his wheelchair he uses a Pentax SLR.[4] Cameras work by slicing off a fragment of visible time. Metonymy is always their action, in causing an eighth-of-a-second, a thirty-second-of-a-second, a hundredth-of-a-second freeze to endure, and speak to the conditions of continuance and perpetuity.[5] As the camera is Jeff's symbol, the movie camera is Hitchcock's. The movie camera gives the *impression* of realism because in its "grasp" it includes temporal extension and movement, even though, as we watch, our sense of time is locked rather firmly in the present moment. The still camera can only allude to movement through space (by means of a blur), and in a photograph we can only imagine the configuration of history, by adding to what it shows a package of information about the world that can be claimed to subtend it.[6]

The relationship between the moving and the still image, which is to say, time itself as it unfolds, is a principal subject of *Rear Window*, as of Antonioni's *Blow-Up* (1966), which is something of an homage. In *Blow-Up*, the photographer lines up a chain of 16" × 20" prints and, walking along their length, produces an impression of the living action the stills sequentially recorded. He is retracing history, mechanically moving backward in time (his camera is a time machine) by filling in the gaps between the shots (imagining more shots per second, or a notably shorter aperture speed). In *Rear Window* we entertain a brilliant, dramatically engaging, optically stimulating illusion of seeing reality for itself over Jeff's shoulder, but in fact what we are seeing is isolated phrases—phrases, because they are filmic, instead of frozen moments: no single frame is suspended for us to linger over—and we imagine our way into the various "stories" offered to the eye by filling in what comes between the moments we are given; filling in what is not actually there.[7] Especially salient is our importing ideas about the previous experience of our many little protagonists: what they must have done and gesturally worried through, prior to our glimpsing them.

The same process applies to our linkage of shots by interpreting edits. As we jump from any shot A to any shot B, how much is elided? This question is a riddle, because in terms of the cinematic diegesis itself, *nothing at all* is elided, as outside the edited configuration *there is no existing corresponding reality*. However, we do imagine a subtending world, and given that imagination (and capacity to imagine) we must ask what has been cut out as the film story jumps ahead. When the filmmaker wishes to make open acknowledgment that he means to find a passage across space or time, between subsequent shots in a film, he uses a signaling strategy (on the historical development of which, see Carey). But here as everywhere, signals may be withheld or abbreviated. Or even neglected. Or faked. Even in the absence of signals we may come to understand that it is *only through its crafted appearance* that our passage forward in film can seem fluid. We use a similar "filling-in" with our ordering of memories by expanding them backward into motivations and forward into eventuations, backward toward origins and forward toward conclusions. If we cannot always understand the symbolic nature of what we see, still we give it rhythm and adjoin it to what we saw once before and what we hope to see soon.

It is wise in this context to remember what Freud taught about the dream, its particular content entirely to the side: that a memory of the past and a hope for the future are fused in a sensation of the present. The structural point is fusing, and how the present is a fusion. Freud was led to inspect the past (like a detective) and to burrow in the ground of desire, in order to make sense of the strange warping of form (the nightmare, the slip, the neurotic symptom) that the present temporal conjunction habitually offered his patients. But more profound than the dreams themselves are the mechanisms of the dream, that time comes to a point, that to make "sense" the temporal frames are overlapped, married.

This kind of marriage, far more than anything that could happen with Jeff and Lisa or any other couple in the film, is Hitchcock's delight. And it illuminates for us the overriding, technical, and philosophical problem that Jeff must confront to unravel the puzzle of his experience: and that we must confront, to unravel the puzzle of the film. This is synecdoche, the willful taking of a part for a whole. As to Jeff's capturing images, and our capturing images of him capturing, consider a typical apartment-dweller's bugaboo, here provocatively represented: that the view through one's window has stark limitations, and is, with apparent interminability (unless the structure of the world outside changes), repeated. Always this frame, always that building, always that sliver of the trunk of that tree; because without getting outside the window this is all that can be seen. And the neighbors living their regular lives, the people one sees keeping on at the same activities over and over again. This prescription must include Jeff, the guy who looks and sees and pictures with such confidence, regularly, even tediously. As to him: his captured vision is of necessity attenuated and fragmentary, only a part of what is "really" going on out there, and every such excision implies—necessitates—an ideology of affiliation, an implicit logic whereby the line of extraction is intrinsically and directly related to the field out of which the extraction is made. (On extractions and fields, read Roland Barthes, who in *Camera Lucida* frames the synecdochical problem as the relation of a *punctum* to a *studium*.)

One way to play out Jeff's problem is to think that in the framing of a picture we establish connections between what we see inside the rectangle and what we take to reside immediately out of view, the shot/countershot formula in which a figure looking off-camera implicitly invokes the presence (solid but unseen) of an interactional partner we do not watch at the same moment. Another tack, perhaps in this case more useful, is to work at understanding the story we see unfolding in a film in terms of a coherent outside world—a universe—taken to generate and support such action. For Jeff in his adventures, then, we add to our restricted view from his apartment the whole City of New York of the early 1950s—downtown in particular: an artistic subculture, such as Greenwich Village actually was then, with Dylan Thomas and James Baldwin writing in the White Horse Tavern; or Merce Cunningham with his dancers working out in Westbeth; or John Cage holed up on Bethune Street. If not locale, we project logical actions. At one point in the film Lisa, Jeff's darling, or fiancée—he is very confused about trying to nail this—sashays out of frame to go into his mini-kitchen (he's in a bachelor apartment, of course) in order to prepare some brandies for the two of them and his chum Doyle, our reliable good-natured police inspector type. She waltzes back after a moment with three filled snifters. *Yet we do not see her fill them.* When she goes off, we conceive her in the kitchen, pouring liquor but also able to overhear whatever is being said on camera in the living room. This making of apparent continuity between the room in which we are tied to Jeff and the second, invisible room where Lisa is at work, is evidence of just such a synecdochical problem as besets Jeff more generally, and of the almost natural solution offered to the audience.

Jeff sees his neighbors in their apartments, but time and exigence force him never to see any one of them for long. These performers, attracting Jeff's notice in their mini-tales, are fairly well known, but a brief rehearsal may prove helpful, especially in pointing to the way information about each of them is cut off from something broader and deeper to which we have no access. From screen right, and circling leftward (as the camera invites us to do):

(a) A composer, in a swank pad with a grand piano and a pleasing mantelpiece with its sedate clock—echo of René Magritte—that our dear maître Hitchcock intercedes to set for him. Struggling to finish a (luscious little) tune, he is having particular trouble with a chord modulation that would permit, if he but solved his riddle, moving the song onward toward its cadence. The actual piece is by Franz Waxman, a pop song of the sort Vic Damone or Tony Bennett might record. Because his piano is a very good one (given the New York location and the company's offices on West 57th Street, I would suspect a Steinway, but look at me extrapolating!), we hear a rich sonority. His working method is to try a few bars, get up and pace around, sit and try again. He is dogged, but frustrated—frustrated, but dogged—aware that he must break from the concentration yet also not lose the string of it. The opulence of his tall glass windows openly suggests that the composer has money, may be the wealthiest of our subjects; yet late in the film, when Lisa ingenuously wonders to Jeff how a man gets the inspiration to write a melody like that, the answer John Michael Hayes puts in his mouth is a wry comment: "He gets it from the landlady once a month." The composer is not casual with his music but very serious; early on, we hear him doing rigorous technical exercises to prepare his fingers for the work. His song sounds like a love ballad. The piano is his instrument, much as the film is Hitchcock's. This musician has been writing songs for a long enough time that he knows the modulation he seeks will come if only he is patient enough. If only there is time.

Keep working, keep trying, don't push it, don't walk away. Suddenly, without warning, the Muse will give a kiss. Where did this man come from, however? How did he become a composer, and how and when did the lyrical inspiration first hit him?

(b) The sunbathers, a pair of young women who have climbed onto the rooftop to expose themselves as the film begins. We don't really catch further sight of them. Are they lovers? Companions, surely. Roommates, harassed by a passing helicopter in which some male is trying for a peachy view. Almost everything in this film happens *inside* apartments, so the sunbathers invoke the dangers of the outside world, perhaps slight dangers, such as relentless openness to inspection, judgment, appreciation, and critique, all of which are curtailed to some degree when one is at home and outsiders can catch nothing more revealing than a glimpse through one's partially blinding window. On the "blinding window," recall the Venetian blinds in Jeff's place, opening so dramatically for us under the credits. (He is asleep at the time, by the way. Who is opening those blinds?)

(c) A traveling salesman, Thorwald (Raymond Burr), burdened with a sick wife (Irene Winston). Tall, lumbering, curmudgeonly, he lives without a smile. The bedridden wife is something of a harridan (and in her incommodious state a parallel of sorts to Jeff).[8] We presume Thorwald's business hasn't been particularly good and perhaps think of him as representing his occupational group, which in the burgeoning consumer society of the time had fallen into decline. Arthur Miller's interesting play *Death of a Salesman* ran for 742 performances on Broadway, ending barely three years before this film's production started, and its script called for a setting of special interest in relation to the argument here: "We see a solid vault of apartment houses around the small fragile-seeming home. An air of the dream clings to the place, a dream rising out of reality" (Miller 5). In Thorwald's bedroom, his wife is ailing—indubitably daydreaming—with an unspecified condition. This is a portrait of marital discontent, inimical squabbling, and also of the imperious invalid and her grumbling factotum (lifted to some degree from *Great Expectations*): invoked are class relations, the desiccation of love, the deep structure of domestic partnership, and smoldering resentment. Is Mrs. Thorwald's affliction her (enforced) powerlessness, or is she suffering from a corporeal disease?

(d) A solitary spinster, Miss Lonelyhearts (Judith Evelyn), named, perhaps, with a nod to Nathanael West. She is middle-aged, climbing against gravity to keep up the vital appearance of youth. She doesn't want to be alone in life, and perhaps we invent the causes of her loneliness: a jilted lover; a spinsterhood that, years before, missed its chance; a psychological weakness of some kind. She knows all the proprieties of femininity and attractiveness in this notably male-dominated, increasingly youth-oriented culture, but because no Prince Charming has come to her door she must play out a huntress's proprieties in desperate pantomime. Finally, she does go afield and lures back a young beast, but things don't turn out well with him at all: he has a sexual appetite she apparently hasn't figured on, in her fairy-tale script. It is romance she craves, not friction.

(e) A middle-aged couple (Sara Berner, Frank Cady) with a tiny Norwich terrier, whom they lower into, and raise from, the garden below in a cute basket-and-pulley arrangement. Puppy is their "child." In reviews and scholarship they are often named The Whistlers. In this torpid heat they sleep outside on their fire escape, not at all an atypical maneuver for New Yorkers in the desperate and unrelieved heat of a Manhattan summer. Their lives are centered around the pup's antics; otherwise they inhabit a forbidding privacy.

(f) A dancer (Virginia Darcy), Miss Torso, frequently seen exercising; she is svelte, perky, young, and, as Tania Modleski has remarked, "suggestive" in her movements (74). Herbert Coleman recollected that he "took her to her apartment on the stage and pointed out the various moves Hitchcock would want her to make. She took the record and left the stage after promising not to make her ballet moves too professional" (179). Miss Torso has a dancer's well-toned body and profound discipline, both physical and moral. We see her with gentleman guests—businessmen of sorts—artfully rejecting their advances. She is not dancing for her own delight, but for some occupational arrangement not directly indicated to us because far out of frame, literally *obscene* (not dirty, but *ob-scena,* beyond the scene). Implicit in this character is the erosion effected by time, since the dancer's life depends upon youthful vigor to a large extent and there will surely come a moment when she is too old for this kind of life; when she is ready to become a second Miss Lonelyhearts.

(g) The Sculptress (Jesslyn Fax), an artist beyond middle age with a sculpture in progress. She does not speak, and makes only few appearances, but she does very perfectly characterize the West Village artistic type, numerous especially in New York's Lower West Side (where the film takes place). We might think of her as a person who minds her own business, since little seems to interest her beyond her own movement and the piece she is working on. Hitchcock has drawn this character with great accuracy. She lives to work on her art. Her art is what demands her attention. It wouldn't be going too far to suggest she is Hitchcock's double in the sense that when he works on his frame, nothing in the world intrudes upon his concentration. Dana Brand has commented interestingly that the sculpture, which the artist has named "Hunger," has a gigantic hole where the heart should be (131).

(h) The Newlyweds (Rand Harper, Steve Forrest), two sprightly young ones, around twenty years of age, who are just, as the film begins, moving into the apartment directly adjacent Jeff's to the left. Very romantic and conventional, these two. The boy insists on the girl walking back into the corridor so that he can pick her up gallantly and carry her across the threshold. The draw-blind is pulled down so that they can enjoy their honeymoon while the film progresses, a Hitchcockian joke, and at one point when the young man raises that blind and tries to gasp for fresh air the new wife calls him back to bed. We may presume one long, more or less uninterrupted heterosexual extravaganza on the other side of that privacy blind; and this bedded female is the very antithesis of the salesman's wife. Has Time attacked the Thorwalds, then? Is their marital strife about Time? It is easy enough to argue that when he hears the repetitive moaning next door, Jeff is being cued to ask himself why he does not "settle down" with Lisa in a similar fashion, but as Hitchcock arranges it, Jeff is bemused by the newlyweds, finds them adorably goofy, not prompted by them to rethink the so-called repressive patterns of his own bachelor life.

As to the rise and fall of the plot that Hitchcock conceived with Hayes (from a Cornell Woolrich short story), and that is composed by arranging the narrative shards involving Jeff's calculations about this array of personae: Jeff is watching them, day and night, sometimes with binoculars, sometimes using his camera, fitted with a long lens for magnifying, sucking in, the view. Although his observations are distracted or blocked by Lisa, who would like his undivided attention, and by the crabby and somewhat moralistic Stella, he nevertheless manages to snag a number of dramatic fragments: the composer obviously has a composition deadline he's afraid he won't meet; the dancer misses her boyfriend, who isn't around; the lonely spinster is verging on the suicidal; and so on. But in the midst of this, and rather suddenly, it becomes apparent the salesman, Thorwald, no longer has a wife. We saw him schlep some suitcases out of his apartment and now we see that the wife has disappeared. At another moment Jeff can see Thorwald fiddling with a large knife. Our photographer-hero becomes suspicious that this man has done something to his partner, something distinctly unpleasant. Called in to consult, Doyle of course rejects such amateur hypothesizing, thinking Jeff loopy for taking himself so seriously (when the police force comprises pros who know how to do their business). But Jeff's doubt in Thorwald progresses. The man has surely sliced up the body, secretly carried the pieces away, distributed them elsewhere. What Jeff has collected are shards: how many ways might there be to assemble and unify them? Embodied by the dignified Jimmy Stewart, Jeff is noble and intelligent, but embodied by the adorably clumsy Jimmy Stewart Jeff is a charming goofball who may easily have miscalculated. How many theories could explain the pieces of action, after all? Is Jeff merely inventing the crime because he needs movement? Consider in light of that supposition Merleau-Ponty's reflection, "I have no other means of knowing the human body than by living it, that is, by taking up for myself the drama that moves through it" (205) and Goffman's keen insight:

> Passive participation is not as passive as one might have thought. If the onlookers laugh when the clown suddenly finds himself falling like a stone it is because they had all along been projecting their musculature and sensibilities sympathetically into his walk and now find that their leaning into his anticipated conduct, into the anticipated guidedness of his doings, their framed prediction of what is to come, is disordered. In this sense watching is doing. (*Frame Analysis* 381)

An exacerbating moment: the dog whistlers have lowered their pup into the garden, where he likes to dig. But now they find that he is dead. As they scream in agony to their unknown neighbors, and as all the "minicasts" of the "mini-films" stick out their heads to show, if not emotional support and neighborliness then at least curiosity, only one set of windows remains dark, with the penetrating glow of a cigarette punctuating the black rectangle: Thorwald's. He has not moved from his solitary chair, in his solitary darkness, whence he looks out on the world from *his* rear window.[9]

Jeff is convinced there is something about that dog and that garden. He has photographed the flowers there before, and comparing his slides with the present reality he sees reason to believe that something has been buried beneath—something the dog might have been digging *for*. He contrives to get Thorwald's telephone number and, ringing him from cover of darkness in his own pad, tells the burly salesman he knows all about the wife and will agree to meet him at a bar nearby and collect some money for his silence. Thorwald can be seen urgently heading out. But Lisa, sent along with trusty Stella to examine the garden, suddenly lights out on her own and makes bold to climb her way up the fire escape and into Thorwald's apartment (no society wallflower she), where, yes!, she finds the wife's purse and wedding ring, a treasure no woman would go anywhere without. But the salesman has returned from his wild-goose chase! He confronts her physically, brutally, while Jeff, frigid and powerless in his watching, even paralyzed as he looks,[10] is forced to see as a "dramatic show" the developing physical aggression upon the woman he deeply loves. Has he learned of the depth of that love, in fact, only now, in extremis? Stella has telephoned the police. In Thorwald's grasp, Lisa manages to twist her back toward his window, and she flashes the wedding ring for Jeff to notice. But

Thorwald notices her gesture and looks past her shoulder out into the darkness. "Who is your audience out there," he seems to be demanding with his gaze; "Whose eyes, fixed upon me, are turning my life into a performance?"

Jeff tries to wheel his chair back out of sight—a wonderfully equivocal moment of cowardice, perfectly evoked—but it's too late; Thorwald has detected him. If Lisa escapes, now managing sufficient explanation in the face of the newly arrived police, Jeff himself is safe no longer. Thorwald is soon at his door, barging in: "What do you want from me?" A monolithic figure, harshly backlit. In a climactic confrontation he struggles with Jeff before being overtaken by Doyle. In the struggle, Jeff is hurled out his own window, and falling into the courtyard suffers his second leg break as the picture floats into its peaceful, slightly comic finale.

STAGING STAGES

As I have suggested, in some theoretical considerations gazing is very typically associated with a kind of brute and disenfranchising masculinity. "Because he is afraid of Lisa's assertiveness and frustrated with his feminization, Jeff denigrates women's knowledge, perhaps as a means of protecting himself from further feminization," writes Elisa Lemire (77), for example. The sculptress, the dancer, Miss Lonelyhearts, the puppy-owner wife—all these presumably threaten something in Jeff's constitution, and he views them in relatively pejorative terms. But does he? Does the film actually show us Jeff looking *down* morally on any of these characters? His apartment being raised above some of theirs, mechanically speaking his gaze has to be from above. Does he look askance at Stella's reproofs as she massages him, and does he think her nothing but a menial laborer with an elementary perspective, or does he take her lesson in and think it through? Does Jeff look down on Lisa, too? She wants to turn and twist in fancy French garments and eat from 21, drink champagne, and think about style and high culture, while he anticipates getting back to adventures in the high Himalayas and other such daunting locales. Is he criticizing her when he demurs against some of her charmingly forward-looking gestures of affection, or is he showing sensible concern and forethought, recognizing how she has not yet shown herself to be part of the active world in which he makes his living? We mustn't fail to see that Lisa herself recognizes what she has and has not demonstrated to Jeff. By film's end she has made a point of changing her performance to show, unequivocally, that his rugged world of action can also be hers. And if Jeff's close-ups of Lisa seem rich as visions, distinctly *present*, fleshed out, thus erotic and suggestive, there is method in organizing them. Hitchcock even includes a complex close-up of Kelly leaning into Stewart's dozing face at sunset—the rich warm light bathing her smooth cheeks, her perfect lips swimming forward toward the viewer, her neck swathed in a delicate chain of perfect pearls—not only as a charming and comic introduction to her character but to provide us with an optical measure against which the views into the courtyard can be appreciated for their challenging remoteness.

As far as Jeff is able to see, everyone in his surround is embedded in some variation of the dance of courtship and sexuality (on this theme, see further Wood 102). The composer of love songs, the half-nude sunbathers attracting attention, the equivocal marriage of the salesman and his wife, the childlessness of the Whistlers, Miss Lonelyhearts's scramble for romantic companionship, Miss Torso's body on show, the Sculptress resigned to the sublimation of her art, the insatiable newlyweds. A typical critical response to this set-up has been to interpret all of this background behavior as a reflection of Jeff's position with Lisa, in short, a reflection (and miniaturization) of our two protagonists thrown into the visual background. I think we may be able to see that the background action, as much as it may or may not touch upon the foreground, has a utility far more profound and effective than mere mirroring. Meanwhile, suffice it to say that down in this little quarter of a Great City, everyone is yearning for—dreaming of—somebody.

Next, and obvious even to the unobservant eye, is that the little dramas are broken apart from one another by virtue of the apartment buildings' brickwork as it functions to keep the various windows separate. This is a reflection at least as much on the apartment-house style of living as it is on Hitchcock's film and filmic intent. One doesn't really know one's neighbors: physical proximity and social proximity are not conjoined, a fact that leads to a possibly chilling situation in which one learns that a violent and brutal murderer is living just on the other side of the: wall, garden, court. More simply, the bricked areas (made of real brickwork) present obstacles to sight, and in this way bluntly announce how the peeping we accomplish with Jeff has its limits.

Further, the penetrating directorial focus on these multiple escapades allows us, by seeing what they have in common, to see what differentiates them one from another. The characters in the various apartments are enacting what could be seen as different *phases* of a single romantic cycle, the sunbathers, for instance, doing more or less what Miss Lonelyhearts tries to do, but at a point earlier in life, when their prospects have not yet deteriorated through aging, pain, rejection, and stress. The newlyweds and the salesman Thorwald and his wife are working through the drama of marriage, and so are the Whistlers. All three childless couples writhe in companionship, the youngest ones by way of pleasure and its fulfillments; the eldest by way of surrender (their dog fully adopted as a member of the family); and the Thorwalds in a tempestuous period where the titillating thrill of being together has dissolved in needy imprecation and boredom. The composer is working to write the music that brings lovers together (the newlyweds probably listened to his songs on the radio a year ago), and Miss Torso and the Sculptress exercise their libidos by investment in their art. Everyone here is in love, was in love, might someday be in love; or is thinking about love; or representing love artistically; or practicing for love; or regretting the absence of love. But in all this, what is crucial to notice is that the phases of enchantment depicted outside Jeff's apartment are out of syntax, rather as though the drama is being presented with all its scenes simultaneously played out on a collection of different stages, all within the audience's (Jeff's) purview. Given this lovely puzzle, what would lead one to choose any particular apartment at any particular moment, as an object of attention? And what cycle of drama and action could be composed, depending on the syntactical order in which one considered these phases of the "life cycle" of love?

Let me suggest what I suspect is the underlying architecture here. Hitchcock and Hayes work out a complex scenario involving, of all things, sex, because it is the most conventional one for dramatic purposes. No adult viewer will fail to grasp the innuendos; and sex, a good audience lure, can be displayed in various ways. But it is a huge jump to conclude that sex is on Hitchcock's directorial mind. The actions of the film are split apart from one another and spread across the apartment complex not to suggest sexual fragmentation in and of itself but to point the audience's awareness to the very idea of the fragment. Hitchcock wants fragments, not sex, but sex and love provide a useful and unconfusing opportunity for fragmentation, a convenient, easily recognizable material out of which to build a tale. The romance tale is well known, after all, so that when we see ripped fragments of it played out with all earnestness, the ripping that makes them fragments can be brought to notice.

Next, and in a higher order of organization: not only are the minidramas in the various apartments *pieces of* a more coherent romantic subtale but as Jeff actually sees them—as they play out onscreen before his eyes and ours—there is never, for any one of them, a complete rendition of any scene from beginning to end. What is visible is a fragment on another order, a metonymic shard that stands for more than it states. In this subtle but powerful way, the apartment action, piece by piece, constitutes a group of metaphors. This concision, this *editing*, goes on all through the film, but in a shocking and frightening set of moments involving Miss Lonelyhearts and the Thorwalds Hitchcock manages to bluntly telegraph the system he is using by drawing our attention exactly to the fact that while we think we see it all, in truth we don't see enough. Every observation cuts in on something that began before, and drops out before the action reaches its peak (this particular fragmentation reflecting a general state of affairs). Miss Lonelyhearts is despondent but Jeff moves away from watching her (through his binoculars) to get a focus on Thorwald, who, he is now convinced, has cut up his wife and deposited her parts around town. But it suddenly becomes clear that the spinster has taken an overdose and is collapsing at her table. A phone call to police goes through just in time, so that officers can arrive to save her. But the point of the sequence is not the incipient suicide of this side character we haven't fully met, it is Jeff's limited attention as he watches her, the sense that as he watches *he* has not met her fully either and does not really care, nor could he reasonably care, since his opportunities to see and know her are now, as ever, so constrained.

Paula Marantz Cohen interestingly points out in respect of *Rear Window* a "tendency to demarcate the look itself. This demarcation appeared in the eighteenth century when the invention of the microscope radically enlarged the possibilities of what could be seen in the natural world" (104). Fascinating in the case of this film (and also, as the film bluntly implies, in organized life more broadly) is the link between the look and the mark; not in the simple sense that observation both points and labels, ascertains and defines, but more complexly, in that a look is confined to a boundary. Jeff's medical confinement and his visual confinement are wedded. And through the limitation of the look, its "demarcation," he comes finally to apprehend the great moral lesson offered by his drama, that perception is piecemeal. Further: the metonymy of sight can be freezing. As a child, Virginia Woolf wrote, "My days, just as they do now, contained a large proportion of this cotton wool, this non-being. Week after week passed at St Ives and nothing made any dint upon me. Then, for no reason that I know about, there was a sudden violent shock; something happened so violently that I have remembered it all my life.... I seemed to be dragged down, hopelessly, into some pit of absolute despair from which I could not escape. My body seemed paralysed" (71).

AN ABSENT MIDDLE

In partial perception lies reason for the abbreviation of the apartment melodramas, for the snatched moments of observation, and for the strained calculation of our protagonist. For his complete inability to see all of the picture (in the way that the filmmaker, the Master, does). For the lingering suspicion he must have—and we with him—when the story is done, that everything is not quite explained, not quite as clear as one might wish. The telling clue to this stance comes from our final view of Lisa, as, with Jeff dozing again, his legs *both* now in casts, she lies upon his divan *in blue jeans and penny loafers*, reading what appears to be *Beyond the High Himalayas* but is in fact, hiding inside, *Harper's Bazaar*! The point isn't wholly that she is who she always was, the society girl hungry for society pleasures, but that she has rapidly metamorphosed, let her gowns evaporate and dressed for practicality, as he would presumably want. How did this happen, through what negotiation, in what process of emotional and physical development? We are left only to surmise, since the shot is meant as a punchline severed from, delivered without recourse to, its joke.

But in this fragmented finale, much is left to be considered:

Moral Position. The moral position of the film hangs in the air outside Jeff's window. Thorwald, apparently, is quite as guilty of slaughter as Jeff suspected, because finally Doyle and company have arrested him and escorted him away. The wife's head was found, as were the other body parts. So the man is a butcher, perhaps even a cannibal. But what made him this way? How did he come to the passion for cutting up people, especially women? What led him to the signal appreciation of dismembered parts? How did the courtship and marriage occur, that brought these two so terminally disparate creatures into that little apartment? Was Thorwald planning murder from the start, from even before the start? The final observation gives us answer to none of this, reflecting, in its optical and dramatic form, just the constraints of that eighteenth-century microscope, which device, when we gaze into it, slices off the remainder of the world to leave only the slide and its contents, only the excerpt from life now taken metonymically as a representation of the whole. For Jonathan Crary, it is "the authority of *an ideal eye*" invoked by the microscope (129; my emphasis). Jeff has had Thorwald under his "microscope," and every "scope" reduces even when it promises to expand. Note Jeff's use of his long lens (that magnifies), and his binoculars: these are teases to his consciousness, because always he must make inference from his selection to the establishing ground around and beneath.

The other figures in the courtyard are, finally, similarly inscrutable. Why is the dancer dancing? We may suspect she is employed in a Broadway chorus line, given the sorts of stretches she endures over and over (some of them constituting what in the early 1950s would have been considered erotic comedy) and given the contemporary show tune to which she rehearses (from Leonard Bernstein's *On the Town*), yet there is no direct evidence. When her boyfriend Stanley returns from his military duty, near film's end, a shortish bespectacled young fellow the very antithesis of athletic heroism, and she embraces him with all the fervor of a Juliet for her Romeo, what can we believe will be their future together? The composer: he concludes his song triumphantly, and has a test recording that he can play in private for the adoring Miss Lonelyhearts, finally now accompanied by a man who might love her. How did she come into his apartment, by invitation? She has, after all, been listening to that growing song. "Lisa," it is called, of all titles on earth. Our own Lisa is listening to it, too, with great affect. Are we to conclude it is secretly about her, that all the time he was struggling at his keyboard the composer was dreaming of her, perhaps even more than Jeff? And so on.

As I regard the film pestered by questions like this, I find myself reminded of a group photograph, an especially handsome one, of the entire star body of MGM in 1943, posing together on a soundstage for a group portrait. Lionel Barrymore, James Stewart, Greer Garson, Judy Garland... fifty-six of them, *and Lassie!* One has a sense of the immediate coherence of the grouping, that everyone belongs—just as, so very strangely, every one of the strangers in this Hitchcockian apartment complex *belongs*—and yet: for each of these persons, as for each of Hitchcock's, a different life is in process, and this moment of the photography is an excerpt with its own value and meaning. The snap perception seems to exist in itself, seems to have its own life. Here is the great Argentinian writer Julio Cortázar:

> One of the many ways of contesting level-zero, and one of the best, is to take photographs, an activity in which one should start becoming an adept very early in life, teach it to children since it requires discipline, aesthetic education, a good eye and steady fingers. I'm not talking about waylaying the lie like any old reporter, snapping the stupid silhouette of the VIP leaving number 10 Downing Street, but in all ways when one is walking about with a camera, one has almost a duty to be attentive, to not lose that abrupt and happy rebound of sun's rays off an old stone, or the pigtails-flying run of a small girl going home with a loaf of bread or a bottle of milk. (117)

Dramatic Construction. The grand story and the lesser stories in the film depend on dramatic construction, the qualities of ongoingness and origination that inhere in the gesture, the action, the tableau. Things lead to other things; things eventuate. While each instant depends intensively on the striking of posture, on a telling gesture, on the affective tone that can be conveyed through light and setting, still the characters develop their presence through a continuity of instants, a chain. In drama any moment takes its full value from what came before and what eventuates, so that here, in a rather radical constructive operation, Hitchcock undoes drama as he spreads the filmic world in front of us. All of what we are seeing has been going on for some time. The routinized, quotidian nature of the action dominates everything else in the film. While in some motion pictures a character might seem to spring into existence in order that the film's story might unfold, here the characters are fully fleshed and fully feeling long before we meet them.

Whatever it is that has been growing between Jeff and Lisa, therefore, is now in full blossom. He's been uncomfortable with something about the relationship for quite a while, and she's been sensing this and trying very hard to overcome what seems to her his stubborn resistance. Again, as with all matters in his films, Hitchcock takes the classical stance and provides us with a signal beforehand, a definitive cuing to the dramatic continuity he plans to interrupt. In the present case, we must see again the photograph of the racing car tire speeding toward Jeff, the picture visible in the camera's first rotation around his room. That tire was on a car; that car endured many races; it was blitzing through this race; something happened and the tire came off; the tire flew toward the camera; we now see something of the result. As a fragment full of unstated implication, that photograph indexes this entire film.

Turn-Out. And then, as we examine the accomplished, if tiny, performances being given in those neatly arrayed apartments, we can note how the various actors, playing their scene pieces, must operate in such a way that Jeff, and the camera, can make head or tail of what is happening with them. We aren't seeing full pantomimes, we are seeing only the smallest shards of pantomimes, but each shard must convey. The actors know that they are being caught *in medias res*, and that therefore, lacking set-ups and conclusions, they must take special care to be readable in fragmentation. Readable, that is, backward and forward in time. This necessity provides an interesting technical challenge. Jeff watches the apartment actions in profile (thus, Thorwald's suddenly staring out at him is compositionally as well as dramatically shocking), a sociological normality, since when people behave at home, they do not make the presumption of living within glass walls, giving a show to passers-by in the street who will see them from the side. Casually and effortlessly they speak to one another face to face, which is to say, with their bodies oriented in direct presentation to each other's. To watch this sort of outplaying is to be very severely restricted, because the gestures of the hands, the shapes and orientations of the bodies, and the expressions of the faces are only minimally visible. In order that they might play successfully in a dramatic context, the actors in Hitchcock's apartments must turn slightly outward toward their windows; enough so that Jeff can see into the action, detect or hypothesize what is going on, yet not so much that their turn-out seems interactionally odd and the characters become reduced to mere show-offs knowingly revealing themselves to some peeper (and the actors reduced to mere performers at work). The particular metonymies staged here are accomplished, then, through a partial turn-out, less than actors would use on the stage, yet much more than people would use in everyday life.

CASTING A STORY

A notable collection of bourgeois objects lards the action space of the film: Jeff's Graflex camera, now shattered (Weejee used one of these, too); the composer's grand piano; Lisa's Mark Cross overnight case, French garments, and gigantic pearls; snifters of Courvoisier and a glass of red; Thorwald's kitchen implements and his wife's golden wedding ring. But of the pieces of the objective panoply, nothing is more glaring, more dominating, more optically brilliant, and more dramatically implicating than Jeff's plaster cast. We meet him through its agency; it weighs him down and pinions him to his positions; it eventually paralyzes him at the moment he most needs—and is denied—freedom of movement.

What is being said to us about Jeff by virtue of his entrapment in this cast—beyond the plain fact that he has been temporarily crippled? The cast is often analyzed, and dispensed with, as an element in Hitchcock's choreographic obstruction: that Jeff cannot get around, that he is glued to his wheelchair, that his wound forces him to depend upon the help of Stella and Lisa and Doyle, that the chair can function for him as an ersatz dolly so that, with his lenses in hand, he can be a kind of on-camera camera, a reference to the very selfsame filmmaking by virtue of which he exists. But all of this notwithstanding, the cast and the wheelchair imply still another dimension.

More than being classifiable as debilitated at present, Jeff is the ongoing bearer of an injury. His body and self have been discomposed. He is engaged in the process of healing. The narrative of the film unfolds as his cure develops. And what this means is that his awareness and consciousness are those of a person who is emerging from a state of profound biophysical stress. As a man in a full leg cast, he has most likely suffered fractures to both his tibial-fibular area and his femur, if not also his patella and its associated ligaments. He has been for some time—the cast itself is a direct, snow white, signal of this—in severe pain, a far greater discomfort than the itch that seems to be driving him crazy inside the plaster. Because of the pain, there can be no doubt he has been medicated, very likely intensely medicated: a broken leg doesn't stop hurting when it's been set. One can presume he's been bearing up in this state of affairs for several weeks, and has weeks left ahead of him (the spotlessness of the cast). It is one thing to distance oneself from him by easily averring that he has a "medical" condition; and quite another to empathetically invest in his experience. He is out of action. He is wounded. If, caught in his wheelchair with his camera, he is something of a metaphor for a camera on a dolly, still he is no camera, he is a human being in pain. While we do not observe him taking medication in the film, no one with fractures this severe is free from needing it.

So it is that this man's perception, structured not merely by fragmentation but also by agony, focuses upon the world around him with a certain refreshing, balmy curiosity for detail, the feeling of emerging from a solipsistic cloud. Poe wrote about this kind of emergence in his story "The Man of the Crowd" (1840). Our hero is bathing in social contact and experience. He delights in seeing others live their lives. And so, while Stella is happy enough to chide him for Peeping Tomism, vulgar fascination with strangers' carnality, he is in truth experiencing the awkward and curious tides of recuperation. He is finding his way back into the world from which his injuries have kenneled him.[11]

Let us add to Jeff's recuperative perception—his receptivity—Hitchcock's artful method, by which all the characters Jeff can see in their plays of life are made notably visible to him only in shards. The Thorwald drama, in particular, seems designed to advertise the fragmentary nature of the general narrative, with this lumbering man continually shuffling out of his apartment and back again, taking a respite we know not where. But all the characters make exits and entrances this way, almost all of them in such a manner that we take their behavior entirely at face value. When Jeff augments his sight with a camera or binoculars, characterological postures and phrases of activity lend special credence to the broad interpretations he makes by expanding his curiosity. About what Thorwald is probably doing Jeff and Doyle are at odds not merely because Doyle's is the inherently more doubting personality, nor wholly because as a professional diagnostician his opinion of Jeff's diagnosing is low; but because Doyle, a perfectly healthy guy, isn't caught up in recuperation and its keen instigations to watching. He isn't carried away by fascination for common strangers, as, in his extremely focused state Jeff cannot stop himself from being. (The painkillers in use here are probably opiates: they dry the consciousness, increase focus, prolong concentration.) Doyle is happy to have a brandy but not really settled into observation as a mode of entertainment. Jeff, however, has only observation; he is seeing *everything* more than Doyle does; and more than Lisa or Stella, too. Seeing with intensified depth and color and moment. His seeing borders on a waking dream, because his perceptual state, only slowly entering the fields of rationality, still lingers in the neverland of his wound. Social life is all a dream. All the apartments he is watching frame the playing out of his dreams.

Hence the extreme power of the film's finale, in which the forbidding Thorwald, having caught sight of Jeff spying on him, migrates across the no-man's-land of the courtyard and barges into Jeff's—into this, into our—apartment. Jeff heard him pounding at the door, gathered his camera and a supply of flashbulbs, wheeled himself around with the speed of a wounded athlete, and switched off the lamps. The figure is in the doorway. Jeff has wheeled himself backward toward the window, his rear now facing the "rear" zone. As he pops his flashbulbs into Thorwald's advancing face, one by one, poppppp—flasssshhhhh (a suffusion of blood red, turning magnesium white) ... poppppppp—flaaaashhhhhh (a suffusion of blood red, turning magnesium white) ... the shock of the flashbulb-illuminated vision of the huge form, Thorwald looming, the light flashing red and magnesium white, red and magnesium white, RED and WHITE!, and as Thorwald takes hold of him, Jeff can only, here, now, and finally after his unbearable ordeal, *awaken*.

For it is just at the point that Thorwald has him hanging from his ledge (a Hitchcockian prelude to another Jimmy Stewart dangle) that Jeff comes fully conscious in the blunt, factual, call it existential reality of his moment. Until that instant, beatifically, he was in a reverie of wavering speculation.

PLASMA

Cinema as screenplay is discussed by William Rothman in an essay called "Eternal Vérités." Before stipulating that "writing is not film," he suggests, "By enforcing the discipline that films were to be 'realized' only after first being envisioned in advance through the medium of the written word, the classical system also acknowledged the power of writing" (*I of the Camera* 289). For all his compositional classicism, Hitchcock's reliance on the written word came from a visual conceit in the first place, not a verbal one. He saw the story. It was to transpose his vision—into a living cast of actors; into a setting; into scenes wherein conversations would occur—that he collaborated with his team to produce production materials in writing. But he foresaw the film as a vision, a dream. Even a cursory examination of his storyboards (produced by skilled graphic artists like Robert Boyle or John De Cuir or Harold Michelson working to his dictated specifications) shows how the film tended to move from a "screen" in Hitchcock's head toward the screen on which multitudes would enjoy it.

In at least one crucial respect, *Rear Window* does not fall under the scriptural classicism Rothman adduces. I refer to the charged and mysterious vision that dominates Jeff and Lisa's charming love affair; and warps more than Grace Kelly's stunning beauty or its contrast, the grisly nefariousness in the neighbors' lives. As all dreams are set in dream space—however "realistic"—filmic dreams are, too, and in this case dream space is dominated by the fabulous apartment structure/courtyard set, built for Hitchcock (at a cost of slightly more than $72,000 1953 dollars) by Joseph Macmillan "Mac" Johnson on Paramount's Stage 18 (with every one of the apartments pre-lit for both day and night [see further Curtis 31ff.]). This stage has a covered pit, typically used for storage, that was opened and emptied to become the "ground-level" of the courtyard, so that Jeff's apartment, roughly on the second story of his building, was situated in fact at real ground level on the west side of the stage. The facility itself measures 185'5" by 99' and is 40 feet from floor to grid, but with the floor removed there are ten additional feet of height; Johnson's set filled Stage 18 entirely, at its time the largest single set ever built on a Hollywood soundstage. "I marveled," wrote the film's associate director Herbert Coleman, "at the way Mac had solved the problem of building an entire Greenwich Village block of brick buildings, a street, an alley, and Jimmy Stewart's second-floor, two-room apartment on one stage" (172). The apartments were most of them in working order, with live electricity and running water. Hitchcock operated his forces from Jeff's apartment, using a specially wired "phone" system, when necessary, to give the performers guidance; "the greatest thing about that system," Coleman told Hitchcock, "is they won't be able to talk back" (175). As we look through Jeff's rear window we can see straight ahead to Miss Torso and the Sculptress and, just left of them, an alleyway that leads out to a street. Across that street are some stores, and real traffic can pass left and right along it. This is West 10th Street. The massive camera[12] was on a dolly arm that permitted the thing to be extended outside Jeff's place, in order to maximize the view into the apartments opposite. Beyond the structures across 10th Street was a painted backdrop, which could be variably lit from front and rear to create temporally accurate effects.

The shooting was a matter of technical prodigiousness, as production manager C. O. "Doc" Erickson recollected to Douglas Bell:

> We had to pour so much *light* into those apartments, up where Raymond Burr was, it almost put him on *fire*. It was terrible. Or you would never have been able to see him, from where we were shooting. As it was, we moved the camera out, as far as we could, to cheat the look from Jimmy Stewart, with his telephoto lens. But, today, it would be *nothing*, it would be a cinch.... The lights have become smaller and more powerful, less cumbersome. Cameras are smaller, with faster lenses.
>
> The sound element is *so* different, you have the mixer sitting at his *tiny* little console, and the sound boom is on a long fishpole, the microphones, *or* they're attached to the person himself, to the actor, with radio mikes, which we didn't have. The sound department, you know, in those days, it was a big *truck* parked outside the stage, and everything was sent to the *department*, across the lot, by cable, an underground thing.

Hitchcock took his set very seriously indeed. It was his delight to give guided tours to invited visitors. And even before principal photography began he was treating the apartments as his private, and restricted, production space. Wednesday, 18 November 1953, for example, Raymond Burr was asked to be on Stage 18 (not in Hitchcock's office, or in the costume department) for a fitting of the eyeglasses he was to wear (that prop crucial for reflecting Jeff's flashes in the finale). Five days later in mid-afternoon Grace Kelly was to appear there for a wardrobe fitting. Everything had to work *inside the apartments* from the point of view obtainable in Jeff's apartment, where Hitchcock would observe.

Orientation becomes an overriding problem in watching. At each moment we align ourselves with a presumptive compass, asking where we are and where each piece of the action is taking place: not within the carefully delimited confines of the screen, but within a topographical spread we take to be subtending the construction of the screen. Beyond the edges of what we see, and beneath the forms, is The City, a resource subject to cognitive mapping even beyond what we see[13] and what, waiting to be seen, sees us seeing. Indeed, the city, as Spengler teaches, is nothing if not a face. "The expansion of the city's 'visage' . . . has a history," and the city's stone visages "are all eye and intellect" (68; 69). As with any filmed drama, the "scene" as it is given strikes us as standing upon some real geographical territory (not the territory of the soundstage where in reality it is to be found). But in *Rear Window*, the New Yorkness of that territory is made emphatic, through the special typification of the characters and through some of their commentary. When Lisa admits she has ordered lunch for two from 21, for instance, she is making reference to the only restaurant on earth of that name, a location at 21 W. 52nd Street (where Hitchcock, on his first visits to the United States, was regaled and loved to dine upon steak and ice cream). The "noted" New York artist Grace Sprague (as opposed to any other graphic talent, available in Los Angeles) was hired to

> work out visualizations of the 15 or 20 apartments for the big, one-set production of Alfred Hitchcock's "Rear Window," then sketch the types of costumes needed by the actors working in them.
>
> Working in conjunction with both Hitchcock and Edith Head, head designer for Paramount, Miss Sprague is sketching the exteriors and interiors of the apartments as seen from the centrally located apartment occupied by James Stewart in the murder mystery. She then fills in the apartments with the types of costuming and clothes to be worn by their occupants in the wide-screen color film. (Finestone memo)

A real space is linked to Hitchcock's filmic space, so that the pedestrians we witness on our fake 10th Street are interpretable as moving not in a movie studio but in New York. That Jeff is locked up in his apartment is the prevention that blocks him from being one of those pedestrians. In his heart and thoughts he is among them, and watches their actions with the pleasure of detachment and imagined involvement. The same is to be said of his neighbors, who all navigated to their homes in ways now forbidden to him.

Watching 10th Street through that tiny alley, we might be looking north or south. The street runs east and west, and when we see the flames of sunset, Robert Burks and his lighting team have cast the entire backdrop with a flush of light, so that it is impossible to determine absolutely whether the west, where the sun is dying, is to our left or our right. To neglect a concern such as this is to see the entire film, as it were, myopically: to bound one's vision and interest only within the (very proximate) dramatic construction without looking beyond to what it suggests and implies. The Bazinian devotion to deep focus—*mise-en-scène*—suggests looking at the setting in terms of SETTING, the city of the film in terms of the City of our world. And when we attempt to do this, we find ourselves deeply and excitingly confused, thrown into dream space, because the two possible orientations of vision are so delicately interchangeable. It is fascinating to note, in this respect, that Hitchcock's team went to lengths, for technical reasons regarding photography, to arrange that Jeff should be pointing to the north as he looks out, pointing, that is, to an entirely imaginary "north" that in practice we will not—need not—read. The sun sets to the left, then. Johnson wrote to Erickson: "Find a rear court of this type in Greenwich Village, with this type of vista (sky and buildings in the background). *This vista has to be north.* The room the shot is taken from is on the south side of the court. This puts the camera in shadow" (Johnson to Erickson; my emphasis).[14] Johnson to Erickson in a private memo, inside a private file, unconnected to the film as screened.

What begs address is a profound experiential contradiction for the viewer. On one side we have the detailed building of a fabular world based strictly on real space, contingency, and proportion; a world in which we look from below 10th Street in the uptown direction, and in which, exhaustively, the "New Yorkness" of the scene as depicted bears witness to, flows out of, a real quality of life in the City of New York in the early 1950s. On the other, we find ourselves in a space where we keep pointing navigationally to one apartment after another, establish the spatial relationships between the neighbors as well as their psychologies and dramatic circumstances, and sense ourselves to be caught up in a vital, but specially fashioned, urban scene. In the first, the "actuality" of the set, its derivation from New York itself, we face diegetic north, as the production team required. In the second, the fabular, disconnected, sacred space of the setting, we do not know at all where we face. Thus, our compass both works and doesn't work; we both know and do not know where we are. What is effected by this disjunction of attitudes is a charged and thoroughgoing dream consciousness on our part, a plasticity of involvement. Because we are in oneiric space, we gain a sense of underpinning pleasure in the gliding smoothness of our proceeding, the cultivated and meticulously *arranged* nature of screened events. If with our dreaming eyes we become Jeff with his dreaming eyes, we become wrapped up in the confusing unfoldings, carried off from dreary rational life. It is similar in dreams, when we simultaneously do and do not know where we are.

This dream state, implies Modris Eksteins, was the way of life in Weimar Germany, where Alfred Hitchcock learned his trade.[15] "He was always taking mental notes," Patrick McGilligan writes. "Although he could be evasive about his influences when pressed Hitchcock would mention *The Cabinet of Dr. Caligari*, Murnau, Lang, even Lubitsch" (all Weimar sources); "and when asked in general about stylistic mentors, his reply was unflinching. 'The Germans. The Germans'" (64). Eksteins adduces Siegfried Kracauer, formidable theorist of cinema, as being "emblematic" of a "shift in focus" away from a "former world, with its cosmic implications—call it Newtonian, Victorian, or simply 'enlightened'" and toward fragmentation and explosion in the wake of World War I, and claims of Kracauer (as paragon of that shift): "He had ascribed meaning to the quotidian and the *insignificant*. The life of the street became for him the street of life" (276, my emphasis). Focus and absorption, not mapping. Jeff Jefferies, as Poe's recuperating stranger, is also obsessed with the street and its vibrant life, indeed himself a paragon of the Baudelairian *flâneur*, who wanders the city in the aimless thrill of observing and classifying people he does not know. Tied up as he is, Jeff is wandering by virtue of his flickering gaze, of his rapt and sweeping attention to his little urban space with its crevice byways, but it is Eksteins's use of the key word "insignificant" that sheds light here. He means to suggest of Kracauer (and, by implication, I would argue, of our Jeff) an obsessive, delirious attentiveness to *what had earlier been defined as "insignificant" but now, suddenly, gains significance* in the fragmented world. This heightening of significance is rendered in *Rear Window* by Hitchcock's elongating, elaborating, extending, and emphasizing the "insignificance" of dream consciousness until it becomes startling and full and real.

The dream consciousness is also an element of Hitchcock's architecture of our viewing experience. At the crisis of the film, a sharp, almost bellicose moment of direct experience—or what seems enough like direct experience to jolt us, as it jolts Jeff—Thorwald looks out and meets our gaze. It is quite as though death rays have projected from the villain's face, and the effect is to stun us awake from the dream, abruptly, shockingly, painfully. *This is actually happening!* Jeff tries to wheel himself back from the window, *You can't be looking, too! You can't be seeing me, seeing you!!!* But it is too late, too late dramatically, far far too late conceptually. This is the moment of dreaming in which the dream fabric rends, and the only available choice is direct perception. Direct perception and, perhaps, darkness. Yet also only a flash. The dream—some dream—can resume. Allen notes in this film "a powerful undercurrent of human perversity," with Jeff bringing a story into being that "expresses, indeed vindicates, his own darkest impulses" (169).

From here, the film races to its conclusion, with Thorwald explosively visiting Jeff, the popping flashbulbs, the crisis at the window. The atmosphere becomes too radiant and too dark in rapid alternation. But in the final moment, the darkness yields to exceptional radiance, with the atmosphere of *cauchemar* that pervaded every moment of the film, subtly, quietly, now magically lifted by virtue of Jeff's sacrifice, and the many neighbors happily reconciled to communal domestic bliss—Miss Torso with her boyfriend returned; a new puppy for the Whistlers (in a joke, Hitchcock wondered whether it should be a Great Dane); Miss Lonelyhearts sitting by the composer's side as he plays for her. To the mounting melody of Franz Waxman's delirious song, we are sent to dream our wholly implicating everydays.

CHAPTER THREE

HIS OWN SENSE OF LIFE

Saboteur

> Here the socio-economic class conflict is vividly posed in burning silhouettes against the walls of the factory and the hinterland.
> —Farnsworth Crowder

Near the beginning of what has often been anointed Alfred Hitchcock's most important film—a work more evidently and unequivocally about mortality than his others—a talented graphic artist lightheartedly entertains an old beau in her studio apartment on Telegraph Hill. She is drawing an advertisement for what he calls a "doohickey": it is a new, radical uplift brassiere, thought up, she informs him, by "an aircraft designer down the peninsula." Full of implication as they are, this claim of the character's and this garment that she is copying from a model on her desk do not constitute, but only (fascinatingly) hint at, the central vertigo in *Vertigo* (1958), with their implication of rising and dropping, the peril of the fall, the connection of a very beautiful woman (in this case Barbara Bel Geddes) with vertical danger, and their tying strategic sexual interaction to military technology.¹

Not only military technology, but military technology in California. By the advent of the 1940s the San Fernando Valley and areas to the south

of Los Angeles had been caught in a "firestorm" of transformation. Pomona of the 1940s, a good example (Mike Davis notes that it had been "so modally middle class—the real-life counterpart of Andy Hardy's hometown—that Hollywood used it as a preview laboratory to test typical audience reactions to new films. In the 1950s it became a commuter suburb for thousands of Fathers-Know-Best in their starched white shirts" [*Ecology* 398]), was subsumed by Hughes Aircraft, falling into prosperity, as did so many other Angeleno communities, gobbled by other aircraft giants, like McDonnell and Lockheed. The aircraft plants were immense and required armies of laborers, people who, shifting to California—still the new goldmine—had to have places to live. It was a time, Davis writes, when "freeways were still applauded as technological wonders, and suburbia was a dream only half unfolded" (419). Real estate developers "could not tear down orange groves fast enough to meet the demand for tract houses for the burgeoning workforce of the aerospace industry. Although what was being built in those huge sheds in Burbank, Long Beach, Downey, Canoga Park, and Pomona was usually an official secret, eight-year-olds imagined that they must include prototype rocketships to the moon and eventually Mars" (420). At this time, the economy of Southern California "was being 'Keynesianized' in its own peculiar fashion," writes Davis, as the "inter-regional capital flows that had been the source of Southern California's prosperity were now institutionalized in national defense appropriations that shifted tax resources from the rest of the country to irrigate the Los Angeles area's aircraft plants and military bases" (*Quartz* 120).

The 1940s utopia, with a footing in the aircraft industry, was yet another version of California dreaming: "No notion is more deeply seated," wrote Carey McWilliams in 1946, "no idea has echoed more persistently

95

through the years, than the theory that a new and vital culture would someday be born in California. 'Here if anywhere else in America,' said William Butler Yeats on a visit to California, 'I seem to hear the coming footsteps of the muses'" (367). But of course the dream would evanesce in the morning. Things would get much worse. Davis notes how "aerospace and defense closures—like Hughes Missile Division's abrupt departure from Pomona or Lockheed's abandonment of its huge Burbank complex" had the "social impact of unforeseen natural disasters. Following the Lockheed shutdown, welfare caseloads in the eastern San Fernando Valley soared by 80,000 in an 18-month period. In the Valley as a whole (population 1.2 million), one in six residents now lives below the poverty line" (*Ecology* 400–401).

Midge Wood's "aircraft designer down the peninsula," a personage working at the heart of the project of lifting toward, ascending into, and finally dominating from the air, and potentially falling, I take to have been an unannounced acquaintance, or at least workmate, of young Barry Kane (Robert Cummings), the heroic protagonist of *Saboteur* (1942). After two films for David O. Selznick, *Rebecca* (1940) and *Suspicion* (1941), both of which, partly to suit the producer's inclinations, reflected the Englishness of the filmmaker's heritage, Hitchcock had arranged to do a film for Jack Skirball at Universal (a film originally intended for Selznick, upon an early story draft for which Selznick made comment). It begins "down on the coast" at Los Angeles, in an aircraft plant where a coterie of cheery young men have been laboring intensively to manufacture the flying machines America sends overseas to bolster the combat against Nazism. Implied instantly at the film's earliest moment is global conflict; patriotism; interventionist fervor; and the persistently awkward delicacy of secrecy and protection associated with war production (in America as in England). This factory is a complex and gigantic one (from outside, the hangar looks roughly like a film soundstage and was built out of storage bins on the Universal lot [Krohn 41]), but as a production site it betokens more than mere capital expansion. It is a cauldron of top-secret military zeal, thus a signal factor in America's war posture (and a symbol of American might and dignity). American aviation was expansive in the tactical, military sense long before it caught on domestically. The air here represents a fighting position; and a factory like this one is to be thought nationally central in its capacity for producing tools of war that can be advantaged by height. Bombs will be dropped from the planes under construction here: an early hint that gravity, both physical and social, contributes vitally to the production of death.

Almost immediately, black smoke signals that a fire has broken out inside the plant. This is shown as a major incendiary event, with workers screaming in flight and vast destruction to merchandise and human life, threatened or actual, on all sides. Barry is handed an extinguisher, but his close chum Ken Mason (Virgil Summers) snatches it from him playfully and heads forward to quash the blaze. Ken's triggering the device produces a colossal flare-up, however, and the young man is instantly consumed in the flames. Suspicion falls upon the innocent Barry, who was seen handing over the extinguisher. He must now flee for his life, setting out on a journey of fear and hope, across America. The nuances of villainy, petty and enormous, that he encounters along the way constitute the main thrust of the film. By convention, he will meet a pretty girl, who begins by thinking him horrible and ends up offering him love. And a major threat against the American war effort will be stymied in a brilliantly shining finale.

The idea of beginning the film in the aircraft factory was a suggestion from Selznick:

> [Come] in on airplane factory where our hero is a mechanic. In a scene of eerie night atmosphere, amid activities for defense, … the hero's best pal is killed by the saboteur and the blame falls on the hero.
>
> Therefore, because of his love for his pal, the hero has the added emotional reason for chasing the villain across the country. (Notes)

In more ways than one our Barry is innocent. He does not bear responsibility for Ken's death, so in legal and moral respects he is blameless, a man "without guilt." As usual with Hitchcock, other people's misperceptions set up conditions in which the hero must recognize that his guiltlessness will not be presumed by the institution of justice: guiltlessness is thorny in itself. Eric Rohmer and Claude Chabrol gave an engaged reading of the Catholic implications of this arrangement, in their discussion of the wronged man in Hitchcock's films:

> The idea is an extremely complex one, the components of which we can successively identify as: that of the fundamental *abjectness* of a

human being, who once deprived of his freedom is no more than an object among other objects; that of *misfortune*, which is simultaneously unjust and merited, like that of Job . . .; and that of *guilt*. (147; emphasis original)

As to freedom and abjectness, the state of being nothing more than an object among objects, more to follow. After original sin, who is not in a position where proving innocence is problematic? Barry's innocence, tender and fragile, is thus quintessentially human, Hitchcock's contrivance being a neat device for metaphorizing a spiritual condition that is both broad and deep, without allegiance to drama or fictionalization for its truth.

But to take a crucial further step, Barry is also, as the film begins, an epitome of the untutored, naïve, happy-go-lucky yet uninitiated man-child much in need of a moral education. The film will show us both the key moments of his development as he comes to a more adult stance in the world and the principles by which his moral commitment is tested. Barry's is a great and enveloping test, a test of the sinews of his spirit, since he surely begins the tale as one of those who are, in Robert Musil's words, "vastly relieved to be left in a position where they can't put their ideas into practice" (312). A factory fire and sabotage could occur anywhere at any time, after all, but this one is set in a war context. And the war is not any war but the global battle against Hitler. Once again here, as so often in his work, the setting is not Hitchcock's theme but it is principally by way of the setting that the theme announces itself. *Saboteur* isn't about World War II. World War II had its saboteurs, but here it is the context in which Hitchcock can most effectively render a story about a sabotage even more affecting, even more profound.

WATCH, I'LL SHOW YOU

Hitchcock's design for this film involves a fascinating leitmotif that will find statement and restatement until in its swirling and magnification it becomes powerfully thematic: the power and debility of looking. Here at the film's beginning we find an early instance, in which if looking is dramatically significant it is also culturally normative so that in a casual viewing focusing attention might receive but little attention itself. In the casual use of the eyes, indeed, the look or the gaze devolve into the glance. Later on, looking will gradually become more pronounced, until there is no mistaking that the use of the eyes, in its relation to the wartime setting and the moral stance, has a central role to play in our understanding: of this film, and of life. But as well as it does the concentrated gaze, conflict also mobilizes the glance. As the stakes of conflict mount and become global, the glance is refined and becomes furtive.

The early instance: Barry and Ken are on a meal break with a third fellow, a smaller, sharp-featured, not especially friendly man. This one happens to drop some money and an envelope and Barry graciously bends over to retrieve them, yet in the process notably *declines to politely avoid* inspecting this stranger's goods. "Frank Fry," he reads. Always, the handwriting on any stranger's envelope might pique natural interest. Yet Barry is being nosy—in a typical, easily recognizable way, just as members of the audience are typically, easily nosy, curious to scrutinize the characters onscreen and learn their private secrets: the formula of fiction approximates us to any and every stranger. Nosy yet not malicious; curious yet not antisocial. I am reminded of Jean-Louis Schefer's somewhat perfunctory self-observation, in "The Ordinary Man of Cinema": "I'm always less the film's reader and more like its totally submissive servant, and also its judge" (110). Barry's instinct is to probe, at any rate. And, aware of the judgmental gaze of his viewers, Hitchcock seizes and dramatizes Barry's judgmental gaze as a way of embracing his viewers' judging point of view.

As Barry takes his judicious peek, the strange man, Fry (Norman Lloyd), whose eyes are round and white, peeks at him peeking.

In his prying—his Fry prying—Barry is amenable, even attractive, casual, and apparently harmlessly quotidian, and this tone of characterization might carry its own import. Virtually on first glance Barry mobilizes our sympathy and Fry does not, though we have been given almost no information about either of them. Perhaps this bias arises on simple, physical grounds; because, like fifteen-year-old Mickey Mouse—the Mickey of, say, *The Sorcerer's Apprentice*—as described by Stephen Jay Gould, Barry betrays marks of neoteny, small facial features in proportion to head size, which is to say, a "cute" nose and diminutive eyes; "when we see a living creature with babyish features, we feel an automatic surge of disarming tenderness" (*Homage* 101). A signally contrasting type, Fry calls up instead the much earlier Mickey of *Steamboat Willie* (1928): "rambunctious, even slightly sadistic, with larger eyes and nose measured against the size of the head." A national symbol, such as the later Mickey and, in his fortuitous development, Barry in *Saboteur*, "was expected to behave properly at all times...," Gould quotes Christopher Finch, a pictorial historian of the Disney enterprise; sweet characters had to assuage the anxieties of citizens "who felt the nation's moral well-being was in their hands" (in Gould, *Homage* 96). Physiognomy (thus, the casting of Cummings and Lloyd) motivates our attention and concern, raises alarm or cues relaxation of the spectatorial gaze. This theme will merit considerable restatement as, in complex ways, it resurfaces in *Saboteur*.

But as to that envelope retrieved and delivered from the lunchroom floor, what must be made emphatic—by me here, but earlier on by Hitchcock to the viewer—is this: Barry Kane's swift-eyed moment is played by Cummings as entirely casual, inadvertent, and unaffected. One hardly pauses to consider his use of the eye here, it blends seamlessly into the cultural grounding of workplace interaction, the forced affability among strangers. Barry's open-eyed approach to the world—his eagerness toward incorporating sights—is a kind of innocent, generalized bent for observation, a bent for surveillance not just here at this moment but more broadly, as the world turns. He "has his eyes open." He "doesn't miss a thing." Yet at the same time there's nothing particular that he's looking for, he's not on a hunt. Our self-consciousness as cinemagoers watching Barry depends entirely on his effortless open-eyed stance, since he is mimicking us. No professional spy, Barry is but an ordinary man of cinema, converted to the task of keeping his eyes open, seeing whatever it is that might be seen. This is a wholeheartedly patriotic, even militaristic posture, to be sure, in wartime: the enemy is everywhere, and is everywhere giving off signals that might have strategic value.

As much as Barry is suspicious of Fry, Fry is suspicious of him. Barry does look sharply at the envelope and retain the information it contains, but more telling than his action is the fact that, as a person with a built-in detection apparatus now geared up for combat, he *can be* observant in this way. He stands as exemplar of the citizen on the lookout, here, there, and everywhere (a figure to be reprised by the detective Graham at the end of *Shadow of a Doubt* [1943], when he claims—with both an intensely moral care and self-serving justification, that the world needs watching).[2]

Under the general social conditions invoked instantly by *Saboteur*, and especially here in this war plant geared to heavy-duty production, no amount of sighting is enough, nor can sighting ever be accomplished with enough care. Michel Foucault places the origin of the surveilling gaze in the military camps, schools, and clinics of the eighteenth century (*Birth* 38–39, cited in Jay 409), and goes on to elaborate the signification of the gaze through the agency of a sort of decoding—my word—that the observer tends to make by observing:

> The clinical gaze has the paradoxical ability to *hear a language* as soon as it *perceives a spectacle*. In the clinic, what is manifested is originally what is spoken.... The observing gaze manifests its virtues only in a double silence: the relative silence of theories, imaginings, and whatever serves as an obstacle to the sensible immediate; and the absolute silence of all language that is anterior to that of the visible. Above the density of this double silence things can be heard at last, and heard solely by virtue of the fact that they are seen. (108; emphasis original)

In essence, astute observation is tactical and productive. Barry's almost reflex gesture with Fry's envelope, casual and unhighlighted, may come to seem an accommodation of self to an overriding, imposing regime of isolation and dismemberment: the Nazi menace is to be located as it lurks and plots on American soil (a soil that still in the early years of World War II certainly harbored a carefully devoted and well-organized isolationist, sometimes even pro-Nazi force) and, once discovered and pinpointed there, is to be severed from its nourishing source in Hitlerian philosophy by way of pointing, diagnosing, open declaration—or even killing. The enemy is here ... Are you watching? Martin Jay adduces Jean-Paul Sartre's rejection of novel-writing as surveillance: "Sartre could still express his rage at the novelist's adoption of the disinterested position of *survol*, that putative God's-eye view, whose deliberate denial he had applauded in other figures like Kierkegaard" (294).

Hitchcock is not, like Sartre, denying the *survol* in this part of his film. First, it is dramatically necessary for him to raise our expectations of significant and horrible eventuality—to be presented and developed later—through the sense that something is already darkly wrong in this factory. Further, Barry Kane's moral callowness, his unmistakable need for an education, will show more clearly if he seems a little insensitive in his curiosity: if not a brute then at least immodest in his invasive gazing. This Mr. Fry, after all, is a shy and unantagonizing little man, guilty here and now of nothing more than dropping his envelope, his—as Henry James put it—"whole envelope of circumstances":

> When you've lived as long as I you'll see that every human being has his shell and that you must take the shell into account. By the shell I mean the whole envelope of circumstances. There's no such thing as an isolated man or woman; we're each of us made up of some cluster of appurtenances. What shall we call our "self"? Where does it begin? Where does it end? It overflows into everything that belongs to us—and then it flows back again. (207)

Nor must one forget the broader historical reality against which this film play is set: that a penchant for alertness, even a program of cautious watchfulness, had by early 1942 been settled in Southern California, not only among military forces freshly mobilized because of Pearl Harbor but also in local civilian life of the kind to be found in the small suburban areas in and around Los Angeles that were enthusiastically supporting the aircraft industry: the Douglas Company headquartered in Santa Monica with plants in Long Beach and El Segundo; Hughes operating out of Culver City; Lockheed manufacturing its P-38 Lightnings at three different plants in Burbank; Northrop in Hawthorne; Vultee in Downey; and North American in Inglewood (on a site later occupied by LAX). Civil Defense authorities let it be known they were on the lookout for lookouts: "workers, husky men and women, who can take it, day and night, come rain, come hail, come sleet, come snow! Let's send a thought of gratitude to those responsible souls who have already taken over these lousy, cold, tedious watchful-waiting, on-guard jobs" ("What Are You Doing for Defense?," *Sausalito News* 53 [1 January 1942], 2). One such responsible soul was Mrs. Frank Steele of 3412 Patten Ave., San Pedro, who "called the Naval Section Base and made the following report; 'At 0630 I heard the sharp report of a gun. Looking out my window I saw a submarine bearing southwest submerging"; the Navy was quick to ask "anyone having such information" to phone in at once, "but not to cry 'wolf!' when there is no wolf" ("'Keep Calm' Is Air Raid Advice Brought to H. P. Realty Board Meeting," *Highland Park Post-Dispatch* 6: 17 [8 January 1942], 1). A generalized sense of caution, precipitousness, and urgency spiced slogans, such as in a 12 February 1942 boldface byline: "A slip of the lip may give a spy a tip" (*Highland Park Post-Dispatch* 6: 22, 3), or "Don't let your guard down!," a piece of advice offered by Lieutenant Paul Schantz of the US Army's Fourth Interceptor command when he addressed "a mass meeting called by the Highland Park Organization for Co-operation in Civilian Defense.... with 200 citizens in attendance." Schantz is quoted as having stressed the importance of a "corps of volunteer workers who keep 24-hour watch of the sky" in an article that, surveying civilian conditions in the Los Angeles area, urged that "at the present time there are 50,000 volunteer watchers in California, under supervision of the American Legion, and more are needed" ("Defense Measures Explained," *Highland Park Post-Dispatch* 6: 24 [26 February 1942], 1). Nor, in the climate of hostility, was watching only a diffuse operation affecting all racial and ethnic minorities and the dominant population, equally. When some people watched, it was a blessing; when others did, it was a curse. The *Palos Verdes Peninsula News* of 2 January 1942 reported a national confiscation order affecting "all Japanese, Italian and German residents," that required the turning-in of cameras ("Aliens Turn in Cameras," 1).

After the fire, our frightened hero—Tifenn Brisset is convinced this type expresses a Rousseauan "égoïsme naturel," an individualism wishing to ensure his survival above all else (9)—speeds off to see his dead friend's mother (Dorothy Peterson), a stalwart and lonely widow collapsed in grief in her tiny bungalow but remaining, in Selznick's words, "the only one to believe in the hero's innocence and who is the one to shield him later in the story from the police. (This will eliminate the character of the boy's own mother)" (Notes). Searching around for some brandy to revive her, Barry comes up empty so he uses her back door to visit the next-door neighbor ("Don't have her [protect him from the police] by merely physically shielding him with her body," Selznick had dictated [Notes]). While he is gone, the police come a-hunting, letting on that Barry is formally suspected in Ken's death. Shocked yet unmoved (she knows her son's friend well), Mrs. Mason tells them nothing. Barry returns when the police have gone—did he see them coming?, and know how to make a dodge?—and soon later, confused to learn that apparently there is no person at the plant named Fry, he leaves Mrs. Mason to grieve alone. The scene at Mrs. Mason's bungalow is important, not only because it shows, up close, the socioeconomic conditions in which war-plant workers carried on their lives in this part of the country but because it bluntly announces a kind of love and acceptance that will later gain prominence in the story but lacks, without this tender woman, a point of reference: Barry is now the closest thing she has to her dead son. He is utterly beyond reproach in her knowing, loving, deeply understanding view (and, like so many other characters here, she *is* taking a view). The ability to see Barry, to take "shells" into account but somehow know what is inside them, is the gift she offers him; but he is too panicked to appreciate it substantially, too eager to be on his way.

Hitchhiking on the highway Barry is picked up by a truck driver (Murray Alper), who is heading into the San Gabriel Mountains north of Los Angeles. If Mrs. Mason's look of acceptance and blessing warmed Barry in his panic, and if in not being especially aware of it he was taking his "membership" in the Mason family more or less for granted, in this truck he is unmistakably not at home. However, Mrs. Mason and this truck driver will turn out to be his first teachers, in his unconscious quest for enlightenment. The driver in particular is a man whose eyes are always peeled: to safely negotiate the roads he must be alert, a true scanner; yet—clear to us before it is to Barry—there is something about this passenger that satisfies his curiosity. This one is all right. This one I can help.

Barry's casual, almost automatic eye-work on Fry's envelope has now been modified, by virtue of Mrs. Mason's tender compassion and the truck driver's polite but cautious glancing, into a palpable feature of the story, a dramatically central, if attenuated surveillance. Barry examines—checks out, determines his safety in the presence of—the characters he meets; and with the shadows of war in the background (as cued in Robert Boyle's brilliant, relentless, high-contrast design) the people around him do the same, generally on the lookout for problem types, in which dubious category Barry might too easily be slotted. When the truck is stopped by a highway patrolman (a minor Hitchcockian emblem) Barry instinctually prepares to flee, but the official problem of the moment is apparently only a faulty tail light (trigger for surveillance on another level, perhaps, but no signal for this cop, with his lesser talent for taking small details as symptomatic of big problems). When, at morning, the truck nears Deep Springs Ranch, Barry suddenly remembers this was the address on Fry's envelope. He begs to be dropped off.

The housekeeper at the ranch house door knows nothing about a man named Fry, but admits Barry to a seat by the swimming pool (a glimmering lure) where Mr. Tobin (Otto Kruger), owner of the place, is tending his infant granddaughter Susie. A gracile, educated, refined, even sophisticated man poised in the vast outreaches of the agricultural wilderness. Tobin confesses he doesn't know Fry either, with a smile that twinkles like the water's reflection. But when he steps out for a moment, the tiny tyke points Barry to an object that turns out to be: an envelope addressed to Fry at Soda City. Now Tobin is back, a very different light in his eye. He menaces Barry with a pistol, naming him as the man wanted by the police for the aircraft-plant killing. But grabbing little Susie as a human shield, the visitor manages to escape into the rancher's nearby field. Tobin's ranch hands corner Barry on horseback—he is but a steer gone loose from the herd, a target for the lasso—and drag him back. The police, summoned by the capable Tobin (who expects their obedience to his status), escort the fugitive away in handcuffs, his feisty energy drained, his prospects dimmed, his adventure curtailed.

The sharpness in Tobin's gaze, and his ability to smoothly shift gears from sociable graciousness to dark hostility, all the while displaying education and a cultivated personality, mark the next station in Barry's moral journey, an undeniably emphatic lesson about the inherent fragility of human encounters; the capacity of the face to mask intent; the way our view of the moment and its implications guides our moral conviction and public attitude; not to say the bitter darkness bounding the sunlit majesty of the American landscape (and notably, the majestic California landscape). To be remembered later: although he was careful and restrained when he saw Barry holding up his grandchild in front of his pointed gun, Tobin showed not a hint of surprise at the cravenness, the horrifying utility, of the gesture. Only the choreography of the moment saves Barry from our condemnation: that he speaks sweetly in baby talk to the little girl, that he is something of a baby himself, that he flies like the wind; and that Tobin may be a threat of prodigious proportion.

Barry's innocence is sharply altered now that he is in the presence of darkness. He becomes—because, in order to survive, he must—more doubting, more conniving, less simplistic. We do not yet have irrefutable evidence for his legal guiltlessness, and he is a man in desperate flight, the forces chasing him relentless and unpleasant. The single unequivocally stainless tag upon his character is something we witnessed that no other character did: Fry placed the fire extinguisher in Barry's hands, and Ken, joking that he wanted to be in on the fun, demanded to have it instead. The extinguisher, then—it lights the fire of the story, instead of dousing it!—came not from Barry but from the mysterious Fry. Fry who collects mail at Tobin's ranch. Fry whom Tobin protests he does not know.

Barry must escape from the police, at the very least because they can too easily be wrong.[3] Handcuffed in a vehicle stalled behind a truck on a bridge, Barry makes a run for it, dropping into the water below. Of all obstacles, the truck ahead is nothing other than his newfound chum's vehicle, that loyal man's, as it happens, who now makes a moral affiliation—whilst, for us, labeling Barry ineradicably—by misdirecting the police so that the fugitive can get away. Barry's moral education is spatially co-present with his freedom; but his identity is also bound with the idea of being free, a theme that will soon deepen. Free, that is, in America; on the road that promises, always, a future; accompanied by the good-hearted worker laboring back and forth across this space in his worn vehicle; and framed gloriously by some of the numerous views in this film of majestic California, the world to which the pioneering spirit moved, where the constraints of class-bound European culture could be undone, where the "footsteps of the muses" would come.

Our hero's increasing awareness is set intrinsically, not artificially, in America's rural space. But if his release now permits him to head away from a debilitating trap, still he has a lesson to learn that must be taught in a radically different context.

DREAM SIGHT

Rain is pelting down in a mountain pine forest as Barry comes upon a lonely log cabin. "The woods are lovely, dark and deep," and Barry has promises to keep. Inside is a watchful, eager German shepherd and his master, a tall and very dignified man (Vaughan Glazer). Did Barry leave his car down on the road? "Why don't you bring it up and put it in the shade? I'm afraid it won't do it any good standing in the rain."

"I don't have any car," Barry demurs, standing just inside the door. "You might say I'm ... traveling by thumb."

"By thumb?" the old eyes squinting and the mouth frowning as the man plunges into thought, turning a little away from his open door so that an ominous shadow of him is projected behind his head (homage to the yawning silhouette grotesqueries in early Disney animation?).

"Yeah, I'm a hitch-hiker."

"Oh," brightening now into a broad and expressive smile, "I see!" As he has turned back a fraction of an inch, the man's shadow now displays the mouth in its warm grin. "I have always thought that that was the best way to learn about this country," both men smiling face to face, "and the surest test of the American heart." He is making reference to an important but, today, in the age of constant conflict and paranoia, much outmoded (if biblical) virtue, kindness to strangers. When one stands at the side of the road, sticking out one's thumb in hopes that a passing driver will pull over (a gesture artfully parodied by Clark Gable for the delight of Claudette Colbert in Frank Capra's *It Happened One Night* [1934]), one places one's safety, one's movement, one's future in the hands of an unknown other; and when as a driver, proceeding apace, one stops to pick up a stranger, one offers the warmth of a traveling home, the personability of a self. Without admitting why he is traveling, then; and without clueing his host as to where he comes from, why he is on the move, and where he is hoping to go, Barry is establishing his credentials as those of a person who needs with desperate urgency to trust and to be trusted, one for whom trust is the signal asset. The "American heart" to which the old man points is the trusting, generous heart, the heart that is implied when, hearing or reading "Give me your tired, your poor," one detects the deep, broad echoing voice, "And I will harbor them."

We have noticed, before Barry, that this old man is sightless.

Come in and warm yourself by the fire. Could you put another log on?

As Barry tries to accommodate, with his host at his side, he accidentally drops his log, hobbled by the police handcuffs. A powerful two-shot, looking up at the men from the hearthstone, the flame's light radiant upon them. Barry's gaze into the other's face, distinctly aslant, is frozen as he waits in panic with the cuffs unhappily in broad sight. But the old face is merely that of a man startled, and he looks forward: to the fireplace glow, not to Barry. "I'm sorry, I should have warned you. Those logs are heavier than you'd think." A gentle face gazing into Barry's alert, fearful face, and without any heed to the wrists, or to the cuffs that gleam too much. "I drop them constantly," a soothing, avuncular tone. But we are staring in close-up at Barry looking off-frame at this man, with eyes opened wide in fear and suspicion, his face and hair moist from the rain, his mouth gravely turned down. On the word "constantly," we shift back to a close shot of the other, but while the portrait of Barry was from our fugitive's level, directly at him as he looked to the side, the shot of the old man is from below, so that the noble head, lifted with dignity, is statuesque in the warm light. From offscreen right, the cuffed hands move forward and sway back and forth across the lined, undetecting face. Even as the man's visage falls into shadow, there are points of piercing light in his eyes. As Barry gets the log onto the fire, his host sits. You should be careful, says he, not to drop the log on your foot; it often happens to me: "You're lucky."

"Yeah," with ironic flatness. "I'm lucky."

"Oh, I was forgetting. My name is Philip Martin." An introduction of self *after* the invitation to enter, *after* shelter has been secured, *after* the firewood is set ablaze.

"Oh, I'm Barry K—... Mason." (Fetching his dead friend back to life.)

"It's a pleasant thing to have a guest sharing the fire, when the rain is beating on the roof." A poetic line. A man definitively in the tradition of Frost, of Whitman, of Thoreau.

"You live alone, do you, sir?"

"Yes ... except I really don't think of it in that way. You see, sounds are my light. And my colors ... my music, for example...." Martin stands up. But as he lifts his body out of the easy chair, his massive head comes very close to the camera. It is as though we have been lingering closer to him than we would normally do to a seated character addressing another character in a filmic story. By the firelight, and talking about hospitality and colors and music, he has become part of the world of our actual presence much more than a figure in a fictional remove.[4] But since Martin *is* a character in a fiction, this illusion of his presence to us invokes an all-too-brief, itself flickering, dream sensation. He is both as real as other real things and an inhabitant of a zone separated from what we would *term* reality. This perceptual confusion passes quickly, like a whiff of perfume in a breeze.

I "rewind" for a second thought about that dark, alert, fearful look in Barry's eyes when he dropped the log. We hadn't seen it before, not anything so close to the grave. The shadowing from the hearth and the camera's angle on the young man's face combined to darken his gaze, convert it to the desperately hungry, terrified expression of the hunted man fearful at every turn that he is at tether's end (there is a brief hint of the malevolent Tracy [Donald Calthrop] in *Blackmail* [1929]). If in Barry's hunted eyes there was a nuance of eagerness to take advantage, it was the eagerness of a helpless man—the urgency of someone who needs any extra ort of beneficence he might finger up from the table of hospitality.

The music that has been promised: Martin charmingly notes, "I compose a little. And there is nobody to tell me that the results are anything but brilliant"—implying wryly that he knows very well, with a convicted modesty, how far from brilliant his work is. On the polished grand piano stand a pair of cut-glass candle holders, pristine and gleaming—"So I live in a comfortable glow of self-appreciation." An important comment, as regards Martin and the America that supports his posture. We might now think him humorlessly narcissistic, while he is everything but. The slightly self-mocking tone implies that there are those who *would* sit in such a comfortable glow, but he is manifestly not one of them: that is, he does not regard his music as special because it flows from, as he might esteem it, some high talent. But the statement also directly points to the centrality of the individual self as a site of moral truth and responsibility. James Baldwin mourns the "nerve-wracking *busyness*" of the American stage—"'Keep moving, maybe nobody will notice that nothing's happening'—and the irritating, self-indulgent mannerisms of so many of our actors.... Sometimes the actor finds that no amount of skill will 'justify' or cover up the hollowness or falsity of what he is called on to do" (20; emphasis original); the "wellspring on which the actor must draw ... is his own sense of life" (22). Here in Martin, affirmed by contrast, is the yeoman spirit, that of the man who knows himself independently of—even in contrast against—what external powers would point him to be. His is the aristocratic personality, protected and separated from society, both by the deep woods and by the faithful hound (the dog performer was Grey Shadow). "I appreciate myself" means I value, esteem, measure, reform, challenge, and finally accompany myself.

I am the man it seems to me that I should be. Martin is a glowing model of the ethical "I."

Barry confesses he used to play triangle in the high school band, but "of course that was a long time ago." A musing reflection from Martin at his keyboard: "It's unfortunate when you let yourself get out of practice on the triangle." This is ambiguous, of course. There is very little refinement required for playing the triangle, so Barry could, if he pleased, play it now even without practice, and since the triangle makes such a pleasing sound, perhaps Barry *should* commit himself to playing the triangle; his having given it up, when it is so simple and delightful an instrument, suggests Barry's faith in the world fell some time ago. But further, this "triangle" is another, grander, deeper, more sanctified triangle, a holy Triad, as it were, that might influence all human conduct to the good were citizens to be mindful of it in their everydays. "The piano can't know that you're blind," Martin says, playing from Frederick Delius's *Summer Night on the River* (in his later years Delius was himself blind), the music something of a soothing, surreal, misty, intuitive lullaby, and Barry gazing back with a little smile, "so it doesn't embarrass you by trying to make things easier for you."

But offscreen right, Barry has seen something, something desirable. He moves that way, reaches out, and the camera slowly pans to follow his shackled hands in their pursuit. It is a silver chaser of ripe fruit. He helps himself to an apple and takes a chomp, the cue to Martin that his guest is starving: "A very interesting effect! Obbligato on an apple!" He gets up and proceeds with the dog to fetch dinner from the kitchen. But throughout, Barry has been looking out hesitantly, suspiciously, fearfully. Is it all right, really, to be standing here? Is it all right to help myself to food? Is this old man going to corner me—and is all his friendliness, all his hospitality, just a lure?

Thus far we have had only half of Martin's great moral lesson, the glowing and enriching half, about the welcoming spirit, gentleness, art, loyalty, and sweetness. For although in his persisting moral blindness Barry cannot fathom this man, we in our sensibility to Hitchcock's carefully composed, brilliantly lit screen, can. Barry's blindness flows from a "time out of joint" that we do not experience, as watchers of this film—the plotting and devising of the sabotage. So, yet another triangle is "sounded": the helpless Barry Kane, the soothing and wounded Philip Martin, and Hitchcock's revealing and limiting camera. Nevertheless the viewer, with sight assured in the republic of cinema, wherein the most refined of virtues finds a happy home, may recognize what Barry still cannot—that he has found peace. But our Barry has one more lesson to learn: the place of caution and prudence in the face of true danger.

As they move to the dining table—a candelabrum decorates it, with a triad of candles—a young woman is arriving outside. With matching alertness Barry and the dog watch her through the window, as she converses with a highway patrolman. Patricia Martin, Philip's niece from New York (Priscilla Lane), who comes every year to spend a month with him.[5] Saying a cursory hello to Barry, she is distraught:

> Uncle Philip, what do you think happened? ... Uncle Philip, there was a car full of detectives down on the road. They wanted to know the way to town. (*Shutting the door behind her.*) They're searching for a man that got away from them. It was on all the radios and everything. They said he's a really dangerous criminal! He—

Martin, smiling nobly at her. "My dear. The police are always on the alarmist side."

"But they said this man is *really dangerous!*"

"I'm *sure* they did. How could they be heroes, if he were harmless?"

Martin is informing his niece, the carefully listening Barry, and us, that the police are no natural collective, sprung from a primordial affiliation of brave, strong, and protective souls who can always, by definition and of nature, be counted on to stand in the way of danger. The police are normal folk lured by ambition or coerced by circumstance into service in an entirely ad hoc, arbitrary social organization with its own internal constraints and operational modes. One does not receive the policeman's identity at birth but accomplishes it, by way of a process of socialization. Part of the policeman's occupational need is a sense of self as heroic, and here now, neatly adduced by someone who couldn't see a policeman staring him in the face, is one formula for producing that "heroic self": find and label someone as a massive threat, so that when an apprehension is made, the apprehender becomes greater on the instant than the threat: thus, glorious. How shabby the police would seem if they did nothing but arrest common folk for doing common things (which, we may take Martin's wry implication to be, they far too typically do)?

It is not only the police of whom Martin is giving warning, however. For him, authority and social control are absolutely, unequivocally, irredeemably perilous. "Pat, dear, would you mind not having any further quotations from the police? Their remarks are always so expected. They kill conversation." And *conversation* is what society is all about, not order. He has moved away from Barry and Pat to pick up the chaser of fruit, in order hospitably to bring it forward into their precinct. Civility, grace, cultivation, simplicity, honesty—these are the values embodied in his radiance and gestures. The police must be left behind for Martin's civilization to flourish. For *any* civilization to flourish.

Pat sits to table and asks "Mr. Mason" to pass her one of those plates. A second characteristic regard from Cummings's Barry now: in medium shot he looks forward to Pat, the eyes moist and tender, the mouth softened, a wayward curl of hair disturbing the blankness of his forehead. This is the look of surrender and imprecation, as though to say, "Oh, please! I will surely pass you a plate, but the act will destroy me." Fumbling for speech, he smiles, turns, and reaches. But as he must raise his body he is unaware that a table knife is being tipped off the table. Hitchcock affords this utensil a portrait shot of its own:

A table knife. Its tip graciously blunted, its cutting edge somewhat dulled—it is for shuttling peas and slathering butter, not hacking through bone. The table knife is a mark of high civilization, which is to say, the cultivation of collaborative social life at a distance from savagery. The knife here rests on a hooked rug beneath the table (a rug with images of flowers), and we see the weak sunlight, that has dropped into the cabin, making pleasing shadows drop there of the ornamental carving on the chairs. It is a solitary image that announces tranquility, rest, peaceability, and refinement, not to say a striking distance from the animal aggression that civility has tamed and corralled. Barry gently looks down, and then, with humble supplication, looks at Pat.

Her eyes meet his. What is it about the eyes that can give the instantaneous impression of their bearer holding her breath? Pat's lovely head gives the tiniest cant. Slowly, slowly, she moves forward (toward the camera), regarding him with increasing concentration. And as she swings over to his territory and stoops, her eyes fall into shadow and thus go dark with what seems a continuance of her (more generalized) suspicion. She ducks below the table surface. Hitchcock jumps to Barry's hands swiftly struggling to pull his jacket sleeves down over his cuffs. Back to Pat's gaze, Pat's defining, controlling, empowered, dominating, and reducing gaze—with her eyes drawn wide open in shock. "Oh!!"

A second vital cut. From below his face, her uncle standing by the hearth, his dark jacket and tie seeming to merge with what now appears a cavernous structure of stones behind him in the fire glow. He is holding his hands together gently, in unconscious duplication of Barry's frenetic spasms a flash ago. "What's the matter, Pat? Have you just seen his handcuffs?" Barry, from behind, now swiveling to face the camera and Martin. Eyes askance, in perfect focus, sharpened, surprised, in pain. Behind him, *but dropping out of focus*, the civilizing table and its chaser and candelabrum. Barry freezes. "I heard them"—Barry rises nervously—"as soon as he came in." The camera has pulled back so that Barry and Pat, side by side, are an uncomfortable pair for the old man to see—but, of course, he cannot see, and seeing, we take his place.

"Uncle Philip, he must be the man they're looking for!" (Barry turns his head to see what's outside.)

"Yes," tranquilly, "very probably." Pat as grim as can be, Barry steeling himself.

"But you should have given him to the police!"

Martin, again from a little below, more light washing his front. The hands folded together, the fingers playing. A charmingly modulated but quiet voice: "Are you frightened, Pat? Is that what makes you so cruel?"

And we are still looking at Martin as we hear her voice: "But you've got to! He's a dangerous man!" Is Hitchcock not saying here, by regarding Martin and not the girl as she makes this "cruel" announcement of her attitude and values, that the uncle is the figure to be attended? His the figure, and thus his the value set. Here is a brilliant cinematological technique for dividing a two-part conversation, so that the moral weight of one side will preponderate.

"Oh, Pat! Mr. Mason may be many things but he's certainly not dangerous. In fact, I'm not at all convinced that he's guilty."

Now back to the two-shot, with Barry a study in release, his body as though easing into its space. Pat's eyes are wide open, her lips parted in dismay. "Uncle Philip, it's your duty as an American citizen!"

Martin's mouth goes tight and serious now, and his folded hands rise up, as they would, here in the early 1940s, in a schoolroom if he were dutifully standing to make a little oration. "It is my duty as an American citizen . . . to believe a man innocent until he's been proved guilty." (Back to the two-shot, with Pat's eyebrows raised—she has been taught a civics lesson—and lips closed—this is the time to listen, not to speak. Barry is holding his head high, looking at Martin behind the camera—I have been recognized to the depth!—and there is a trace of happiness on his lips.) "Pat—don't tell me about my duty. It makes you sound so stuffy." Barry turning to Pat with a smile of—what? Criticism? Triumph? The recognition that he finds her attractive because she is not as stuffy as she is pretending to be? Or because he cannot imagine why she might be pretending to be stuffy, since clearly Uncle Philip is no fan of such nonsense. "Besides. . . ." Pat is now doubtful of herself, and has turned to look at Barry less judgmentally, "I have my own ideas about my duties as a citizen. They sometimes involve disregarding the law."

"What are you going to do with him!?"

"I'm going to turn him over to *you*, my dear." A pleased expression on Barry's face. Finally, something to look forward to. "You're going to drive him down to Tim the blacksmith and have those preposterous contraptions removed from his wrists." The language: yes, stand back independently, and regard the invention of metal cuffs linked by chains, nothing but contraptions, and nothing but preposterous, to deny a person the use of his hands! (Hands for holding and striking a triangle; for playing Delius's *Summer Night on the River*.)

"Oh, Uncle Philip, how could I do a thing like *that*?"

"Because you know I can see a great deal farther than you can. I can see intangible things. For example, innocence."

Innocence a matter of the spirit, not an appearance. Innocence, not the performance of innocence; not the impression. True innocence, which is, per Philip Martin, visible to those who can truly see. Barry, listening to this ostensible lesson directed at Pat, is receiving instruction, too. Much later on, as the film reaches its apotheosis, he will commit an action that offers irrefutable evidence he has learned the lesson here. He will see intangible things. But for that, we must wait some.

At the doorway Pat moves off to her car and the two men say goodbye. "Go ahead, and do the things I wish I could do," Philip Martin intones, and turning to him, with his two cuffed hands, Barry clasps his mentor's. Hands upon hands, the human gesture—made difficult for Barry but with a constraint not untranscendable.

There is a notably wry earlier moment, before Barry and Pat go to the table. "Mr. Mason" is being told he has probably seen the face of Martin's niece before. "As a matter of fact, you've seen her practically everywhere. I'm told that billboards she adorns would reach across the continent, if placed end to end." Pat stands beside the table, grinning with embarrassed pride. "But I can't imagine who's going to place them end to end, nor why they should consider it the thing to do." Here, indubitably, is a critique of the money impulse which now (during the war) raises its head across the country. The image of the American continent—wild, untrammeled, unexplored, Godly—necklaced now by billboards, craven even if they display the unquestionable beauty of this beautiful man's beautiful niece. But more than critical, the line has a hilarious ring of parody, pointing at the pure ridicule of multiplication and extension for their own sakes, as when one conjures some megalomaniac design freak placing billboards end to end across the country, gigantic dominoes (on roads that are not yet the interstate highways they will become in the decade to follow). Hitchcock offers an ecological critique, too, and far ahead of its time in popular thought: the very conceit of turning the wilderness into a platform for commerce. But in Martin's lines is there not a curious echo, too, of a much-repeated Dorothy Parker riposte: "If all the coeds at the Yale prom were laid end to end, I shouldn't be in the least bit surprised." This scene—something of a knowing homage to the blind hermit's cottage scene of James Whale's *Bride of Frankenstein* (1935)—was written by Parker. "Suddenly, the writing took a leap and I wondered how the hell that happened and it was Dorothy Parker," Norman Lloyd recollected to me (Interview).

Parker's arch comment about Pat's billboards reflects a sour, suspicious attitude toward the glamour of development, then, and toward the glittering promise of economic prosperity that this seemingly unending chain of advertisements reflects. Philip Martin's commitment to honest labor and soulful truth is missing from lures like these, that in sum constitute an affront to and denial of the myth of yeoman labor. The Western yeoman, writes Henry Nash Smith:

> had become the hero of a myth, of *the* myth of mid-nineteenth-century America. He no longer resembled even the oft-praised English yeoman, darling of poets and social theorists. The very word had changed its meaning in American speech.[6] The Western yeoman had become a symbol which could be made to bear an almost unlimited charge of meaning. It had strong overtones of patriotism, and it implied a far-reaching social theory. The career of this symbol deserves careful attention because it is one of the most tangible things we mean when we speak of the development of democratic ideas in the United States. (135; emphasis original)

That myth is a dream, of course, like all myths. Call it the American Dream:

> MOMMY *(offstage)*: Who rang the doorbell?
> GRANDMA *(shouting offstage)*: The American Dream!
> MOMMY *(offstage)*: What? What was that, Grandma?
> GRANDMA *(Crossing to arch left. Shouting.)*: The American Dream! The American Dream! Damn it! (Albee 33)

Presenting himself to Barry (at the door), our Philip Martin is one distinct embodiment of that dream. And because of Martin's prominent placement in it, Hitchcock's voyage across America becomes a dream voyage, one in which truths are revealed that cannot be seen in daylight. "In dreams we never deceive ourselves.... Our truest life is when we are in dreams awake" (Thoreau, "Week" 79).

INTANGIBLE THINGS

What, in practical reality, can Philip Martin have meant by "intangible things," those things "a great deal farther," that he can see and Pat cannot? Surely, obviously, human feeling and possibility, of which, being considerably older than his niece, he has a finer view at each instant of life. She is still learning the ropes of interaction. And that the contemporary culture being fresh, vibrant, stimulating in her eyes does not mean she possesses the means for placing her appreciation in context. But Martin isn't just adulating his own maturity. If Barry's innocence, a matter of the heart, an inner matter, is apprehendable to him, so must be other inner matters, such as fear, illumination, and the movement of cultures through time. Martin is telling us that in provocative moments he apprehends more than the surface of action gives to apprehend. He dwells on a planet of spirit and desire, not just one riddled with conflicting lines of action and bluntly stated antagonisms. Take this as a guide to Hitchcock's work more generally. Playing his Delius, Philip Martin sees the river, and the fall of the light, the draping willows, the glint of sunset in the ripples, the movement of leaves in the breeze; and also—*Summer Night on the River* was written not long after the funeral of Edward VII—the waves of uncertainty and freedom approaching the beach of culture, the improbable dawn.

War culture and war work—the "backdrop" of this story—are technical and calculated, indeed a beachhead for the growth of technology and the calculating mind. By contrast with the America in which he is presently living, then, Martin is in a waking dream. Alive for him are melodies inconsistent with the present struggle, marching tunes, perhaps, for a greater and earlier struggle of the hopeful and tenacious spirit against both unforgiving nature and emptiness. Hitchcock never elsewhere poses a character so dramatically and uncompromisingly bold, noble, and brave. Martin's is a historical memory and a vision of the future, a utopia and an archive but also a dream, because he persists in seeing beyond the superficialities that engage those who, only scrapping at life from beneath the dark threats of storm clouds, nervously point and alienate, locate some enemy—whether of "Freedom" or of their personal competitive intent—and move to kill. As he states and implies it, Martin's world is what America could become again, if it did not forsake its history and the dream that brought that history to life. "Who rang the doorbell?" "The American Dream!"

In *Saboteur*, two distinctly opposing forces are represented: Barry Kane, a humble aircraft plant worker (read, member of the working class), and Tobin, an eastern industrialist baron moved all the way west to California, now a landowner, rancher, and representative of the new wealth. In *Where I Was From*, Joan Didion writes evocatively of the western trek (in the earliest days; and by implication also in the days of people like Tobin), its hardships, the many deaths along the route, the pioneers moving steadily, courageously, toward the Donner Pass and beyond, and of the way that, in decades that followed the advent of the Southern Pacific—in short, railroad money and, tightly linked to it, bank money, real estate money, development money—development came to alter and evaporate the dreams of the early settlers, evaporate the dreams and replace them with subdivisions that stood where orchards had spread. The "crowding of people into immense cities, this aggregation of wealth into large lumps, this marshaling of men into big gangs under the control of the great 'captains of industry,'" Henry George had written in 1868 in the *Overland Monthly*, Didion shows, "does not tend to foster personal independence—the basis of all virtues—nor will it tend to preserve the characteristics which particularly have made Californians proud of their state" (88). "Personal independence—the basis of all virtues": the abstraction which in Philip Martin is admirably embodied.

The aircraft industry dominated the economy of Southern California in the early 1940s—McDonnell, Douglas, Hughes, Rockwell, TRW, Northrop, Lockheed, companies that believed themselves "consecrated to what they construed as the national interest, and to deserve, in turn, the nation's unconditional support" (Didion 135)—as did the hovering cupidity of the big ranchers, who had already sold out the San Fernando Valley but would continue to see federal and railroad money as a lure to dividing and selling off more and more land. People like Barry and his chum Ken Mason, among so many other young hopefuls, "were fairly but not entirely homogenous in their ethnic background. They were oriented to aerospace. They worked for Hughes, they worked for Douglas, they worked at the naval station and shipyard in Long Beach. They worked, in other words, at all the places that exemplified the bright future that California was supposed to be" (Donald J. Waldie, qtd. in Didion 106). The town where Barry and Ken lived, now or earlier in their lives, was no doubt one of the "breeder towns for the boom ... these were the towns that proved Marx wrong, that managed to increase the proletariat and simultaneously, by calling it middle class, to co-opt it" (115). And as Barry was inevitably proletarian, his adversary, the lurking Nazi imperialist, was fruit of the Eastern American aristocracy. The tension in the film is a class tension, notwithstanding the very foreignness of that term generally for Americans devoted to the thought that class qualified only the Europe their ancestors left behind. Californians were especially allergic to thinking about class:

I asked my mother to what "class" we belonged [recollected Didion]. "It's not a word we use," she said. "It's not the way we think." (128)

Aircraft-based California was not simply a wartime fountain, but lasted through the market crash of the late 1980s. "Even when the defense plants started closing down off the San Diego Freeway and the for-lease signs started going up in Orange County, very few people wanted to see a connection with the way life was going to be lived in the California that was not immediately identifiable as 'aircraft'" (Didion 129). But that more modern, easily identifiable California where 'aircraft' was in the air remains the California of *Saboteur*. Barry, Ken, temporarily Fry while he has his job in that plant, are "the last of the medieval hand workers," and in years to come "the spaces in which they worked, the huge structures with the immaculate white floors and the big rigs and the overhead cameras and the project banners and the flags of the foreign buyers, became the cathedrals of the Cold War," writes Didion, "occasionally visited by" (as at the beginning of this film) "but never entirely legible to the uninitiated" (136). In the decade beginning 1940, the population of California increased 53 percent, Didion observes, and we can surmise much of this hike, early in the decade, was linked to war production. Tobin and his class, meanwhile, were profiting from the war and hungry to profit more. Didion shares a more recent elegy about the San Joaquin Valley from Victor Davis Hanson's *The Land Was Everything*:

> We have torn up vineyards and now have planted the following crops: Wal-Mart, Burger King, Food-4-Less, Baskin-Robbins, Cinema 6, Denny's, Wendy's, Payless, Andersen's Pea Soup, the Holiday Inn, McDonald's, Carl's Jr., Taco Bell, four gas stations, three shopping centers, two videotape stores, and a car wash. (qtd. 178)

Before Barry meets him, Martin is already outside all this, in his dream California, his dream future. And because of the glow on Barry as he takes his leave, we can reasonably believe he has entered Martin's dream and now lives it, too, committed to battle not only the Nazi threat (which rather perfunctory adventure the film now shows in detail, all the way to the Statue of Liberty) but the blind unfeeling forces that would render the garden waste, even in the name of virtue. With Martin, Barry sees himself "heir to the freeholding yeomen farmers who, in [J. Hector St. John de] Crèvecoeur's and his own view, 'created the American republican spirit'" (Didion 175). Here is de Crèvecoeur, Martin's antecedent:

> At home my happiness springs from very different objects: the gradual unfolding of my children's reason, the study of their dawning tempers attracts all my paternal attention.... But these are themes unworthy of your perusal, and which ought not to be carried beyond the walls of my house, being domestic mysteries adapted only to the locality of the small sanctuary wherein my family resides. Sometimes I delight in inventing and executing machines, which simplify my wife's labour. I have been tolerably successful that way; and these, Sir, are the narrow circles within which I constantly revolve, and what can I wish for beyond them? I bless God for all the good he has given me; I envy no man's prosperity, and with no other portion of happiness than that I may live to teach the same philosophy to my children; give each of them a farm, show them how to cultivate it, and be like their father, good substantial independent American farmers—an appellation which will be the most fortunate one a man of my class can possess. (22)

A TUMBLE

Why should the film end with an escapade upon the Statue of Liberty? About which, with pardon, a very brief interruption from the heart of the moment. Norman Lloyd took time to correct for me a misapprehension many viewers and critics of *Saboteur* have about the filming of Fry's climactic drop from the Statue. "Fry" was a part he had eagerly wanted:

> I had been in the original Mercury Theater with Orson Welles and John Houseman. Houseman was an equal partner with Welles. John and I became very good friends. At one point, the Mercury went out of business and John got a job with David O. Selznick who had Hitch under contract. Hitch was preparing *Saboteur* and in the middle of his preparation he asked Houseman if he knew of a young actor, preferably unknown, who could play a saboteur. And John recommended me.

And I was ordered to go to the St. Regis Hotel at 8 o'clock one morning and there was Hitchcock dressed in his dark suit. We introduced ourselves to each other. We chatted—I think he told me what the picture was about, because he loved to tell the stories of his pictures. "Well, we'll have to test you." He had to go back to California, and he had someone else do the test. Hitchcock said, "Pick a scene you want to act." I did a scene from *Blind Alley* chosen by me. It starred Roy Hargrave.[7]

When it came to the on-set filming of his portion of the matte through which the figure falling would be made palpable (the contextual shot looking down from the crown of the Statue had been filmed independently), he found himself

> on a saddle—to the eternal argument with Bob Boyle, who was the art director. Boyle insisted I was in a chair. I insisted I was in a saddle-like affair. As I go, they had built above me a platform, and this platform had a hole. The camera shot through that hole, with the cameraman on it. The piece of the Statue of Liberty that I was holding onto was removable and attached to the bottom of the platform—and on a cue, this platform went up in the air as I did beautiful balletic movements down on the saddle.
>
> As it went up, my hand slid off the piece that was attached to the bottom of the platform. The saddle was on a pipe and the camera went up and up and up all the way to the ceiling. I didn't go, the camera went. (Interview)

A 17 November 1941 memorandum listing exterior shots required for the Statue sequence indicated thirty rear-projection plates required for studio composites or mattes that were to include two of Fry in actual fall and numerous others to be used alone as establishments or in partnership as images of action with the Statue or the surrounding area behind.

Yet the central conundrum stands: if we had to be in New York for the finale of the narrative, there would have been numerous heights available there for Fry to climb, assuming the villain must tumble away from some notable potentiality. Was it Liberty because Tobin and his controlling class would have been claiming to stand for America itself, no matter the results of the war? (Whether or not he is actually fronting a Nazi cadre, the Nazis have guaranteed him wealth and power, with which to turn ranches into subdivisions; other antagonistic powers could do the same.) Should the Nazis invade, Tobin would be a principal "American" for them, a leader in the "New America"; should they be defeated, he can still claim his "American" birthright, as long as his connections are in the dark, as long as he has a flunky like Fry to take the fall for him. Tobin, that is, stands next to the flag, buys up and markets the territories where the flag flies. His foe is Liberty itself; the hope and raised torch, the proud gaze, the welcoming stance, the as yet unresolved future.

To turn on a harsher, but less confounding light, also about choice of setting: assuming that Barry is wounded through Nazi action (the set-up at the aircraft plant) and sets out on a quest to find the guilty party, defeat the Nazi threat, and make America safe on its war footing (a simplistic reading of the film's plot, but not an inaccurate one): why in such a case would there be need for, and value in, a scene in the woods with a blind philosopher? Why Philip Martin at all? There are plenty of ways Barry could meet Pat (meet straight; meet cute), without her being the niece of a yeoman farmer type. When we take Martin as crucial, intrinsic to the film, we must come to understand the nature of the America for which he stands and out of the history of which he is born, and see Barry's affiliation with him as announcement of his commitment in terms greater than the war itself, terms linked to the economic history of which both he and Tobin are irrevocably a part.

The Statue of Liberty quickly and fully signals this tightly woven fabric of freedom, danger, threat, and possibility. If he tumbles from Liberty it is perhaps less, as some have suggested, that Liberty herself has defeated him than that Fry might seem not to merit ascent to the heights of Liberty. Yet this reading is peremptory. He does reach those heights, and Liberty *is* offered to all the tired and poor who claim Her, including our destitute, deplorable Fry. He, perhaps, is the quintessential example of the "wretched refuse" from a "*distant* shore," who requires, who craves what America can offer, but who, in this eventuality, seduced by the conniving Tobin, seems left out of the bargain. He deserves to be at the top of the Statue just as Barry and Pat do, and he promises to cling; but the threads of his garment have come apart.

The cabin sequence represents a double seclusion. In purely diegetic terms, Barry has been racing from one problematic moment to another, constantly conscious of prying and misdefining eyes. Here, without anticipation, he finds himself safe, quiet, respected, even admired. He can take advantage of the cabin for catching his breath; but the audience can catch breath, too; feel the coziness of this hearth against the chill of the (diegetic) forest outside. On quite another level, however, the cabin represents a sacred island in a turbulent sea, Prospero's magic cell, with the dog his proper Caliban. Its tumult and its conflagration proceeding indefinitely, the war has entirely disappeared here; at least for the moment. We are in a zone of the Emersonian moral perfectionism adduced by Stanley Cavell (and later by William Rothman). If we can be thought to inhabit a Kantian Realm of Ends, ends, that is, not things, we might be heading for what Cavell calls an "eventual human city"—and where, he proceeds to wonder, "is the entrance to the city?" (46)—in the concrete forest of which the civic and personal duties of one man to another outweigh what are now clearly visible as lowlier institutional strictures and demands. Here in Martin's cabin is the yeoman farmer in his own land, his virgin land, as Henry Nash Smith had it, master of his surround, if blinded, and responsible—in the keenest biblical sense—for offering hospitality, kindliness, and refreshment. The traveler on his road is wearied in spirit; he is to be uplifted and born again.[8] And every American is a traveler on that road, because America is the road.

> To draw a new circle, in Emerson's understanding, requires us to awaken to powers we had not been conscious of possessing, to open our eyes to the reality that we are not who we had believed ourselves to be, that our being is not limited to who we have been. It requires us to abandon an old self so as to enable a new self to be born, to acknowledge that the old self is now as dead to us as a heap of brontosaurus bones. (Rothman, *Must* 9)

When it faces him, Philip Martin recognizes a moment in which pedagogy is the only hope of salvation. The moral foundation upon which he has built his life (and his cabin) does not glorify the generalization *America*; nor does it the fragile institutional arrangements (the police, the advertising culture) by which hegemonic power is retained and maintained by unthinking myrmidons in the interests of a greedy few. He believes in what the founding fathers upheld, the dignity of the individual soul; the rights of the individual man; the honor of honesty, simple work, and natural beauty. Let us say, simply but meaning to point to a deep complexity, that this man sees his country, his home, his family, and his life with special eyes. On the instant he would recognize the heart and generosity of Mrs. Mason. He would acknowledge the trust the truck driver finally achieves for Barry. But Tobin he would reject, and the police, and war machinery, and the war itself. That is why in his cabin there are no inklings of the war; why the war, in Hitchcock's representation, has not penetrated the sacred pine forest where in "moral perfectionism" Philip Martin lives. And it is why, finally, Fry must fall from, rather than easily perching on, the Statue of Liberty.

SABOTAGE

A widespread belief is evidenced in much critical appreciation of Hitchcock's work, as well as in untutored everyday discourse between fans commenting on his films, that he possessed, and worked from, a fairly simplistic, wholly rational approach to experience. Hitchcockian films should therefore, finally, be understood as tales evoking precisely and only the themes they superficially announce—taken up in the most practical and mechanical sense possible. For example: *Vertigo* is about the fear of heights, especially one man's fear, as, dangling from an eavestrough, he witnesses a second man fall to his death. *The Lady Vanishes* is about a lady who vanishes. *The Lodger* is about a lodger. *I Confess* is about a man who makes a confession to a priest, thus, the priesthood. *The Birds* is about a bird attack, which is to say, nature (or nature gone amok). *The Wrong Man* is about an honest gentleman who has been wrongly accused of a crime. And on and on. In *An Eye for Hitchcock*, I suggested that the vertigo in *Vertigo* has to do with falling through a story, and with falling through the very broad story we call history; thus, Hitchcock's posing a man hanging from an eavestrough is a symbol (a stand-in) for something much grander, much more disturbing than the hero's troubles with height. All of Hitchcock's films are grander and more disturbing than they are typically taken to be.

In this light we must ask: Who is the saboteur in *Saboteur*?

Frank Fry, of course. A man who plots a great destruction in order to assist the Nazi war machine. A man who is pegged, pursued, trapped, and caught, and who finally, even despite a good man's attempt to save him, perishes in what might be called a divine accident. To say this even more simply: to have a film called *Saboteur*, Hitchcock needs an actual saboteur (just as Lloyd recounts), and so he constructs Fry, who will do well enough in the role. But can we say the film is about Fry? He meanders through it, yes, and his appearances—thanks to Lloyd's startling performance—are all sharp and affronting, all incitements to concern, desperation, finally terror. However, Fry is not the center of the film, nor is any aspect of the plot that can be taken at face value: the German cadre operating out of New York high society; the journey across America.

When we stand back from the story, but not from the film; when we gaze at, more than the chain of happenings, the graphic construction of the thing, its movement, its lightnesses and darknesses, the tones of the talk (which we can "see" with our ears), the presentation of sightings repeated again and again and again, the ocular puzzle which is social life—when we do all this, we are in a position to understand how a certain *sabotage* is present everywhere in organized life: call it a destruction of the spirit. And Fry is nothing more than its souvenir. A charming and beautiful soirée in an elegant Fifth Avenue ballroom, with an orchestra playing and couples swirling around the floor—yet all of it only a mask to cover murder and profit. A vista of the Hoover Dam, majestic accomplishment of man's engineering skills and governmentally supported infrastructural financing through the WPA, a splendid intervention upon nature by way of, as David Nye terms it, the technological sublime—yet at the same time, only a potential target for havoc-making destruction. A quintessentially beautiful model of youth and freshness, spread on billboards across America as a perduring icon of optimism and cleanliness— yet also a font of suspicion, fear, distrustfulness, even panic. A sincere and loyal male friendship, boundlessly forward-looking and playful—but, in the judgmental eyes of authorities and strangers, only a site of jealousy, rivalry, desperate hatred (else why would anyone imagine Barry as the killer of his chum?). Barry Kane experiences moments of salvation, but this occurs in the presence of the bereft and destitute of society, not its empowered or normalized citizens: the safe haven of Mrs. Mason's little house; the safe haven of Philip Martin; the safe haven of the circus freaks he and Pat meet along the road, virtually every one of whom is in some telltale way a blatant contradiction of the values touted forcefully in wartime capitalist America and among the enemy spies.

To find a mere adventure tale here, we must discount. Mrs. Mason is finally just one more in the countless list of mothers who have lost their sons in the war. Martin, in the end, is nothing but a lonely hermit. The citizens of the circus caravan discountable—objectifiable—as mere entertainments.

But these alienations of spirit are precisely Hitchcock's point of focus—that devaluing people, stepping away from them, can be a typical, even unconscious mode of operation, a typical part of normal everyday life in this place at this time. The true American values—as Hitchcock sees them—of kindness, openness, optimism, thrift, assiduous labor in the creative spirit, generosity, care, and humility can be systematically trodden upon, even evacuated from the culture, logically, in the name of military watchfulness, attentive suspicion, and fearful defensiveness. Then the great ship capsized by sabotage is America itself, the true America of inclusiveness, promise, and rich possibility. The saboteur is anyone anywhere who operates out of negativity when the human spirit is imperiled.

In a culture riddled with negativity a creature like Fry will pass unnoticed, not merely because he is got up as an "ordinary" type of fellow, his features retreating from his own face, but because so many of the people among whom he shuffles already resemble him. At the Statue of Liberty, for example, it is only for Pat and Barry that Fry stands out; the crowds are busy sabotaging American liberty through their nervousness and doubt, their anxiety toward the future, and Fry is only one more among them. The same, we might see on reflection, could be said of the aircraft plant, where aside from Barry and Ken, lost in their youthful dream, the multitudes are hooked on war work, that is, building killing machines to keep other killers at bay. Hitchcock—I would argue—is not meaning to suggest that the war is futile; only that in the face of diligence and defensiveness, now spread across the country, a certain conviction in what America is most authentically about, has been slain. Unconscious murder.

Saboteur is thus an accusation, or a warning, in the very truest spirit of a man who did not want to see America destroyed as America fought to win a war. The America of the industrialists—the warmongers who owned the aircraft plant, for example, and profited by every airplane manufactured there—are represented by Tobin the megalomaniac and Mrs. Sutton (Alma

Kruger), his blithering benefactress. The America of the working class has a more complex representation: the doubting Pat is a worker, albeit glamorized, as is the trusting truck driver; the dutiful but somewhat imperceptible henchmen are workers, as is the malignant butler on Fifth Avenue: what all of them share is a sense of obedience to forces above them, forces that appear sensible and well-meaning and that don't get subjected to critical view. Even pathetic Fry is an unquestioning, dutiful sort, perhaps not really a bad man in the end so much as one who has taken his instructions too seriously, admired with a passion too fervid the monsters above his head.

In Hitchcock's view, the America that lies under threat in *Saboteur* is considerably more than a democratic bastion at war with Hitler; it is a condition and potentiality, an arrangement of attitudes and hopes, an hypothesis. The American social fabric is itself—Paul Goodman wrote a poem to this effect—"homespun of oatmeal gray," made by the people, ongoingly. America is thus what the social fabric *could* be if people regarded one another with respect and accorded one another dignity; if poverty were overcome; if health were made possible, both at the individual and the national level. Infection or degradation are possible—and easy—all the time, virtually anywhere; and the film works as an admonitory text to show pertinent cases where citizens who might have all the reasons in the world to suspect strangers, fear strangers, even abhor strangers, make the choice instead to be generous. The spiritual conviction in American possibility is at the heart of the country. It was a quest for enlightenment without power and control, freedom without measurement, experience without obedience that founded America, and it is for this quest that the yeoman nation strives. To think America is its capitalization—its buildings and highways, its bank accounts, its displays of wealth, the overarching New York skyscraper in which Barry and Pat are held prisoner, and from the window of which they contrive to fly a note imploring help—to think of America as money, is already to capitulate, already to be sabotaged. Thus, in this film, the portended material destruction of the ship at its launch in Brooklyn is only a signal about the saboteur's much broader power: to be corrupting, to make ordinary people think twice, to make mere surveyors of those whose eyes have gazed on beauty—"Albert Bierstadt saw Yosemite in 1863 and came back to do the grandiose landscapes that made him for a dozen years the most popularly acclaimed painter in America" (Didion 66–67)—and to have them always on the lookout, eyes narrowed, never finding enough and thus always sufficiently dissatisfied to look further, across the next frontier.

FREEDOM

Writing of the proclivity of its citizens, old and new, for more than a hundred and fifty years, to entertain a glorious vision of their state as utopian garden in the face of the agonizing journey westward, in the presence of rivers surging, and with population increasing through the immigration of zealous easterners who were eager to divide and sell off land; to cherish ideals through the troubles with water and troubles with manufacturing as the aircraft industry dwindled away, Didion remarks of California that it "likes to be fooled" (86). It may serve a deeper understanding of *Saboteur* to consider some of its villainous types less as a deeply and essentially malignant force than as well-meaning workers taken in by glamorous promises and a handsome smile.

Yeoman farmers or workers as they may once have been, the dream of bounty and sustenance from the work of one's own hands may have failed for them, so that in desperation they sought a different, more equivocal kind of labor; or, indeed—more ironically—they may have become entirely convinced that their work to help detain Barry and Pat, or to destroy parts of the American military establishment, is itself a noble endeavor, a guarding of America's truest, deepest interests—old interests, agrarian interests—from the incursion of a high capitalism that would erode the national spirit. We are given no details in the film of Fry's engagement on the side of evil; or of Mr. Freeman's or Neilson's, the two gracious henchmen Barry and Pat find at Soda City and with whom they voyage eastward in flight from the law.

But of the ringleader Tobin we are given a very sharp portrait: brief but telling. When we meet him at the ranch, there is a sun-tanned glow upon his features and a genteel polish to his language and manner. It is unmistakable that he is wealthy—that he represents the claims of the super-rich. When we meet him a second time at Mrs. Sutton's home on Fifth Avenue, he is a dignified visitor, a man who does his business in back rooms but surrounded by Aubusson tapestries and gilt. Perhaps a few hours before, he took a lunch of kangaroo-tail soup at Fortnum and Mason, on Madison Avenue nearby, so that he would be fortified in schmoozing with some of the sixteen or so thousand names in New York's social register this evening (see Worden 304–5; 307). Tobin's telling feature, however, the quality that strikes a viewer instantaneously and always decorates him, more than his power, is his polished charm, his glow. He is the shining future the workers at the aircraft plant think could be theirs someday, if only they struggle forthrightly and keep their noses clean. More importantly, he is the sort of knight who might very easily, and very swiftly, mobilize the loyalty and adherence of losers such as Fry and Neilson, and even of a more arrogant loser such as Freeman, boasting of his son's golden hair and admitting, with some slight equivocation, that he had hair like that himself as a little boy. Certainly this is an open advertisement for Aryan purity; but it is also a confession of a diluted masculinity, the stigma that, as Freeman came of age, would have brought on the aggravated self-conscious feeling of powerlessness, placing him under the dominion of an understanding (thus, always potentially mocking) Tobin. If I was girlish once, I am not girlish now, thus a man like Mr. Tobin looks favorably upon me.

I mention these curious, and only dimly sketched, portraits of two lesser, very minor, characters because of a subtle semi-musical theme enunciated through their presence again and again. It is the theme of freedom, and man's ability to act in freedom's spirit under straining circumstances. Consider first Tocqueville: "The slave, among the ancients, belonged to the same race as his master, and he was often the superior of the two in education and instruction. Freedom was the only distinction between them; and when freedom was conferred, they were easily confounded together" (355). And then the yeoman farmer as illuminated by Henry Nash Smith's citation of Charles J. Faulkner: "Our native, substantial, independent yeomanry, constitute our pride, efficiency and strength; they are our defence in war, our ornaments in peace; and no population, I will venture to affirm, upon the face of the globe, is more distinguished for an elevated love of freedom" (134). The hard-working man of the land is associated with freedom and an inherent nobility, and with the prospect of gaining, by virtue of that freedom, affiliation with the master and liberty from the master's power, however glorious. Our bomber in this film, the man who leads the chase and who, in his final breaths, shows his simple humanity, his vulnerability, his deep-set innocence, is, of all possibilities, Fry, which, as we enunciate it—the name is articulated many times in the film—sounds not only somewhat, but precisely, like the German (read Nazi) pronunciation *frei*, which means, of course, "free." And the chief honcho who was blond as a boy is Mr. Freeman, that is, a free man.

Could Fry and Freeman (and Neilson, as Freeman's "free man") have been Californians "fooled" by the glitter of Tobin's luscious promises? Is Fry a converted yeoman, a worker who wants very much to believe in a less humble world than he is forced to occupy before the film begins? Tobin, after all, has eminent power to be convincing, with his shining good looks, his smooth tongue, his hypnotizing voice, his twinkling but also mesmerizing eyes. Freedom is what it is all about, in California history, in the film's plot, in Hitchcock's filmmaking. *Freilichkeit*, Freemanship. The freedom to work and to grow, the freedom to move across the continent, the freedom to be fooled. One more time: "The Western yeoman had become a symbol which could be made to bear an almost unlimited charge of meaning.... The career of this symbol deserves careful attention because it is one of the most tangible things we mean when we speak of the development of democratic ideas in the United States" (Smith 135).

By the agency of yeoman morality and yeoman labor, and by virtue of the freedom implicit in the symbol of the yeoman farmer, Fry and Freeman are linked to Philip Martin: but Martin has not been fooled. Martin would know Tobin for what he was, and it is through the introduction of Martin into the film that we can unambiguously identify Tobin's evil for ourselves.

Because Fry is Fry, that is, *frei*, it is on the Statue of Liberty that he must die. And he must die by losing his Liberty, becoming factually and symbolically *unfreilich*.

JOINING IN

Thoreau describes the particular pleasure of joining a countryside party and finding himself, soon, "in the midst of a huckleberry field, on one of our highest hills, two miles off, and then the State was nowhere to be seen" (*Civil* 16). What he had blissfully lost was the surveilling censure of the cultural press, as well as an especially pernicious symptom, goading admonishment and titillation that, working in tandem, pump up belief in glorious impossibility. Again come to mind Didion's Californians, marshaled at every level yet eager to be fooled, workers throwing themselves into the aircraft plants all through the 1940s, building the great aerospace economy of the state—the economy that decades later would shrivel, crumble, evaporate under their feet as one by one the great makers of the future pulled stakes and shuffled off to Louisiana, Georgia, anywhere the taxes weren't so high. They rushed in 1941 and 1942 to assemble those F-18s, had lunch in the cafeteria with men like Fry and dinner in their little bungalows in the newly built subdivisions serviced by the newly built malls. Behind them, behind and propping up the State, were the great landowner types, Tobin and his ilk, pleased to dole out freedom to the population. Pleased to set eyes on a man like Mr. Freeman and *designate* him as free, so long as he served placidly as a smiling serf.

And nestled, too, within the State that for Thoreau was suddenly "nowhere to be seen," was our Fry, the shy little rodent-man with the beady, starving eyes. Fry, who works freely but without commitment, another California dreamer. So that when we find him transplanted in New York, nose down at his nefarious work, rather than being energetic and excited, thrown into passion for a cause, he is depressive, sullen, drawn into himself, furtive, precisely as gray as he looks in this black and white film. The shine has worn off the promise, but he has nowhere else to go.

A kind of freak, perhaps, is our Mr. Frei, a person condemned to eternal presentation of the self on the side show of life. Weasly and small, he nevertheless cannot stop commanding attention; indeed, his very uncertainty is a performance. But he is only metaphorically, only by analysis, freakish. A startling and realer congregation is especially important to the moral structure of *Saboteur*. This congregation of outcast "free" civilians is the small family of the freak show at the traveling circus, whose trailers Barry and Pat see on the nocturnal road by night, and race to hide in.

All the typical types are here: a pair of Siamese twins (Jeanne and Lynn Romer), a challenge to our understanding of self and world, as Leslie Fiedler has it in his masterpiece *Freaks: Myths and Images of the Secret Self*, because too many people are inhabiting a single body; a bearded lady (Anita Sharp-Bolster), open acknowledgment of the riddle of gender bifurcation; a tall strongman and his fat-lady wife, Mr. and Mrs. Jack Sprat, as it were (Pedro de Cordoba, Marie LeDeaux), tender and wise, compassionate and loyal, hospitable to strangers and able to see, with a kind of dream vision, how Barry and Patricia are in love; and the midget (Billy Curtis), a *monstre par défaut* whose diminished body and diminished soul seem appropriate to each other. This last is an anxious Judas, ready to give Barry and Pat away to the highway patrolmen who have made entry with their brave flashlights. The probing lights in the dark trailer constitute defining vision, quotidian vision, to contrast with the dream vision of the freak array caught, as the cops slowly pan their beams, in the momentary burn of denuding publicity. The twins cannot come to a unified point of view (like a politically divided nation, with isolationists bonded to, and at war with, interventionists). The bearded lady is maternal, which is to hint, originary. The "giant" strongman—he is taller than the other freaks in the caravan, but hardly a pituitary case—sees from a higher perspective, takes a longer view.

At least some of these physical specimens are on display in the film in order to emphasize, for Barry and Pat—whose moral education is herewith in progress—the importance of what I have been calling dream sight: a mode of inspection and understanding that surpasses the surveilling eye, has no truck with easy labeling, is not seduced by promises of glory and wealth, has no straitjacket of sentimental conviction in its own extensive rightness and superiority. If Philip Martin was sedentary, everlasting as a sequoia in his forestial domain, these are perforce mobile types, movers and shakers, whose only homestead is the present moment in some unknown spot upon an unknown road. Moving across America in the way that Mr. Freeman will, they make connection for us with him and his colleague, on one side a group of individuals who remain true to themselves (because their physical conditions require it) and on the other a pair of men who have sold out their principles for a birthright in what has been sold as a better future.

Finally in the caravan, while Barry hides away, Pat allows herself to be seen, got up as a snake charmer. Barry has entered the hidden bowels of the circus; Pat has joined the company. The police are stymied on their hunt for human treasure, and Pat, who has been suspecting Barry ever since she met him, is finally shamed, by the honesty and warmth of her new circus friends, into accepting him for the innocent he is.

Bill Krohn carefully shows how, in the nighttime circus truck sequence, when the bearded lady peeps out to ascertain the strength of the police force that has stopped the caravan, a skillful fakery was used to give the effect of the vehicles stretching far down the road:

> A perspective shot was created on a desert set using trucks of different sizes, then shifting to miniatures further back, and finally to cutouts.

Hitchcock filmed the shot two ways to show the police searching in the distance while full-size actors playing policemen approach the freaks' truck: one take with cutouts of policemen at the back of the train holding tiny lights that could be moved up and down like puppets, and one with midgets, a trick probably suggested by [producers Frank] Lloyd and [Jack H.] Skirball, who had used midgets to create perspective in one shot of *The Howards of Virginia* (1940). (46)

What Hitchcock does here is to fake size. Inside the freaks' truck he played upon that very theme, by introducing us to people of notably varying size, all sufficiently "abnormal" or "incorrect" to solicit profitable attention and thereby rationalize their being displayed as oddities. The body oversized or undersized, the head too close to the ground or too far away, the doubling of personality inside a single corporeal frame, the body whose beauty rests outside the social designation. Pat, by contrast here, is the epitome of the freak, anything but the socially constructed "beauty" displayed on those billboards all across America. Here, the epitome of beauty is the bearded lady, without compare. She has the tender heart, the wise gaze. Hers are the eyes that see, the heart that understands.

So, just as he does in the exterior shot with graphic construction, inside the trailer Hitchcock manipulates size, appearance, and proportion to confound our estimation. In the same fashion, he suggested of Philip Martin an ocular deficiency that was truly not present; blind, Martin saw better than anyone else, saw "intangible things." The coda of the circus scene is a moment's reflection that brings us to a position from which we can acknowledge that "handsomeness" and "beauty," understood morally not graphically, are more important than superficial glimpses. Emerson: "The ingenuity of man has always been dedicated to the solution of one problem—how to detach the sensual sweet, the sensual strong, the sensual bright, etc., from the moral sweet, the moral deep, the moral fair; that is, again, to contrive to cut clean off this upper surface so thin as to leave it bottomless" (159). The moral sweet and the moral strong: desperately important, because a force devoted to sabotaging this yeoman coupling might be in operation everywhere. Anyone might be doubtfully free, *frei*, the saboteur. And we are all of us, in truth, freaks of nature, blind in the night, needing to reach out.

CHAPTER FOUR

REBECCA'S SHADOW

PRAELUDIUM

A stunning shot interrupts Michelangelo Antonioni's progressing tale in *The Passenger* (1975). A man and woman have met in Barcelona, fallen into the net of interest in one another. But suddenly they must flee, and in a used convertible they are speeding along a Spanish highway in broad daylight. "One question," says the woman, young, mysterious, and resting in the back seat. "Always the same. What are you running away from?" His eyes on the road, the man tells her to turn her back to the front of the car. She kneels on the plush red seat, gazing at the receding road, a solidified wake as it disappears. They are moving at great speed and the road is empty. Plane trees border the paving on both sides, their emerald leaves receding, receding, receding, receding. For a brief instant the filmmaker gives us a shot of the woman taken from the rear hood of the car and gazing up into her face and long curly tresses, the lush sunlight dappled through the trees smacking her and evanescing, her eyes wide open, a smile of wonder on her mouth.

This sequence does not really contain information about the events that enchain it within the film's plot, but it does convey a complex—and

very filmic—idea that may well seem an underpinning of everything to be seen in the film. We are always looking back, at the unfolding past. None of us can ever see where we are going. With the woman, the orientation of the body makes the situation plain and simple. But the man, too, is looking at the past. Each image he draws in is an image of where he just was. This is true of the human condition: because we have eyes in the front of our heads we appear to navigate, but we are being navigated. The dream is a memory, altered from everyday perception so that it can speak with a greater fullness. But in the dream, we also see the past; so the dream is memory clarified, just as waking memory is a confounding dream.

MANDERLEY

In thinking about Alfred Hitchcock's first American film, *Rebecca* (1940),[1] it is wise to keep in mind that the entire story is recounted by an unseen female narrator about a dream she had "again" last night. We will wonder, both caught up in her tale and swirling in her memory, whether the recounting is an imprisonment. The recounting is the film, set in a nostalgic paralysis. The voice is giving over a recurring dream, then, and we may imagine, having had recurring dreams ourselves, how on each occasion it changes a little, yet also remains the same. As she regales us—with a lulling, intoxicating voice—we travel back in time to understand how she came to the enchanted place—Manderley—of which, as she says, she dreamt and dreams again; what that place is, what it meant to her when first she arrived; and later on, what it has come to mean to her now. Time is confounded. While her voice is sweet and clear and feminine, she may be a newborn Caliban:

> Be not afeard; the isle is full of noises,
> Sounds and sweet airs, that give delight and hurt not.
> Sometimes a thousand twangling instruments
> Will hum about mine ears, and sometime voices
> That, if I then had waked after long sleep,
> Will make me sleep again: and then, in dreaming,
> The clouds methought would open and show riches
> Ready to drop upon me that, when I waked,
> I cried to dream again. (*The Tempest* III.ii.1533–44)

But we never quite grasp what "now" is for our "voice"; indeed, we never grasp how far separated her "now" is from her "then," the temporal setting of the shared dream. For all we can tell, the dream space was real for her a mere week or month ago, so that, very soon afterward, when we are transported to see her as protagonist in her own dream, and when we take this figure to indicate the figure behind the present voice, we think it younger by only a little. Although of course, the dream may have had its reality in another life, and as we hear her our recounter may be in old age. If the dream refers to events that occurred a very long time ago, a time now very long gone, and if the present speaker no longer resembles the figure we meet in the extended flashback that is the film—and this we can never know—she is a true phantom. She speaks from across an impenetrable boundary.[2] True, the present voice sounds very much like the voice we hear inside the recounting, but it is true that as people age their voices very often do not. She may now be very old indeed, our narrator, thinking back to something that happened in her almost forgotten youth, yet thinking of it hard, with the keenest focus, so that what she remembers seems crystal clear and shocking. But, again: we cannot know. And we cannot know where she is going with her story, nor can she. It is all a looking back. A looking outside of knowledge.

The whole thing is a looking back.

"Just as [the Greeks] taught that all knowledge is recollection," writes Kierkegaard, "thus will modern philosophy teach that life itself is a repetition." But "what is recollected has already been and is thus repeated backwards" (3).

And if this episodic backward glance isn't yet clear enough, I should emphasize that we never actually meet—never actually see—the dreamer who is recounting the dream of *Rebecca* in her present (narrational) condition. She is the epitome of the *acousmêtre:* "When the acousmatic presence is a voice, and especially when this voice has not yet been visualized—that is, when we cannot yet connect it to a face—we get a special being, a kind of talking and acting shadow," writes Michel Chion of the *acousmêtre* (21), and further, "An entire image, an entire story, an entire film can ... hang on the epiphany of the acousmêtre. Everything can boil down to a quest to bring the acousmêtre into the light" (23–24), and still further, "*The acousmêtre is everywhere,* its voice comes from an immaterial and unlocalized body, and it seems that no obstacle can stop it" and then, at last, "*The acousmêtre is all-seeing,* its word is like the word of god: 'No creature can hide from it'" (24). But in this case, because the acousmêtre speaks from memory, we have a direct filmic statement of Mircea Eliade's "myth of the eternal return," that fundament of culture East and West. All of history is an embedded chain of returns. All of our action is a repetition. All of our thought is a remembering, a recollection that, for Kierkegaard, "makes a person unhappy."

In truth we are not even being told that the dreamer is *presently* dreaming Manderley "again." We are told that "last night" she dreamed of Manderley again. Already, even in her invocation, she carries us back.

And Manderley: well, there lies another riddle, another dream.

BEFORE

As we watch the film, our young woman—I am going to follow some critical convention and also Hitchcock's procedure in dealing with the problem of pointing to her (since she never for one instant has a name) and call her She—encounters the Lord of Manderley spending some time on the Côte d'Azur. He becomes besotted with her, they run off and marry, and soon she is, as it were, at the palace. We are there at the moment She meets the staff—quite a large staff, some of them intimidating—and when She explores the vast halls of the enormous mansion perched atop a cliff in Devonshire or Cornwall: crashing surf, huge rocks below; sedately balanced Gothic architecture, a house in several wings; yawning ceilings (typical of no real English house, but entirely suitable for an American audience's dream fantasies); rich carpets, huge fireplaces (worthy of Charles Foster Kane), long tables, paintings inside gilded frames, you name it. We see all this, but in passing, as though we know we will see it because we have seen it before, as though everything is already accepted and understood. The action of the film gives a striking appearance of involving personages, not spaces, because it is the faces and the postures that come forward and linger. Personages who are perhaps less than ideally visible in these spaces; spaces that seem to command those who scurry around in them. Manderley has the character of a temple. Manderley—

But we ought to begin with Rebecca, because in this dream within a dream her name is an undying echo. Manderley is Rebecca's temple, her cathedral, her tomb.

The Master was married to her, *before*. She is, unfortunately, dead. Our "She" has become the replacement. Rebecca was a Presence, a Form, perhaps popular, certainly very popular with some people. Might she have been one of those women who, like Proust's Princesse Mathilde, "gave many people the satisfaction of feeling that she was on intimate terms with them, that she would gladly have come to their houses, and that she had been prevented from doing so only by some princely obstacle" (364)? One has that sense, by virtue of a kind of invisible yet palpable perfume she has left behind. Rebecca had a pup, a charming jet-black spaniel named Jasper, who continues to pad around happily and shows, by posing staidly outside her rooms, that, like pups everywhere, he is loyal in spirit to the One who is Gone. Rebecca, it seems, was indeed Singular: the whole establishment revolved around her Whims and Desires. Mrs. Danvers (Judith Anderson), the housekeeper—an austere and apparently haunted soul—was close to her in oh, so many ways, and now never ceases reminding She of that conceivably disturbing fact. The butler, Frith (Edward Fielding), is taciturn and accommodating, perhaps, we are led to surmise at one point, more Mrs. Danvers's factotum than anyone else's. The Master, Maxim de Winter (Laurence Olivier), has an estate agent, chummy, efficient, practical, genteel, and modestly withdrawn: Frank Crawley (Reginald Denny). And de Winter's sister and brother-in-law (Gladys Cooper, Nigel Bruce) are epitomes of the upper-class type, jocular, direct—if not too direct—sensible to a fault. The sister is older than Maxim: we can trust her guidance implicitly. Her husband, Giles, is an entirely well-meaning goof (Bruce will recreate this type a year later in *Suspicion*). A lurking roué named Jack Favell (George Sanders) was—or claims he was—a staunch chum of Rebecca's (could he have been her lover?). Certainly, if Favell is telling the truth, and we are given no reason for supposing otherwise, his is the sort of personality that would lead a reasonable observer to conclude Rebecca's friendships were what could be called *louche*. He seems to know his way around too many cabbage patches, and perhaps Rebecca was the same. And so on.

Rebecca went out sailing, her boat capsized, she drowned. The seas are rough near the rocks.

Maxim grieved. A typical inheritor of European charms, he grieved inconsolably, so people say, most notably the American dowager Mrs. Van Hopper (Florence Bates), down in Monte Carlo—"Monte"—doting upon him rather too much. We see him being noticed by She (Mrs. VH's "paid companion") while standing poised atop a precipice and gazing out to sea. Our young girl instantly fears he is going to throw himself off in desperation. Fears *something*, at any rate, and this is the cataclysm of their meeting. It is said that he grieved without limit. That everyone grieved. Down on the beach beneath Manderley is Rebecca's tiny stone hut, where she was wont to retreat—Jasper the pup still goes there. Ben (Leonard Carey), a strange gaping beachcomber—not wholly in his senses: "Those are pearls that were his eyes"—wanders the area, perhaps imagining he can speak to Rebecca across the Great Boundary. And so on.

All pure Daphne du Maurier (daughter of the very great British thespian and stage manager Gerald du Maurier [1873–1934], who played, among many other roles, the original Captain Hook): sentimental, haunted, evocative, romantic "balderdash" aimed at a vast and sympathetic audience of sentimental, haunted, evocative, and romantic female readers around the world, who, David O. Selznick was certain, would relish seeing onscreen a faithful rendition of the traumatizing love story they had adored in print.[3] They were his pre-sold audience, and the film needed only to speak to them, to bring these hopeful female viewers into the past.

In the middle of the film there springs a fateful—haunting, evocative, romantic, sentimental—storm, recalling, perhaps, Shakespeare:

> You are a
> counsellor; if you can command these elements to
> silence, and work the peace of the present, we will
> not hand a rope more; use your authority: (*The Tempest* I.i.25–28)

and as the sea vomits up its treasures and secrets, part of what floats to the beach is none other than Rebecca's skiff, which, now that people can examine it, makes open demonstration of strange foul play. "Ask your heart what it doth know," because in its bottom is a gaping, an undeniable hole. Rebecca didn't just die.

For the story beneath the story within the dream, later.

Because in truth (Rebecca herself, we will learn, was not such a very nice woman), my focus is on something far less linear, far more visual than a sense of events following one another through some logical line. It's that, improbably, with all these variegated characters (and some others I haven't taken the trouble to list), with all these craftily written and articulately spoken melodramatic exaggerations, each one of them played by a performer of the greatest talents (Gladys Cooper!, Judith Anderson!), somehow, still, one doesn't approach the heart of what the film offers. Because it's that monstrosity of a mansion, that Manderley, the city upon the hill, the tower upon the precipice, that has gripped and held us from the start and that grips and holds us all through ... and that, when the movie is done, grips and holds us onward. It's that confining dream-space. Guy Davenport writes of Pound's Canto LXXVI, "The sun's periplus is fused with the poet's memory ... so that the poem's heroes appear in the memory as a vision of stars" (92).

A HOMELY CAVERN

"Every people," wrote D. H. Lawrence, "is polarized in some particular locality, which is home, the homeland. Different places on the face of the earth have different vital effluence, different vibration, different chemical exhalation, different polarity with different stars" (17). Manderley is the picture in the frame of Hitchcock's screen, always Manderley, the house in its park, the house upon its cliffs, the great rooms, the immense staircase leading to passages and sepulchers unknown. The place is home yet, peculiarly, how very much it never feels like that. Mrs. Simpson visited a vast country estate: "'What fascinated me,' wrote Wallis later, 'was the architectural wizardry that had been exercised in imparting to the interior of this sprawling fort such an atmosphere of warmth and informality'" (Tinniswood 277). There is a sociological observation buried in Hitchcock's depiction of this place: our She is a middle-class girl, unfamiliar with the aristocracy and its haunts, but suddenly now, thanks to Love, not only inhabiting this palace but reigning in it. She is never for a moment completely comfortable. There are beautifully choreographed instants—the most celebrated involves a Cupid statuette that She inadvertently drops and smashes, but then hides so that the daunting Mrs. Danvers won't find it (and punish her)—in which we see how She is swimming helplessly in the great shark-infested sea of Manderley. So the *unheimlichkeit* of the place is a token of class boundaries and their prohibitive culturations: that She doesn't fit, has never fitted, will never fit. (In England, one doesn't attain class.) She manifests a kind of dream presence, that sense of recognizing one's terrain while finding it entirely unfamiliar, of moving without a map, neither fully conscious nor fully self-conscious.

Also at play is Hitchcock working for the first time with an American crew and in an American studio (Selznick International), under the baton of an outspoken, domineering, and blustering American (David O. Selznick), now contracted to portray for a largely American audience the delicacies of British upper-class life with which he is familiar in ways they aren't, have never been, will never be. America, by definition, is "not at home" in England (thus, the adventure of the Pilgrims), and so our sense that the spirit of place inhabiting Manderley is not a welcoming spirit is entirely fitted to a pervading alienation we are meant to feel with the story and its characters, even as we "inhabit" the diegetic space and care deeply—as deeply as moviegoers can care—for the love relationship between Maxim and She.

Very notably the film's presence is at Manderley; and when we are not there we are thinking of being there, by way of anticipation or reflection. There are no visions at Manderley, even character portraits, where the mansion is not invoked sharply by some detail in the composition. At Monte Carlo, when Mrs. Van Hopper cupidinously points Maxim out to She, with an obvious thirst, even in her dotage, to become his concubine and be whisked off to his dreamland, we are led by her too friendly imagination to dream for ourselves a magical castle where this forlorn prince makes his home. The Maxim we see in Monte Carlo is thus, in retrospect, only a shell, only a figuration, of a deeper persona who does not come alive until he is back in Manderley—or who *came* alive there, until Rebecca, soul of his soul (as we are cautioned), left him. We wonder about Manderley, and thus grasp intuitively what the young She must be going through as she wonders, too. Of course She knows that the employer who first told her of Manderley is American, a woman with somewhat inflated conceptions; yet, what if Manderley really is a dream castle?

And when we see it, a dream castle is precisely what it seems to be.

Because for us Manderley is quintessentially Rebecca's space, the space of the Dead, that is, the harbor of Rebecca's presence, when we finally arrive a gaping emptiness appears at its center. The camera's perspectives on the atrium and staircase convey this sense of emptiness.[4] Yet, at the same time, it is an emptiness that is not empty, an emptiness with proportion and form. Perhaps the house still vibrates. Perhaps Rebecca is still there? In this way is opened the double riddle of the film: on one side, that the title is an absence (Rebecca does not make an appearance); on the other, that the title and the absence refer less to a person than to a place, the presence or meaning of Rebecca being constantly invoked by way of the house and those who inhabit it with her memory. It is not quite Rebecca on the surface of the earth who is gone; it is Rebecca at Manderley. Rebecca was always at Manderley, and still is. Manderley was the space occupied by her. She was its mistress and is, still.

A charged moment takes place in Rebecca's suite in the west wing. Beyond the double doors that guard it, outside of which Jasper stands as sentry, is an atrium winged off by sheer curtains that drop down from an ineffable height, unseen and incalculable. Our She is hesitant fingering these sheers, parting them, but Mrs. Danvers, who follows shortly thereafter, is confident to spread them and gain entrance. Inside is the "outer" chamber, with its matching spectacular windows curtained over, its fresh bouquet sumptuously exploding from a crystal vase, the dressing table with the photographic portrait of the observant Maxim, the silver hair brushes like little soldiers all in a row. And then the "inner" chamber, the *sanctum sanctorum*, only for the priestly caste, with the drawers and closet, the sumptuous four-poster bed. We move through all of these spaces, first alone with She and then under the direction of the stern guide Mrs. Danvers, reproving but at the same time informative, perhaps too informative. "This is where she . . ." Mrs. Danvers is reliving her time with Rebecca, walking She through the old rituals, sitting She down at the dressing table and taking up the hair brush and almost brushing the girl's (already well-brushed) hair. It was like this. I did it this way. And then she. . . .

We are led to imagine Rebecca undressing for Mrs. Danvers. With Mrs. Danvers. For, with, for, with. With Danny and for Danny, and then Danny helping her to bed. "Come, Danny." It seems natural, unavoidable—there is in social fact nothing natural about a voyage into privacy—that Danny should bring She to the closet and withdraw a fur coat to brush against the girl's cheek and her own; and to the underwear drawer to show the panties arranged in a quarter-circle (the drawer opens out like the moon in one of its phases). The panties were stitched personally by the nuns at the Convent of St. Claire. A comment here about the delicacy, the holiness, and the privacy of those panties; yet also about how Danny is willing to part the curtains of that privacy in order that She have a direct experience of the innermost Rebecca, of Rebecca's "innermost." We move to the bed where Danny withdraws a dark peignoir to show how fine it is—how fine it always used to be: time collapsing into itself—and slips her hand inside to reveal the sheerness (and her own capacity for delicious invasion). "Look! You can see my hand!" Seeing is touching.[5]

If in the film's first act, that precedes the shipwreck, there can be said to be an inherent story, it's a question: against the pressure of Maxim's businesslike cool, his personal stiffness, and his preoccupation with the place, can She overcome her deep discomfort at being his new wife and come into her real power, her real feeling and action as a self, at Manderley? Since what we are watching is She thrashing in her own insecurity and unselfconfidence, buffeted by Danvers's virulent nostalgia and outreached at every turn by the extensivity of Manderley, then the sequence in the west wing, opulent and even awe-inspiring in its visual formation, offers almost nothing to further that plot, beyond a kind of ornate formalization. We knew already that Danvers was a formidable woman, too formidable. We knew that Rebecca had prominence of place, and could therefore have suspected she would have bedrooms of some notable proportions, like the rooms we see. The magical hair brush is finally a hair brush, the gorgeous flowers finally flowers, the broad, sumptuous bed finally a bed in which a body went to sleep, the delicate, even tantalizing panties finally panties. Mrs. Danvers, like the camera, is notably interested to see She's detectable interest as the panties are exhibited: in our greatest privacies we are all not only like one another but indeed only the beings others could have imagined us to be, yet we wish to sniff out the evidence, put a foot to the ground.

We are given opportunity to learn She's erotic secret, then. And to annotate, up close, the frigid, fearful quality of her posture and movement, definitive evidence of not only a personal and physical, but a broader social discomfort. And we are given to learn, in case we had not yet supposed it, the strange depths of Danny's bond with the dead woman. This bond could be framed in sexual terms—hardly an original thought: Danvers was not only mechanical and servile in peeling away Rebecca's clothing every night, she was one who liked to put—or dream of putting—her hand inside that peignoir. A lesbian love at the heart of a country estate, a love now shattered by death. But—

The passion of such a love as Danny's for Rebecca, the physical contact of the women however perfunctory, is something Hitchcock could have felt no pressing need to express or imply. In being carried away by intrigue about Rebecca we tend to forget that Hitchcock was not. The film is not about Rebecca herself. A far more involved knot charged Hitchcock's fascination, a knot of which sexuality of any kind is a mere token, if present at all. And that is Danny's bond with death. The Rebecca we see her metaphorically "touch" is, after all, not only a remembered Rebecca of the flesh but, indeed, a memory. And for the pretty young She, also a body secreted inside clothing, a wearer, too, of panties that could be held up for demonstration, Danny has no desire whatever, although Danny might, were sex on Hitchcock's mind. Our She is too alive to the moment to be sexual; she has not relaxed into her own muscularity enough to feel the throbs or tickles of desire, which is to say, the pungent and evasive perfume of memory.

In talking of Danny this way I mean to be adducing here not necrophilia, but communicative urgency and helplessness. Speaking with the dead. The sense of being caught in a conversation that can never end and never be certain. It is, finally, not a conversation *within* a dream as much as a dream conversation, a conversation *that is itself* a dream. Mrs. Danvers is the great dreamer in Hitchcock. Her dream is a very great dream.

VIVACIOUS TALK

Talk is life, we may think. Motion pictures from and about Britain tend to be on the talky side, but in *Rebecca* Hitchcock establishes verbosity early on, as an important underlying theme in itself. Less what people say than their bent for saying, the mouthy charge, the bubbling spring. Mrs. Van Hopper's most ostensible characteristic—albeit she is an American overseas, she has been imagined for a British context as a middle-aged Daisy Miller—is blabbiness.[6] As soon as we arrive at Monte Carlo we find her ensconced there, regal in habituation. This is the kind of (monied) tourist who, returning to a beloved locale again and again and again, year after year after year after year, accrues, at least in her own mind, a certain feeling of ascendancy, a certain command. She uses her voice to show off a (false) familiarity with the territory (no one who lives in Monte Carlo calls it "Monte"), a certain casual intimacy with other regular visitors of wealth and distinction—people, like Maxim, with whom she has absolutely nothing in common and in whose view she does not occupy a bethroned position, if any position at all. When this dowager takes to bed, with either a flu or a digestive attack from having gorged herself too heavily on the delights of the Côte d'Azur—her performance of need is so intensive it becomes a challenge to diagnose her frequently displayed "symptoms"—Maxim steals the girl off and soon enough asks her to marry. Mrs. Van Hopper discovers at what is for her the worst possible moment, having packed up and dictated to her girl that they are leaving for America. Maxim has rushed his proposal (interrupting his morning shave) and now finds himself obliged to inform the self-important employer that her companion is a companion no longer. He does this by asking that, before getting into her limousine, Mrs. Van Hopper come up to his rooms, which, sycophant that she is, the lady is only too tickled to do.

But when she enters and is confronted with the impending marriage, her self-worth is utterly punctured and she becomes the resentful, conniving climber that always rested beneath that gilded surface.

Mrs. Van Hopper is introduced in order to convey bluntly, if indirectly from a narrative point of view, the idea that situations are established by talk, even talk that is pure drivel. Characters and their import are signaled by their talk, its quality and directness. The dowager is imperious in Monte Carlo in much the same way that Mrs. Danvers is imperious at Manderley: in fact She transports to Manderley some of her feeling of subservience and timidity gained in the presence of the domineering American. But Danny has a different voice (east coast Scottish), an almost perpetually sealed mouth, a way of enunciating with piercing eyes. Confronted by her, we may note the impeccable grammar of her utterances, their thoughtful succinctness, their linguistic punch. Yet while Danny does not say a lot, when she speaks there is to be seen in her eyes, often camouflaged by the cassock-like gown she ports and beneath the sternness that She seems always already expecting to hear and feel, a look of wet-eyed tenderness: toward She, or toward Someone Else who inhabits the state of Memory. Or do we only imagine it? Danny seems dominating in a continuation of Mrs. V's well-rehearsed domination, but more silently so. Is a wordy dialogue progressing in the silent spaces that surround Danvers? The incessant spieling has opened us to the possibility of spieling, and thus to noticing how at Manderley such a thick pall of silence has descended.

We might also notice Maxim's florid, if clipped, orality, his generally taciturn personality (Olivier borrowing from his own Heathcliff), his extremely suave bearing and perfectly apposite posture in every situation coupled, perhaps provocatively, with an unknown—"Unknowable?," She must wonder—facet that is perpetually unlit by the sunbeams of cordiality and friendship. He is a moon, and day after day, as the month ticks by, he reveals only one, silvered, side.

At Manderley vocality is presence. The presumptive, preoccupied Maxim, with a voice perfunctory and proper, never fails to mean what he says, yet does not mean to embrace; or at least She can fret that he does not mean this. The stuttering elliptical Giles, so unequivocally well meaning yet entirely out of bounds. The somewhat haughty voice of the sister—well, she means to protect and to educate, and only with She does the sister become charming and real. The chillingly telegraphic Danny. The virtual silence of She: such a silence that when we strive to imagine the voice inside her head, we cannot hear a trace of even that.

The dampening space of Manderley envelops She, which is to say, the dampening nostalgia for a time thoroughly lost, of which She can fathom no part (or: of which she can fathom no part. But *She*, we must note, would never simply be *she*; that is, referent of a narrational pointing toward character and act. Always She would be the identifiable and identified She, self-conscious, nominal, highlit, subject to judgment.) Each bright room is a labyrinth unto itself, this state of affairs made clear through Hitchcock's neatly contrived contrasts: too-blithe Favell, for example, is far too much at home in a territory that belongs to She by right, and yet is not She's by fact. Or the gliding silent sudden presence of Danny, who would seem to occupy all space, every space, all the spaces, because like a dark smoke she filters through air, passes through walls, slides under doors, present in fact or in implication in all of Manderley: Danny who knew Rebecca. Danny who clothed and cleaned Rebecca. Danny who confided with Rebecca. Danny who, for all intents and purposes, *was* Rebecca. And now that Rebecca is proclaimed dead, Danny who is dead, too. Dead in life. Not really speaking.

DEAD IN LIFE

Regarding the possibility of death in life, let me divert if only briefly to Robert Jay Lifton's startling account of that condition, on the far horizon as Hitchcock made *Rebecca*. In Hiroshima, following the clearing and reconstruction after the A-bomb, many survivors experienced what Lifton termed "death-in-life," a status, a condition, and an extension of feeling and sensibility summarily encapsulated in the label *hibakusha*. The *hibakusha* was somehow closer to death, while being alive, than other people, who also moved and acted with a sense of mortality. "Death-in-life" implied a mortal weight, a damnation, a sentence that was deeply and eternally present, while also calling up the future and the past, and thus, as Freud would have been one of the earlier scholars to suggest, a dream state. "The dream originates from the past in every sense. To be sure, the ancient belief that the dream reveals the future is not entirely devoid of truth. By representing to us a wish as fulfilled the dream certainly leads us into the future; but this future, taken by the dreamer as present, has been formed into the likeness of that past by the indestructible wish" (Freud 443). The *hibakusha*'s body is effortlessly penetrated. Relations and activities are sharply provisional. Having been present in the blast zone one achieves a kind of supernatural transcendence, a Being superior to, but more vulnerable than, normal being. "Exposure to the atomic bomb changed the survivor's status as a human being, in his own eyes as well as in others'. He became a member of a new group.... Nor is this identity of significance only for atomic bomb victims" (Lifton 165).

Danny is not *hibakusha*, of course, but she is a kind of prototype. She moves in Manderley, and in the world at large—since this film is a diegetic microcosm of a diegetic "world at large"—as a member of a special (and restricted) class, a person associated with mortality in an irregular and always challenging way. We would be diminishing her significance, for us and for Hitchcock, if we concluded she was a protagonist in a ghost story, a tale-within-this-tale, where Rebecca was the ghost and Danny was her human interlocutor, the only human who could see (and interact with) her. It is more that she is filled with a capacity for love that transcends the grave, because for Danny Rebecca, however dead she may be on paper, is continually, interminably present in Manderley.

Because of the radiation and the directness of their experience with the bomb, an atomic future is always present, always here, for the *hibakusha*.

For the *hibakusha*, the world suddenly, shockingly, preternaturally dissolved away, so that space became at once vastly expanded (where buildings had stood, there was nothing) and contracted to the point of the self. For Danny, something oddly similar has happened, not on the vast social scale of the Hiroshima/Nagasaki attacks but similarly shaped, analogous, to such a degree that in comparison the atomic bombings could be understood not merely in military terms but also as providing a new scientific context for the interpretation of mortal experience. For Danny the Rebecca who was not merely her point of contact but indeed her entire world was suddenly gone, suddenly evaporated. *Not merely her point of contact but her entire world.* We know nothing of Danny outside of Manderley, outside of her relationship with Rebecca, except that through the new Mrs. de Winter she is in some way reliving that relationship, or aspects of it, reconstituting the razed city. Manderley was Rebecca; Maxim was an attachment to Rebecca; every room was Rebecca's space, every drawer in every closet a repository of Rebecca's secrets. For Danny, not only was there nothing of significance in Manderley that was not Rebecca but all of Manderley became significant because of Rebecca. When I say that Manderley was Rebecca I mean that for Danny, when Rebecca died Manderley died. Manderley is now dead. A dead zone, dead space, dead city. Bruges-la-morte. And Danny is living in that death.

Danny is inhabiting that death.

And in a way, so is She, because timidity and bullying have made her quiet as a mouse, have diminished her physicality (a physicality elegantly donned and then dropped away by the unfathomably skillful Joan Fontaine) so that, moving around the place with her voice turned off (her voice not found) she is the equivalent of the old mistress now, still, for Danny, drifting Danny, sleepwalking Danny, filtering around the place without a voice. Hippolyte Bernheim: "The hallucinations of somnambulism are really nothing but dreams that have been provoked; the image that is produced is more or less alive, and one's awareness of its identity can persist, more or less confused, in relation to the dream, without the dreamer being struck by the contradiction" (94; my translation). Absent the character of Mrs. Danvers, conceived as Judith Anderson conceives her, *Rebecca* is but a thin tale of a man who marries a girl quite unready to become his wife, socially speaking. Not an uninteresting tale, perhaps, especially when it turns out that Maxim may well have murdered his first wife (not only the boat but a body is found, and this leads to an inquest). The film becomes nothing but a murder mystery. But as we have it, *Rebecca* is about forms of love, multiple forms, of which one striking variant runs through the veins of the housekeeper—a woman apparently so cold there is nothing running through her veins. (Danvers is recapitulated by Kubrick in *2001: A Space Odyssey* as the unfeeling, all-knowing, and jealous HAL9000.) In the very ornately decorated, stone-cold Manderley, the great empty city of Manderley, two ghosts wander, one given limbs and breath through the body of the woman who cannot stop loving her and the other embodied by a child-woman who has nothing to forget.

She, we ought not forget, has no one to talk to, not even the chummy farm agent, who means to befriend her but honestly has no time, obedient as he must be to Maxim's command. Not even Maxim's dear sister can help, who would be embracing if she could, but one has the sense that for this kind soul it's all become a little too much, and besides, what could one do? She is understandably already under Danvers's spell, always, unendingly puppeted, because She is lost in the Tunnels of Love, to which Danvers has the key.

Danvers, who looks like a priest.

SURVEILLED

"You wouldn't think she'd been gone so long, would you," says Danny, interrupting She's flight from the bedroom suite. Here are the doors, just pull them open. But the gliding Danny has She cornered. "Sometimes, when I walk along the corridor, I fancy I hear her, just behind me. That quick, light step. I couldn't mistake it anywhere. Not only in this room ... in all the rooms in the house." The word "room" is queerily pronounced: *rhume*. (Danny is an immigrant from the North; Judith Anderson came from Australia, and said *rhume* again in *Kings Row* [1942].) "I can almost hear it now," she goes on, turning to glare into the frightened eyes of She—the frozen animal eyes—with her bony, placid servile hands folded together as in a little formal elocution, "Do you think the dead come back and watch the living?" Schoolmarm, High Priestess, concièrge in some ancient dilapidated hotel of the spirit. The last words about the dead coming back to watch, and other phrases in Danny's speech, are taken verbatim from du Maurier, who has She now continue in her first-person narrative recollection:

> I could not take my eyes away from hers. How dark and sombre they were in the white skull's face of hers, how malevolent, how full of hatred.

Fontaine's She is quite beside herself with terror, and her tongue has slipped half-out between her lips. "I don't believe it!" she murmurs, with tears.

Danny's face approaches, and Hitchcock has his camera operator, George Barnes, slowly zoom in, to effect a head-and-shoulders paired close-up. "Sometimes, I wonder if she doesn't come back here to Manderley... to watch you and Mr. de Winter together." A stark reversal of *surveillance*, the keeping watch over the tomb, with the dead now using their dead eyes to seize dead visions of the living lovers. The present as a betrayal of the past.

The quality of this moment, chilling, invigorating, otherworldly, set in a space away from waking life, is central to the film, since it leaks into She's consciousness and is thereby spread through the space of Manderley and the space of the plot. But it would be seriously erroneous to take the closeness of the bodies in this powerful shot as physical intimacy or warmth. The very point is that a certain chill has entered the room, or an unworldly "warmth" brought by a figure who is not a figure in the normal sense. Thus, in her "priestly" garb, Danny makes something of a confession, giving over wholly and in a kind of troubling generosity a secret of the very greatest magnitude, that she takes herself to be the object of Rebecca's perduring oversight.

In reflection we may see that secrecy is all over *Rebecca*. The film is itself a great secret, made up of an arrangement of lesser secrets. The real nature of Rebecca herself, known now only in retrospect (do we ever know a person's nature in any other way?), the secret connection between Danvers and Rebecca, the secret connection between Rebecca and her husband. There is a portrait of a woman in a party gown, hanging atop the main staircase: Who was the woman posing for that? What spirit is caught therein? Originally She was being charitable in watching Maxim at Monte Carlo—a man to whom something enormous and grave had happened. Then she was caught in his spell. Now she has been imported to his royaume. What kind of kingdom is this, anyway, with its vast interlinked corridors, its endless rooms, and the sprites who fly about? Is it a Wasteland?

A bond between secrecy and the pervasive air of grief, nostalgia, and perturbed memory can be discerned in every shadow. Manderley—it exists no longer, as we will learn—was a grand secret in itself; those who lived there lived on secrets, fed on them, nourished themselves with secrecy. Once again Hiroshima—not that the destruction there could truly be likened to what we see in this motion picture, but that with Lifton's subjects, the *hibakusha*, one finds a somewhat analogous spread of grief, grief all-invading and endless, grief for tomorrow. A further observation of the events in Japan notes that in 1946 (the year of my birth) the Americans instituted a vast net of censorship, so thorough that "there were to be no film or newsreel pictures of GIs; no pictures anywhere of American soldiers and Japanese women. No pictures were permitted of soldiers in jeeps: no reports were allowed of any criminal offences by GIs.... References to hunger and rationing should not be 'overplayed.'" Further, strikingly:

> One of the biggest taboos was mention of Hiroshima and Nagasaki. No pictures could be published of the devastation of the cities caused by the atom bombs. John Hersey's superb book *Hiroshima*, which originally appeared on 31 August as a long article in *The New Yorker*, was published in the US in November. A Japanese publisher wanted to translate it into Japanese. SCAP [Supreme Commander for the Allied Powers] refused point blank and the book was banned in Japan until late 1948. In well-educated circles of Tokyo a few people who read English passed round smuggled copies of the US edition, like *samizdat* manuscripts behind the Iron Curtain. (Sebestyen 359; 360)

To summarize: the devastation could not be directly addressed. The supreme commander mandated information blackouts. Yet in *Rebecca* even the name of the supreme commander was a secret. Maxim de Winter is occupying the role of a British country landowner, but is this truly his land? Given the meticulousness of Danny's care in maintaining the house, continuingly, in its pristine condition, may it have been Rebecca herself who dominated in Manderley, everywhere? May it, indeed, have been the utterly secretive Danny behind the throne, given that regardless of social position a great deal of force can be exerted in human lives by the avenue of emotional strength and control?

WINDOWS

The cloistered quality of Manderley raises the issue of windows, and of light. The entire prefatory Monte Carlo sequence is shot for brilliance: sparkling daylight by the sea, or gaudy internal light at the hotel. We have a sense of comfort, relaxation, spaciousness. But at Manderley, first a copse of trees hide the castle, then we are startled by great stone walls set with a myriad windows, into which we cannot see. Inside, rooms with proportion and décor, yet hardly a sense of the outside world peeking in—except with the one tall window through which the nefarious Favell smarmily crawls into the study. If there is a perduring memory of Monte Carlo and its glitter, that might be a window onto the Manderley world, yet the Manderley world is so absorbing, so undefined and unexplained for She—whose sensibility we inherit as we watch—that thinking of what came before is unlikely and unhelpful. As She and Maxim go walking on the clifftop, the bouncy Jasper unendingly invokes the dead Rebecca, who also walked him there. So even this ostensibly invigorating hike is a cloistering. The same can be said for the dark, recursive interior of the cottage by the surf. Inside the great house itself, there is a glorious multi-paned high window at the landing leading up to the west wing, but the light filtering through is only enough to make She's blouse glisten in her anticipation. The bedroom suite is about fifteen feet high, and the matching high windows, revealed when Danvers pulls the draperies, show a stunning flood of light. But this light is diffuse, not clarifying, with tree branches making exciting but also confusing patterns. At a climactic moment we look out a high window to see the flurry on the beach during the storm, but it is night. And at another climactic moment Danny encourages She to jump to her death from a high window, held open. Once again here, the terrifying encounter with this agent from the past, this agent of Mortality, overwhelms a sense of an exterior and possibly salvational world.

Near the film's conclusion there is a visit to London, the suite of a Harley Street medical professional (Leo G. Carroll), who will open an envelope of secrecy by revealing some information about the dead woman that, as it were, "brings new light." Yet the scene is brief, in a fairly dark closet, at night, in a darkened city. During the inquest scenes, the interludes outside the courtroom that pose Maxim, Favell, and She in or around an estate car refer, in short, to encapsulation and cloistering, with Maxim encapsulated and cloistered by impending guilt in a horrible crime, and She trapped in bond to him as his loving and loyal partner.

But there is one brief moment of relief from the prison of darkness into which this bright young girl has been cast by her act of love: not an actual window but a narrative "window" that lets narrative "light" stream through. It is a moment of lambent and lighthearted play, of springtime blossoming, of cherished and brilliant delight, and although it will be sharply curtailed and poisoned by darkness soon enough, it remains a signal beacon of natural light. Maxim and She are dressed in evening clothes, tucked away in a private study—small, embracing, perfectly right—with the lights turned off. They are caught up in watching his home movie of their wedding and honeymoon. The hotel where they stayed, something possibly Swiss, enchantingly obscure with hanging flowers. Maxim mugging childishly in front of the camera. She a paragon of demureness, still retreatingly shy, but clearly a flower in bloom. He a man who has thrown off the dark harness of grief so as to swim in feeling once more; the open delight on his face, the youthful abandon: after seeing it here we never see it again. For Olivier's Maxim, it is a moment in front of his camera when he can openly proclaim that the Lord-of-the-Estate mask has been tossed aside. "I am not acting": which is to say, for Olivier himself, it is a moment in which he proclaims, "I am acting that my thoroughly acted Maxim is not acting." The remainder of Maxim's appearances are thus defined by the actor beneath him as comparatively performative: Maxim's surface; Maxim's obligatory Iron Mask. Maxim is thus generally hiding himself, experiencing the brittleness of masquerade: his true feelings are tucked beneath the proper façade he is obliged to wear as master of Manderley. We can hope, having now all too briefly glimpsed those deeper feelings of liberation in the home movie, that alone with She, Maxim might regularly exhibit his real self again, the light of his real self.

But in seconds She is complaining that everybody at Manderley looks her up and down like a prize cow, that, in short, she is never free. He is blithe: What if they do? But in his joy, Maxim is being inconsiderate: he is quite used to being looked up and down like a prize bull, he has spent his life at Manderley in that condition. His self-consciousness has been well trained in the repeated patterns of the place, so that he needn't feel himself anymore as the object of a gaze. For her, things are new, disorienting, displacing. And in only a moment it will become clear that still, so early in their union, Maxim is one of those who looks her up and down, too, because the business will arise of the small Cupid statue that She inadvertently broke and hid away from Danvers. Frith the butler stands accused. She will confess to Maxim what really happened, but he will not hold himself back from chiding that She should not run around in fear of these people, should have come straight out with what happened. She should stop being herself, in other words, and become the "Mistress of Manderley" just as Rebecca was—as he has never had a moment of doubt She would eventually—hopefully with speed—proceed to do. A look back at that mocking face he showed the camera in the home movie: freedom for Maxim to play in the privacy of the honeymoon, yes, but also a very put-on face. A mask; a "what-if-I-wore-an-entertaining-monkey mask," the one we very self-consciously apply when we are actually *not* feeling the liberty simply to be.

The viewer's hope is that the trapped She will find a way out of her prison, and that Maxim will show true spirit and bravery in escaping, himself, from the bondage of class position and place in order to show She the way, in order to take her hand. If their love can be real, realer than the reality of Rebecca and whatever it is for which she persistently stands, the jailer can be made to hand over the key. But as the film progresses, what we see is the multiplication of layers that constitute Maxim de Winter. Who is the man beneath the roles, hiding away in only mercurial light?

TAKING STEPS

Maxim is throwing a soirée in order to introduce his new wife to the community. It will be a costume affair. Danvers has offered to help She—in secret—with a suitable garment modeling Lady Caroline de Winter in that lovely portrait at the head of the stairs. The bright idea is that the portrait will be brought to life, with She elegantly embodying the form. We see the emergence from the bedroom, the slow and unsure march to the top of the stairs, then, catching the portrait and the living form in shot together, see the vivacity, the vibration of the masquerade. She puts a hand on the banister and begins to step down. Hitchcock's camera is on a crane, elevated at first so as to share a position near the top of the stairs. As She slowly descends, so does that camera, following every step and recording the shifting patterns of expression on the smooth young face. Hope, definitely. Fear, or trepidation. The burning desire to be liked and accepted finally, to be regarded as belonging. And what better way to belong than as an incarnation? An ingratiating smile, as though to say, "I can shine with glamour, just for you, dear Maxim, just as always happened in your wonderful life." Maxim is waiting at the bottom of the stairs, turned away, in conversation with Giles and Beatrice, whose eyes look up past his shoulder before he turns—whose startled eyes perhaps anticipate by half a beat what is to come.

He turns in a blaze of happiness, and it is as though a pall from hell has, with leaden weight, darkened him forever. Then anger. Then the fury of lightning.

Rebecca wore that dress just before she died! This was entirely the wrong approach, She suddenly knows. More: it was in all likelihood a damaging, if not a fatal, move, a provocation to the husband she adores, an attack, and yet, how? How???? In only one way. Danvers was not her ally but her enemy. Her capable enemy. This much must now be taken as certain. Not her ally but her *mortal enemy*. This enterprise was all wrong from the start. All . . . wrong. She is all wrong. Her desire, her hope, her prayer—all wrong.

But that moment on the staircase: it demands serious reflection. We must not neglect the circumstances in which a small-town, middle-class girl like She, raised by morally upright parents (one of whom, at least, may have been professional) and taught the proprieties of loyal British female life under wartime conditions (stiff upper lip, prudence, thrift, eyes open), may have come to leave home and take up employment in service of a traveling tourist, without possessing the social tools that make for easy adjustment to high-class circumstances and fluid mobility there. After all, were She to have had such tools, there'd have been little reason for her to take a companion's position, nor would She likely have been looking for work at all. The fact of her status, as first we meet the girl, says much about her capabilities but even more about her class. Graceful, articulate, literate, sensitive, considerate, attentive, and generally as sweet as candy, She is also a person who has never had the experiences upon which one can establish and mount a landowner's self-confidence. Thus, when She comes to Manderley, we find exemplified, in one artfully staged scene after another, that she doesn't trust herself in this surround. She has feelings but she doesn't rely upon them with surety; fears and anxieties, but She doesn't feel confident in these either. She is afraid even of her own fear.

If we look at the chain of interaction between She and Danvers from their first moment of encounter through to the staircase moment, we find She constantly withdrawing into herself, freezing, being incapable of articulate speech, stymied by terror but at the same time aware that no real threat is being put forward by the housekeeper, no real weapon being readied for use. Thus She suspects herself of overreaction in being fearful. In her withdrawal, her freeze, she is pulling away not only from Danvers but also from her own rigid trembling, from what she recognizes as a kind of dramatization. Learn how to trust. Relax. Stop being afraid of your own shadow, or the many shadows that inhabit this place. Turn on the "light." Make yourself at home.

Thus, She's commitment to accept Mrs. Danvers's offer of help with regard to a costume for the ball is far from casual and far from slight. It is an offering of the deepest, most vulnerable, tenderest self, an opening of the chamber of fear and self-regard. A step forward.

And it is into this very private chamber of tender receptiveness that Danny has insinuated the poisonous idea of the dress, the great straw hat (as in Elizabeth Louise Vigée le Brun's self-portrait), the perfect reconstruction of the Impossible Queen. Danny's idea, Danny's tactical stratagem will be accepted wholly and graciously, rapturously, hungrily by someone who so desperately needs a friend and has feared that she will not find one. Danny has her own cluster of motives here, some of which will occupy us in a moment; but surely a deep and central one is bringing back the dead. She is positioning the woman on the staircase, as it were, *d'entre les morts*; making a soul return to life; animating a ghost. She is entering the dream space between life and death, where phantoms gain bodies and bodies evanesce. Rebecca will live again by her hand, she will be the mother and the father of the new Rebecca.

What is at stake for the new Mrs. de Winter as she walks down those stairs is, all of this: She's desire to give Maxim the figure she believes he has been obsessed by in all his distractions, the beautiful sylph; her desire to flower in a kind of sunlight—his adoring gaze; her desire to unify with this mysterious, ineffable specter, so that Rebecca, whoever she was, can gain, at least for the moment, for a whisper, some materiality, because does She not intuit, somehow, from the air in her nostrils, that the portrait was important, some jewel of Maxim's memories and hopes, jewel of the estate, the glow of which she might now happily reflect; and finally her desire to make peace with Danny by allowing Danny to—by convincing herself that Danny can—be her friend. The nervous chin, not confident. The calculated steps, step—step—step—step—not confident. The preposterous hat, swank, gay, but not confidently worn. All of it not confident but hopeful, desperately hopeful. In a prayer.

But then suddenly the pall of the blackest night, a night without morning.

What Danny wanted, of course, was to drive between his new wife and the regal Mr. de Winter a wedge irremovable, to make the man fear this impetuous and very silly child whose impulses would never make sense. He needn't want to send She away; so long as he could be made to cease loving her. Perhaps—this has to have been one of Danny's deep fantasies—perhaps to think fondly of the very dear, the very cherished, the untrammeled Rebecca once again. To think of the supreme Rebecca and find this distinctly lower charlatan wanting.

She, for her part, has gained a useful piece of knowledge: that one can never trust Danvers again. That Danvers has never been her friend, and that in fearing Danvers—more precisely, in fearing a condition where Danvers was not her friend, her ally—She was not being misled or mistaken, She was being sensible. In this moment of pain and humiliation, self-confidence is actually born. She is going to be able to stand, to stand up, to rise up, to come to Maxim's height. What was erroneous was not her fear of Danvers, but her fear—her shame—of that fear.

How does Hitchcock convey this?

The answer is both simple and profound. He uses his camera to concentrate on the girl; not, that is, merely to frame or to watch She but to refrain strictly from even the slightest wavering of attention, to make She the very hub of the visual universe. As we watch that descent on the staircase, the camera mimicking the girl by descending at her pace, and as we are given to note the very tiny adjustments of her facial muscles, the adjustments of her head cant, the intensification of her gaze, we come to realize how vivid and quaveringly *alive* is this organism, this frightened little thing caught up in a puzzle world so oceanic in proportion. In its utter devotion to She, the camera does not shirk its duty to follow every modulation of gesture, any more than She herself shirks the duty to present herself perfectly to the finally judgmental perception of Maxim. The devotional gaze upon the descending figure, which mirrors her devotional fixation upon the body of Maxim at the bottom of the stairs, perfectly aligns our sensibility with hers as regards the man with his back turned, gives us the opening whereby we can enter She's consciousness in that act of stepping down to him, become her body and presence, grasp the confinement of her condition. "Love me! Love me!"

A shot like this is a courageous step for Hitchcock—special crane arrangements were required on set—newly arrived on the American working scene and with a substantial reputation to uphold under Selznick's often bitterly scrutinizing gaze. Hitchcock knows his character from the inside-out, because he, too, has been brought into a wealthy and enormous estate (Selznick International), imported from afar; and is under the control of a man who could be sincerely beneficent if he did not perversely exercise so much taste over the work of his minions. Hitchcock by this shot is showing the world—and showing David Selznick, who will see it before anyone else does—the condition of innocence being watched. But he is also deviating from cinematic convention by spending so rich an attention on an action that might in anyone else's hands be treated perfunctorily: get the girl from the top of the stairs to the bottom, move the story forward. Here, in place of that, a miniature dream sequence, a lifting of the viewer's attention away from the propulsion of the story for a breath, with a focus on the biological-ecological unity: a body with all its emotional outgivings placed in such a way that it must attend to itself (to prevent a fall) and see where it is going (prepare to meet Maxim at the foot of the stairs). Nowhere in the film is the beautiful Fontaine—now, ironically, dolled up as an "object of beauty"—treated with so little regard to her general sweetness, as here. It is not her sweetness Hitchcock is following, with surgical intent. It is her ongoing transpositions of feeling and sense, the very pulse of her life.

Two little Hitchcockian tricks to border this dream shot:

First, we saw the girl march along the balcony and pass by the portrait oil painting, of whose subject She is now a walking doppelgänger. A little set-up joke, invoking doubling, authenticity and fakery, image and substance. The technical operator, Mrs. Danvers, is hidden in the darkness off-scene, where technical operators belong.

Secondly, Hitchcock has Maxim in conversation at the foot of the stairs, his back to the staircase dramatically, but when he turns we see him from She's point of view, his glare of—what?, shock?, hatred?, disappointment?, outrage?, despair?—directed fully and only to the camera. Now, then, the camera is She. And because of the dream descent and our involvement in it, the camera is also, perhaps more distinctly here than at other moments, us. The thrust of his negativity comes as a jab, virtually military in form, because we are inside the young woman at whom it is directed.

TWO *REBECCAS*

There are two dramas in *Rebecca,* one nestled inside the other. The more superficial drama is embedded in the unwinding plot: a man was married to a woman now dead, the event of her death being somewhat unclear, and his feelings and guilt are interwoven with the life of an innocent girl attached to him through a new marriage that sails through the wake of his past. "Neither law nor sexuality (nor, by implication, progeny) is sufficient to ensure true marriage," writes Stanley Cavell, and—eerily intimating *Rebecca*'s odd but poignant construction—"what provides legitimacy is the *mutual willingness for remarriage,* for *a sort of continuous reaffirmation,* and one in which the couple's isolation from the rest of society is generally marked; they form as it were *a world elsewhere* (*Pursuits* 142; my emphasis). Maxim and She know this marriage is nothing other than a remarriage and are mutually willing it; the early marriage that needs replacement or reconstitution is now phantasmal. What, at any rate (this drama asks), was the actual story of Rebecca, who was she, what did she want? And how and why did she die? In this rather dark and cloistered tale, a tale essentially without windows, as I've suggested, a blinding shaft of light comes through one of the strangest windows of all, the nocturnal session in London with Rebecca's physician confiding a secret that changes not only the history of her life and death but also the lives of those who were connected to her: Maxim, Mrs. Danvers, Favell. This radical illumination allows for an ending to the story in which Maxim and She can find a loving life with one another, safe at last from the haunting shadows of Rebecca and Manderley. Mrs. Danvers, we learn, loved Rebecca either madly or too much, with a commitment too fierce and a will too directive, or helplessly, mortally, in agony.

This first *Rebecca*, this exoskeleton, is, I think, the film that has taken the attention of most audiences, most critics, and most lovers of romance. Even of most Hitchcock fans, who remain, at this writing, swept away by the magic of this film. The exoskeleton is of course a noir setting of a Victorian love story, character-based and swirling with passion and despair. Reading the passionate invective in his correspondence, especially to his new employee Hitchcock, it is hard not to believe Selznick himself was caught up in the swirl. There can be no accident that Maxim is a Heathcliff, that the soaring music of Franz Waxman storms and sweeps us through the scenes, that at the margins of the action, just as at the margins of Manderley itself, there is a "sea" crashing against rocks. The homosexual tonality of Mrs. Danvers and her constant toying with the new wife's sexual innocence adds provocative spice to the conventional love story, a story here duplicated so that one version takes place before our eyes and the other in a secret oneiric space of memory, desire, enchantment, and questioning. As I say, all of this has been seen and seen again.

But there is a second *Rebecca*, the story of a spiritual confinement within monumental strictures. At play in this second film, this inner film, is a somewhat different set of game pieces. Our She is a well-meaning but unknowing child confronted with not merely a social world that is strange to her but a social institution, indeed, an institution that looms throughout as the dominant character. This institution is Manderley, Manderley the dream zone invoked by Mrs. Van Hopper, Manderley the daunting prospect seen on our first arrival, Manderley as class statement, Manderley and its servants. The house fills the screen in so many ways, seen from without and within. Moving from room to room is like wandering an endless labyrinth. Du Maurier's novel spells it out by *not* spelling it out:

> Yes, there it was, the Manderley I had expected, the Manderley of my picture postcard long ago. A thing of grace and beauty, exquisite and faultless, lovelier even than I had ever dreamed, built in its hollow of smooth grassland and mossy lawns, the terraces sloping to the gardens, and the gardens to the sea. As we drove up to the wide stone steps and stopped before the open door, I saw through one of the mullioned windows that the hall was full of people. (71)

Manderley is the persona to which, to whom, our She is enfiefed. Abstraction following abstraction is Manderley, until we come to the mullioned windows, something real, something to touch. Most everything about it is beyond the mind, beyond perception.

Maxim, too, is caught in Manderley—tethered there by his loyal estate manager Crawley, who just does his quotidian job with efficiency and no intent to cause harm. If the Lord of this estate, as we learn, has been tormented in his marriage, and tormented much worse by his wife's death; still his position on the estate requires him to show courtesy, equanimity, sanity in the face of an insanity of feeling. Crawley supports Maxim; but Maxim cannot let himself be other than the figurehead Crawley is willing to support. "Each child grows up in an adult world that is specified by both politics and social existence, and they are reared by adults who consciously know and who unconsciously manipulate the particularities of the world that shaped them" (Steedman 123). Was Maxim the flamboyant lover with Rebecca, or was the marriage as hollow as the castle? Such marriages existed in the English higher class. "The Marlboroughs' unhappy marriage:—He spoke so rarely at meals that she took up knitting to pass the time between courses" (Tinniswood 223).

Worst off is Danny. The institutional *Rebecca* is the story of how this woman's passion overcame her duty. As Rebecca's housekeeper and personal maid, she owed fealty to Manderley, always Manderley. Rebecca could claim her only by virtue of being Lady Manderley, this an arbitrary position falling to her upon marrying Maxim and terminating with her death. Danny rationally knows all this. At one point she uses the house telephone to ring "Mrs. de Winter" and ask about a menu. But our She, confused, stutteringly anxious, retreats, unaware of who is on the other end of the line while explaining sweetly that unfortunately Mrs. de Winter is dead.

Danny knows that she answers to whoever is, or has become, the current Mrs. de Winter. But in her heart of hearts, her dream zone, there is only one Mrs. de Winter and will never be another. And the timid little She thinks the same! Danny overstepped her boundaries, allowed herself to form an attachment to a particular person, whereas in the institutional view there is never any actual person acting on the estate's behalf, only the keeper of a title for the time being.

Hitchcock was fascinated to see played out the tension between the compulsions of people's needs and desires—biology, history, destiny—against the requirements, the legalities, of institutional structures and arrangements. So for him Manderley is two things always in this second, more pulsating *Rebecca*: it is the glorious, twinkling, sparkling, universe of an essentially incomprehensible romantic dream and it is a stony, well-run, routine-based, landed institutional structure.

In the superficial *Rebecca*, the love story, Manderley is the woman we never meet, the first wife, and the diligent housekeeper who loved her. When it burns in the finale, when Danny perishes, the past is ashes, and Maxim and She can go forward to a future. In the second *Rebecca*, the film of the institutional prison, the burning of Manderley is a kind of deinstitutionalization (shown, to be sure, in grand proportion, a tumultuous blaze, that calls to mind the paintings and etchings of the fire of London, 1666). Maxim at the end is only a man. She can love him with no thought of his position in society, because what dominates is his position in life at the moment: and his position in life at the moment is that he is alive.

UNSPOKEN LOVE

A concluding, very brief word about Danny and her attachment to Rebecca's Manderley, Manderley's Rebecca. Danny, the servile cipher:

> Someone advanced from the sea of faces, someone tall and gaunt, dressed in deep black, whose prominent cheek-bones and great, hollow eyes gave her a skull's face, parchment-white, set on a skeleton's frame.... I could see that black figure standing out alone, individual and apart, and for all her silence I knew her eye to be upon me. (du Maurier 72–73)

For the romantic *Rebecca*, it can seem logical to imagine the dead woman having harbored with her own dear Danny a secret love, one her husband could never have understood. It would have functioned as yet one more great secret that Rebecca was not confiding to Maxim, a kind of sealing wax upon the empty document called "Rebecca" that he was never able to read.

But for grasping the institutional *Rebecca* there is no inherent logic to this idea of forbidden love. What needed to be shown, finally, was a servant eclipsing her station, regardless of motive. Danny is no reprobate; she is conflicted. Among other qualities, she shows a certain under-stairs realism if also a stern asceticism: "The housekeeper [in the upper-class house] wore a black silk dress, sometimes relieved with lace" (Lethbridge 52), her asceticism a constant reminder that "the duty of being respectable fell heavily upon women.... Respectable servants were more likely to uphold the service status quo" (99). Lucy Lethbridge mentions a sixty-year-old housemaid, "tall with an aristocratic bearing," who had

> absorbed, seemingly without question, the tastes and mannerisms of her employers. For pleasure she read the *Tatler*, travelled first class on her holidays and stated that she liked "to work for people who have breeding.... When I started you were really a servant, whereas now you're more of a friend. They come and thank you more." (312)

Perhaps Danny's secret life was that of an avid reader; "We could not have talked of escape except within a literary framework that we had learned from the working-class novels," writes Carolyn Steedman (15–16). The sexual allusions merely put a cause before the effect, an arbitrary cause; they heighten our awareness sharply as to the housekeeper's forgetting herself, or, perhaps more controversially, show how she avowedly denies servitude in the name of free relations. But Danny is not really free, systematically. What Manderley stands for institutionally is the British class system, another giant structure in which one can wander to no end. Manderley is not only an example of upper-class wealth; it *means* class distinction. Thus we must see servants in plain display. And the butler who never for a moment steps outside his servile role, by contradistinction to Danvers who dared to love—or now dares to suggest she loved—not the Lady of Manderley as an institutionally secured personage but *the individual* who was playing that lady before she died. And the local citizens' general upward gaze at Maxim in the courtroom. The form—the vertical form—of the system.

We may presume that for Danny, then, all of Manderley and all of the class structure of England were but a grand, ostentatious performance, beneath the painted flats of which, if one was but free and sensitive, one could see, hear, even touch the actual beings who wore the robes. She is the ultimate Hitchcockian dreamer. That one could put the hand *inside*. That there existed for her a "backstage," where one could penetrate to encounter the nobility in fact and as plain persons, without the drawback of their titles and the etiquette attached. And of course it is true that, in preparing her, in the upstairs bedroom, to make that historic descent down the staircase, Danny *was* touching the actual person acting presently as Mrs. de Winter, touching perhaps more than ever she had touched or wanted to touch or dreamt of touching, but didn't know it.

CHAPTER FIVE

CATCHING
TO CATCH A THIEF

> To surrender means to take as fully, to meet as immediately as possible whatever the occasion may be. It means *not* to select, *not* to believe that one can know quickly what one's experience means, hence what is to be understood and acted on.... By "catch" I mean the existential or cognitive result, yield, harvest, *Fang* (catch), *Begriff* (concept, from *con-cipio*) of surrender, the beginning (*Anfang*), new conceiving or new conceptualizing which it is.
>
> —Kurt Wolff, "'Surrender' and 'Catch'"

In the third week of June 1954, while photography was being completed on the Cours Saleya flower market sequence of *To Catch a Thief* (1955) and pressure was mounting on the cast and crew to be done with Cary Grant's participation in order that he be freed to catch the S. S. Mauritania back to New York (Erickson to Caffey, 22 June 1954), Alfred Hitchcock was paid a visit on set by the French *père de critique*, André Bazin. There, and in an extended subsequent interview at Cannes' Carlton Hotel a few days afterward (translated by Sylvette Baudrot), Bazin worked to plumb the Hitchcockian technique, noting with a little surprise (as Baudrot herself had

already done [16]) the apparent ease and disattention with which Hitchcock greeted the actual photography of his films: that he would lay back in his chair while his diligent crew maneuvered to get the shots, apparently not watching except for the rare brief glance. "I'm essentially interested very little in the story I'm telling," Bazin heard Hitchcock say. "Only the means of telling it: that alone is important to me" (28; my translation). Of the Bazin interview, which appeared in *Cahiers du cinéma* as "Hitchcock contre Hitchcock," Hitchcock's rather arch biographer Donald Spoto claims that it

> began the critical debate over Hitchcock as serious artist that has prevailed internationally. One of the proximate results was that the French directors Eric Rohmer and Claude Chabrol joined forces and started writing the first extended critical appreciation of his films (a 1957 work more important for its provocative and seminal suggestions than for any sustained depth or factual accuracy).
>
> With Bazin, Rohmer, and Chabrol, there was sounded in the community of critics and filmmakers the call to take sides about the value of Alfred Hitchcock's work. By the time of Bazin's death, in 1958, the critical bibliography had begun in earnest. (377)

One may surmise that, its importance as a story (a "suspense," as the French loved to call Hitchcock's films) entirely notwithstanding, and even if one chose to pay little attention to Hitchcock's storytelling manner, still, *To Catch a Thief* has enduring historical importance on the basis of its having functioned as setting for the meeting of those two great artistic, philosophical, and, I would add, religious minds.[1]

Failing to attend to this challenging film would be folly. It apotheosizes the problem of interiority, essential to cinema, and also points up

167

a reflection of François Truffaut's: "Civilization has become so protective that we're no longer able to get our goosebumps instinctively. The only way to remove numbness and revive our moral equilibrium is to use artificial means to bring about the shock. The best way to achieve that, it seems to me, is through a movie" (201n).

TUMBLER

The story, at its most perfunctory: John Robie (Cary Grant), an American expatriate who worked closely with the French underground during the Second World War, is settled luxuriously in Nice, suspected there, by his friends as well as by the police, of being the notorious "Cat" who has been burgling the big hotels of their aristocratic guests' fattest jewels. As Grant himself was an acrobat once, Robie was once a burglar. Haunting the case now is H. H. Hughson (John Williams), a stodgy but loveable insurance investigator from Lloyds; and an American tourist duo, the outspoken Jessie Stevens (Jessie Royce Landis) and her spectacularly attractive, not overly modest daughter Francie (Grace Kelly), both of whom succumb to Robie's charming Cary Grantish personality. We also meet Danielle Foussard (Brigitte Auber), daughter of one of Robie's Résistance cronies and something of a tomboy, eager to steal him away—in reality or only in play—from the amorous attentions of the deliciously uninhibited Francie. Since the robberies are continuing unabated, police pressure mounts. Will Robie be caught? (By the authorities or by Francie, surely: but which?)

Much of *To Catch a Thief* is shot on genuine locations on the Côte D'Azur, both in and around Nice and on the beach and in the Carlton Hotel at Cannes. Thus, audiences may take a touristic pleasure in seeing the screen filled with luscious views and intimations of intoxicating aromas and rich adventure, or, as *Variety* had it, "an aura of sophistication, that goes well with the scenic values of the Riviera strikingly, if a bit self-consciously, displayed here in VistaVision" (Brog., "Review of *To Catch a Thief*" [20 July 1955]). As to beauty and beautification, Grant and Kelly are as handsome a couple as ever graced the screen, with Landis and Williams providing the richest, but also the very subtlest, character support. Robert Burks understandably took home an Oscar for his cinematography. Edith Head made

Kelly so alluring it could hardly have been a shock to Hitchcock when Rainier of Monaco fell in love with her and took her away from Hollywood, although for his legion fans Grant was the more princely gentleman, at least onscreen. He plays a scene with Kelly that is often commented upon, for all its relative innocence: Robie and Francie are cooing on the couch in her suite, and in the night sky behind them, as they kiss, fireworks (presumably from the annual *Bataille des fleurs*) explode with what *Variety* called "a saucy implication" and an enthusiasm the Production Code Office took pains to dampen.

As the *Times* noted, the visual richness of *To Catch a Thief* owed much to the then-still-young VistaVision process, originated at Paramount by the studio's technical head Loren Ryder in 1953 in order that a first production, Michael Curtiz's *White Christmas*, could debut in 1954.[2] With film stock passing laterally rather than vertically through the specially modified Technicolor camera, the image frame's final negative size virtually doubled. For *Thief*, not only principal photography but also background plates for rear projection were shot in VistaVision, the camera having been imported to France from Hollywood and indeed temporarily left behind there, once the company had retreated back to continue with interior work, so that further background plates could be made. As the unit manager "Doc" Erickson noted, "This picture is going to have considerable transparency[3]—much more than we originally intended" (Erickson to Caffey, 13 June 1954). The effect of a VistaVision image, if, as the studio urged exhibitors, it could be projected in 70mm on a very large theater screen, was to offer a thoroughly stunning representation, virtually grain-free, with Technicolor's trademark saturated color now springing out in grandiose proportions to provide an effect of unmitigated reality. In an America getting back on its commercial and cultural feet after the war, and with the profusion of a new appetite for seeing the Europe that the fighting men had defended and about which they accordingly felt they possessed some expertise,[4] this kind of cine-tourism proffered enormous box-office appeal by the mid-1950s; and among a number of big-studio touristic offerings of the time, including, for instance, David Butler's *April in Paris* (Warner Bros., 1952) and Jean Negulesco's *Three Coins in the Fountain* (Fox, 1954), *Thief* stood out boldly for the richness, wit, and dreamy enchantment of its depiction.

The film's central figuration, enlarged in aspect and brought into crystalline focus, is without question the Cary Grant audiences had learned to love, or the John Robie who seems to be isomorphic and synonymous with him. Early in the film, and for some extended time, this character sports a horizontally striped French maillot in the mariner style, a garment that in its visual representation dazzles every time he twitches a muscle. Indeed, with its narrow, alternating navy and gray horizontal stripes, the maillot is a virtual optical illusion, seizing and holding attention in its every appearance. Robie is instantly given over as a person from whom the gaze cannot easily be shifted. Further, the audience's presumable previous affinity with Grant renders him even more seductive and elusive, this case being an instantiation of Hitchcock's strategy to blend performer identity, or star persona, with the character in which we find it: there is a kind of textual slippage, a not at all infrequent phenomenon in film construction considered more widely yet also one to which Hitchcock brought the special consideration of fleshing out his star as not just a type but a rounded personality that had to be sandwiched with the personality of the character.

There are four Grant appearances in Hitchcock. Robie, the third of them, stands upon and calls up the cagey, entirely unpredictable Johnny Aysgarth in *Suspicion* (1941)—*was* he trying to murder his wife?—and the suave, coldly duplicitous, but finally heroic Devlin of *Notorious* (1946). One need hardly comment that Roger O. Thornhill of *North by Northwest* (1959) will follow suit quite obediently. This Grant-as-star—well known to Hitchcock's viewership, but also to inveterate film watchers more generally (such as Hitchcock was)—tended to incarnate adorable connivance, as with irrepressibly conniving but adorable Walter Burns in *His Girl Friday* (1940), irrepressibly conniving but adorable C. K. Dexter Haven in *The Philadelphia Story* (1940), haplessly goofy but adorable David in *Bringing Up Baby* (1938), noble, tactical, and adorable David in *Holiday* (1938), intoxicating, irrepressible, and adorable Mortimer Brewster in *Arsenic and Old Lace* (1944), and a platoon of other folk. Something about Grant made him seem almost "naturally" appealing—his bone structure, his dignified posture (self-mocked in *Baby*), his ultra-crisp, curiously twangy diction (like many pirates, he sailed from Bristol). Yet an air of equivocation surrounds his performances, a foxiness, as though he were perennially whispering, "I have still one more little trick to slide out of my bag." He was the embodiment of the Trickster, having created and solidified the screen persona of a man who would lure us to take him seriously but make us know, if we succumbed, that we ought to have known enough to hold back a little. A fellow not quite to be believed at first hand, not quite what he seems to be, "at once insolent, mocking, inept, clownish, and emphatically ribald," as Enid Welsford describes his lost progenitor Harlequin. "I believe that he was extraordinary agile, and he seemed to be constantly in the air; and I might confidently add that he was a proficient tumbler" (*Fool* 290). Jack Moffitt touches upon Grant's subtle equivocation when, in his review of *Thief*, discussing Hitchcock's lap dissolves, he writes that especially when they go out on "rueful close-ups" of Grant, they "carry a note of humor over into the succeeding scene" (*Hollywood Reporter* [15 July 1955]). Perhaps we might think of this "note of humor" as a "tone of uncertainty." One need but see Grant to lose one's balance.

Robie's exquisitely awkward grace, his stalwart poise that makes us lose our own poise, is *the* central structural form in the film. We can never see with full certainty either what he is or what he means to be. He requires us to take much on faith (thus introducing, rather directly, the problem of faith into a story of criminality and modern life). It actually makes good sense to think that he is the Cat, of whose secretive thieving we snatch glimpses as the film opens; yet it also makes good sense to think—certainly to hope—that he is not. We note his odd double nature: that the war cronies stuffed into positions at Bellini's seaside restaurant (Robie's hangout, where one senses he is not made to feel particularly welcome) remember his heroism with pride and gratitude but at the same time have decided to loathe him. Do they "see" something the eye cannot catch? While the police don't trust him for a minute, he seems blithe and carefree around them, as though they are but mice in his "cat's play." Or his unfathomable layering: that as "Cary Grant," one of the Hollywood screen's great sex symbols of all time, he should be so taken aback by Francie's very direct physical approaches: when she seizes his face and plants a kiss on him in the Carlton corridor outside her room, he seems to blush like a virgin. That with the coy and agile Danielle he seems at first big-brotherly, then paternal, then avuncular, but cannot handle her decided desire, her "teen crush." Most grandly, that the film's surface is so densely crammed with glittering references to affluent luxury—the twinkly jewels, the grand villas on the hillside, the sports-car ride along the corniche, the opulence of the Carlton, the soirée with its men and women of untold means dressing up like children and drinking themselves silly; and the gorgeous views of the Côte, the sea, the landscape—yet at the heart of the structure is Robie, organ of trust and innocence or of duplicity and greed—we cannot manage to affirm which—a waif almost invisible, because so equivocally visible, turning and turning through the dream landscape of a heightened everyday.

ROBIE'S ANGLE

From the very beginning of the film Hitchcock introduces duplicity, ambiguity, and moral doubt by using his camera with a calculated mixture of forty-five-degree angled shots and face-on straight ones. Does Robie have an angle, the camera murmurs, when he looks at the world? Is he hiding something? Is he setting something up? But if we ask whether this central figure looks at the world face-on or with an angle, objectively or with a bias, Hitchcock ensures that we must ask the same of our own view in watching him watching; that is, we must note the camera's perspectives in offering us opportunities for a view.

At the travel agency vitrine where the story opens, for example, the angling is dramatic and definitive, yet among the angled travel posters in the window, one—"France," featuring a Dufyesque painting of palm trees on Nice's Quai des États-Unis—has been twisted for presentation (adjacent a model steamship and a mini–Eiffel Tower) so that it faces us head-on. On top of the angled shot appear the opening credits, with the lettering also angled—narrowed in angular perspective toward the right (a tactic that will be followed again in the next Grant-Hitchcock collaboration). As Hitchcock's camera continues to dolly in through the credits, we are finally confronted with only that right-side straight-on poster; thus, the screen configuration seems to be rationalized subtly and we are lured to looking "directly." We cut to a matron with cold cream on her cheeks, screaming into the camera: her jewelry has been stolen (presumably in "France"). She is facing us straight-on, too, or at least, given the full frame, as straight-on as that poster did: her head is turned slightly to her right, but her shoulders are turned slightly to her left. What can we say she is delivering? Agony, to be sure, but also a sense of being affronted, that we are present to watch her before she has even laid on her face. Recursion, bluntness, the felt presence of the camera, itself *being felt in its presence*, and thus, might I say, truth?

Let us consider in greater depth Hitchcock's two distinct ways of showing: angled and straight. If the straight shot is functionally invisible as such, unmarkedly conventional, we take its content to exist plainly and uncontrivedly before us. The camera is a window, and merely looks out on what is *there* (in technical terms, a pro-filmic event), something that is to be taken as having happened or as currently happening, so that thanks to the filmmaker's "magical" presence (and prescience) we can be there to witness. The straight shot seems factual. Take that "France" poster: France *is*, and one can travel there; the poster *is*, too, as an advertisement for the country and culture. The straight shot refuses to wink, does not seem to tell, or hint at, a lie. Especially when it is counterposed against angled shots, the straight shot seems newsy and unadorned.

The angled shot, by contrast, seems to "take a slanted view of" a situation. It stands to the side spying, or peeks from a corner, catching, as Ortega suggests of Impressionism, one of those "side views 'from the tail of the eye' which represent the height of disdain" (123). What we gain is a squinting, wondering, riddling, perturbing, doubting view. The angle on the shop vitrine says, in effect, "*You may think* this is plain and simple but it is not." Or: "France appears to be a lovely place full of pleasures, *but look again*."

Let us treat the two forms of looking, straight and angled, as "accepting" and "suspicious." An acceptance of the world as seen; a suspicion of that world, and even of seeing it. An engagement by incorporation, or a skepticism coupled with analysis.

At the beginning of this film, Hitchcock confronts us with neither France as an objective space nor only a promise of such a France but with an alternation between acceptance and suspicion, a manipulation of our perspective that both depends upon his authorial presence and announces it, destabilizing our ability to take what he gives us to see at face value. "France"—the setting, the image—is a mere marker in his game, an entity that can be presented to the camera (by way of the travel poster) in such a fashion that the mode of showing gains precedence over the object shown. Once again (and here openly expressed by way of the imagery itself), "I'm essentially interested very little in the story I'm telling, only the means of telling it."

What follows is a forty-five-degree angle on an empty jewel box seen from above, followed soon after by an exterior, straight-on, almost architectonic display of Nice's Quai des États-Unis (exactly the view from that poster), showing the Baie des Anges curling around on the left, turquoise and alluring, the line of palm trees, heavy traffic, blazing sunshine. But now without warning night has fallen (catch, if you would, the abrupt toggling between radical alternatives, in a pair of visions that must alarm the senses because of the gaudy sunlight of rationality succeeded by the green-tinted moonlight of dreams). We are hiding on a rooftop (terra-cotta tiles spreading away from us) and watching a black cat, no less, striding confidently our way. The shot is a forty-five degree angle. The cat is sleek, silent, shall we say malevolent? It could creep into a matron's hotel room without her knowing.

Now an elegant reversal shot. Still forty-five degrees, but angling left, not right. The green suffusion of light washes over the bureau of a (hotel) room. We are very much in a dream zone, the artificiality of the light an inducement to reverie, imagination, musical movement. A jewelry box is open and a black-gloved hand is reaching into it (echoes of the subway car purse robbery in Sam Fuller's *Pickup on South Street* [1953]). The inside of the jewel box is magnificently upholstered in shimmering emerald-green silk *moiré*, a dream surface. Back to the angle view of the hotel rooftop, with the cat now (successfully) striding away. In daylight again, and straight-on to the camera, a reverse view of the Quai des États-Unis, the bay now onscreen right. Night again, and that rich green suffusion: the cat coming straight to the camera, but a different rooftop, angled to the right. After the next robbery, an *angled* view of the hotel in daylight. A slightly angled view of the police commissioner nervously giving a press conference in his office. An angled view of inspectors hopping into their car outside, heading to Robie's house (because he's a "usual suspect").

At the house—Robie's personal lair—a complexly angled view of circumstances. Whitewashed plaster floors and walls, the downstairs rooms built on three distinct levels with a staircase finally leading up rightward and off-camera toward the bedrooms. The entire construction is angled to our view, with three stairs ascending forty-five degrees toward screen-left, where there are some wing chairs; then three more stairs ascending forty-five degrees toward screen-right, where a housekeeper has just come in through a door that leads outside. Next, a startling left-angled view (forty-five degrees) of a black cat spread on a rose pink sofa. Robie's cat? The cat from the hotel rooftop? A black cat on a rooftop analogous to a black-handed thief. Robie is perhaps the thief.

A slightly angled face-on view of a newspaper with Art Buchwald's column, "The Cat Prowls Again?," slightly clawed: "Is it true, or just a rumor—that John Robie, former cat burglar of Paris before the war, is once again on the prowl? Fashionable resorts on the Riviera are being regularly looted by a skillful jewel thief. Robie, once a hero of the French Résistance Army, was said to have reformed—however, the style of this new crime wave is certainly his." Buchwald's byline is: "EUROPE'S LIGHTER SIDE." Now, from a left angle, the cat upon the newspaper. Cats do love to perch on newspapers, but this particular cat has been "reading" Buchwald. An angled shot through an upstairs window of Robie in his sunny garden, with the hillside beyond all dotted with villas: his body is straight-on to the camera, the line of the hillside is at forty-five degrees to him. Is his "gardening" a façade?

As we move into the film, with the police visiting Robie to arrest him; Robie eluding them on a local corniche bus; Robie showing up at a restaurant on the Nice waterfront, encountering his old Résistance cronies, and finally zipping off in a speedboat with Danielle, we see a continual alteration between straight and angled views of this protagonist and his world. "Here is how it is" counterpoised repeatedly against "Here is how one could (be led to) believe it is."

In a legion of motion pictures, the forty-five-degree angle shot is employed for establishing space, especially its depth, and articulating character movement with verve and dramatic implication. The angle both facilitates and implicates. In compositions for a standard 1.33:1 screen ratio; or even for the 1.85:1 of VistaVision, lateral movement can be augmented and freed if the performer advances at an angle to the camera. That is, he can appear to cover a greater lateral distance, sometimes useful in conversational moments. It was partly in order to facilitate greater breadth of space for such movement that Darryl Zanuck opted for his CinemaScope process in 1953, where with a 2.55:1 frame the actor, alone or with several others, could traverse much greater latitude without going out of range and without angularity. As to implication, when part or all of the performing body enters the frame at an angle it seems in part to emerge from the viewer's space. In *To Catch a Thief*, therefore, as the black-gloved hand of the "Cat" enters the frame to work upon the silk-lined jewel box, it is a hand from the company of viewers as much as one from the province of the filmmaker. We all turn to thievery; or, every looking is a theft.

But the presence of the angle shot in *To Catch a Thief* is not signatory in itself. What must be investigated is a certain latent proclivity and energy in this shot—which I am calling "suspicious"—that is counterweighted by straight-on presentations artfully intercalated with it. Any form of shot can serve the mere purposes of identification, but the alternation of angles in a single narrative space—even more, the rhythmic back-and-forth between two particular angles—begins to establish a subtle dynamic of feeling and intensity, not to say a provocation to thought. "I am about to tell you a story," Hitchcock's camera is saying, "a story involving seeing from an angle. A story *about* angles." Not only Robie will have an angle. The police will have theirs. The Résistance fighters, resentful and unable to forget their past horrors, have another. Francie will have hers, and of course her angle will turn out to be not only straight, but straightforward, and winning. Her canny mother will of course have an angle, maternal, cynical, hilarious. And Hughson will have an angle, too, cagey, calculating, loyal, picky. In some cases, the angles will be financial, in some cases, moral and/or political. Robie, a man of honor, has an ethical angle. Danielle, young and insecure, has a psychological one. One might cogently argue, I think, that the Côte d'Azur—the film's setting—is an angle in itself, buried away from the civilian everyday in a corner of France, bathing in the tropical sun, its beaches tranquilly washed and its denizens tranquilly self-congratulating in hilltop villas, lavish beachfront hotels, and the generally delicious atmosphere of haute-bourgeois decadence. If dream space is "at an angle to" everyday waking reality, then the fabulously luxurious Côte D'Azur, presented so thoroughly here through optical angles and the agglomeration of characters' angles, is a dream zone, and the lush green illumination of the dream-time thefts symbolizes its fabular lushness and separation from the normal. Green vegetation (a tropical dream), dream wealth (green with greed). In the escapade that is the story of this film, we move in and out of this dream space, a space in which cats travel with ease [read the newspaper by claw] but ordinary humans fumble.

The angle shot puts the viewer in the position of looking somewhat askance, not really taking a point of view for careful study but snatching glances for examination later. Looking at the angle shot, we become cat burglars, prepared and activated to "steal" the story. By alternating angled with straight shots, Hitchcock makes it possible to offer two claims in juxtaposition: that *this* is the scene itself, and that *this* is how you (the viewer) are suspiciously watching it. If we consider the dynamic of the narrative—and here I give nothing away—the film proceeds to its penultimate moment before we learn whether our friend Robie is or is not the "Cat," and what will eventuate from the fact once it is made clear. If, like a true-blue Cary Grant fan, you are convinced that *of course he must not be the thief,* and that underneath or behind most of the other characters' too sharply critical view of his guiltiness—even, at one point, Francie's—he persists as a stalwartly innocent, noble, well-meaning, and self-sacrificing bloke, still the film offers plenty of reason to doubt him and adopt a suspicious attitude, including that optically challenging striped maillot, his squinting defensiveness, his ambivalent comments, his lithe, even athletic prowess, and his inescapable—which is to say, seductive and confounding—charm. Add to this that Hitchcock often gives us an angled view of Robie himself, openly suggesting that he is more (or less) than the figure we may be taking him for. In a sense, then, the use of angle shots reflects the casting, since Hitchcock had knowingly to play to his audience's preconceptions about the performer. The idea had to be insinuated that Grant's Robie could be, at once, a paragon of sophisticated charm and social grace *and* a mischievous anti-social criminal whose comfy existence was built upon mocking and humiliating the very people he smiled at. Is he not even like the Harpo Marx described by William Willeford: "forever chasing girls" and yet "a virile and lewd Shirley Temple" (180)?

In the sense that performativity is invoked by the film—Robie as an ultimately insincere claimer of sincerity—there is a virtually natural allusion to angle, because when he is in role the performer takes an angle upon his own character. (This is why Laurence Olivier's Hamlet and David Tennant's Hamlet are different Hamlets, though they mouth the same words in the same syntactical order.) As is the case with other actors, Grant cannot fully become, for camera, a person he is not (John Robie) without mobilizing a conviction—his own conviction, his own temporary conviction—in the fullness and integral sanity of that character's being. Whatever his character does, he understands himself doing in the context of a private but entirely logical rationality. Yet at the same time, if he loses himself entirely to his conviction in the character, he then actually *becomes* that character rather than merely playing it: *becoming* is, indeed, losing oneself entirely to conviction. The performer must emulate Hitchcock's camera, standing slightly at an angle to the being he incarnates so that whilst this being is energized and finds space, at the same time the performer retains the capacity for a straight "view," in which he knows himself to be outside the drama. The majestic culminating masked-ball sequence of the film (a real testament to what Technicolor lab work and the VistaVision format were capable of achieving together, to seduce the viewer's attention) is a mini-essay on this theme.

SOIRÉE

As an imitation of eighteenth-century magnificence, this gala ball partakes a little of the quality of sport, in the particular sense adduced by Wolfgang Schivelbusch when he writes of carriage riding, a "traditional" mode of travel before trains, that its fate "was to become the amateur sport of the privileged classes" (*Journey* 14). By the mid-twentieth century it was possible for the rich to *play at*, rather than committing themselves to, disguise in order to find entertainment, given that the royal power that lay behind (and above) earlier court masquerade had been replaced by capitalism. Early court masking worked as a conveyance; but the modern masked ball was only for fun, only a sham or sport. In Hitchcock's ball scene, the guests, somewhere around a hundred of them, are garbed to the hilt—as though visiting Versailles in order to sip champagne with, and curry favor in the retinue of, Louis XV. As though visiting Versailles, but only *as though*. Nobody is actually engaged in the social climbing we may think to see. Opulent and flagrantly colored garments swaddle them, an Aladdin's chest of heavy jewels hangs upon their necks, make-up or masks hide their faces, all the accoutrements appropriate for those who "tend to judge the importance of what you say by the style in which you dress to say it" (Durrell, *Mountolive* 245) accompany them, with unlimited bar service, giddying music, twinkly light. Mrs. Stevens marches in dressed as a doyenne (joke: she *is* a doyenne), and leading the way is her Nubian slave bearing an enormous palm frond as "umbrella": the heavy cares of the world must not be allowed to fall upon the mistress. The Nubian is, of course, Robie, another little joke, since of all Hollywood performers who were available for work on this film in 1955 (or at any other point), the very least like a Nubian was Cary Grant, though as guardian he is perfect: gallant, canny, and incapable of violence, at least on his biographical record. At a key moment Mrs. S. remembers that she forgot something in her room at the château so the slave excuses himself to go retrieve it, a perfectly unobtrusive demonstration of proper servility. He returns soon enough, silent, obedient, dignified, very much on the watch.

During the soirée, police officers have been spotted around, disguised as barkeepers in livery (!) because there is rampant suspicion the "Cat" will make a big hit on the château (every room, presumably, being occupied by some society matron as a backstage—the sequence invokes the idea of a constellation of backstages—so, doubtless there are jewels galore). But they find their professional services unrequired—*dommage!*—as there are no screams, no breakings of decorum, no disconcerting events: the scene in fact troubles to show one event notable for its uneventfulness: it displays display.

When at evening's end Mrs. S. and Francie return to their "dressing room" with their loyal Nubian in tow, this latter removes his mask to reveal: the shocking vision of *doppelung*! He is not Robie but a doppelgänger, the gasping Hughson, virtually prostrate from having had to spend the entire evening inside the hot costume. How long has Robie not been behind that dark mask? Since the switch, of course, effected on that false little "errand" (false, that is to say, invented by the participating supporting player got up as a star, Mrs. S.). This second Nubian was in the "dressing room," ready to go, had rehearsed the slave routine (no gigantic problem for a flunkie of Lloyd's, himself a bureaucratic slave nine-to-five). A performer in the wings, ready to step onstage.

Doppelgängers inevitably invoke a Manichaean split, one twin being the quintessence of evil while the other is good. If this good twin—helpful, attentive, concerned, devoted—is the unimpeachable Hughson, Robie must be the "bad" one. Hitchcock is raising the ante on our speculation, since if the twins are divided conventionally, Robie's pervading charm must fade in the face of the insurance man's uptight rectitude. The narrative point of the switch, as we learn, is that it was all Robie's plan. He made an open declaration: *not being the thief, he is intent upon discovering who is*. But the doppelgänger strategy also makes possible completely unfettered thievery on Robie's part, and Hughson, no fool, knows this only too well. As an element of scenic construction, the doubling participates in, aggravates, the angularity of the tale. Indeed, as both Hughson and Robie are now shown as participant to the doubling, Hughson's careful performance-within-the-performance is no more fully supportable by Francie and her mother, more contributory to catching the thief, than the release of Robie from the social bondage of the soirée.

But when we see the social gathering as a form of stricture, we must acknowledge that Robie may not be the only straitened subject mingling here tonight. Why could not a great number of the costume acts of this soirée be covering secondary costumings, unheralded motives, secret adventures: even the acts of a thief? Anyone who can wear a costume could be here in costume, or, at least, anyone here in costume could be planning an incongruous, illegal act. After all, the scene is carnivalesque.

Here is Lawrence Durrell's commentary on the carnival, in *Justine*:

> The whole temperature of life in the city alters, grows warm with the subtle intimations of spring. *Carni vale*—the flesh's farewell to the year, unwinding its mummy wrappings of sex, identity and name, and stepping forward naked into the futurity of the dream. All the great houses have thrown open their doors upon fabulous interiors warm with a firelight which bristles upon china and marble, brass and copper, and upon the blackleaded faces of the servants as they go about their duties. And down every street now, glittering in the moonlit gloaming, lounge the great limousines of the brokers and gamblers, like liners in dock, the patient and impressive symbols of a wealth which is powerless to bring true leisure or peace of

mind for it demands everything of the human soul.... But what stamps the carnival with its spirit of pure mischief is the velvet domino—conferring upon its wearers the disguise which each man in his secret heart desires above all. To become anonymous in an anonymous crowd, revealing neither sex nor relationship nor even facial expression.... And concealed beneath the carnival habit (like a criminal desire in the heart, a temptation impossible to resist, an impulse which seems preordained) lie the germs of something: of a freedom which man has seldom dared to imagine for himself. One feels free in this disguise to do whatever one likes without prohibition. (189–90)

CARNIVALE

In *To Catch a Thief,* the carnivalesque is always already implicit in angularity. The angle hints at a "disguise which each man in his secret heart desires above all" (Durrell 190); gives the required torque for undoing the "mummy wrappings of sex, identity and name, and stepping forward naked into the futurity of the dream" (189). There are so many angles at the masked ball, every character hiding for a particular effect; and so many camera angles for showing the angularities. "Carnival offered temporary liberation from the prevailing truth and from the established order," notes Mikhail Bakhtin; "it marked the suspension of all hierarchical rank, privileges, norms, and prohibitions. Carnival was the true feast of time, the feast of becoming, change, and renewal." And then an explosive thought: "It was hostile to all that was immortalized and completed" (10). We must permit ourselves not to forget Kenneth Tynan's splendid, I would like to think carnivalesque, invocation: "Sex is essentially undignified, an act of reciprocal abandon *in which poise and solemnity and 'what other people think' are forgotten*" (193, my emphasis). Freed here in time-bound form, then, is hostility to received ideas, to conventions; to definitive conception, to certainty, and to moral assignment. Something, perhaps, of an experiment with rejection, since the dawn would arise and the carnival end, order be reconstituted or reemerge from the gaudy masquerade in which it was hiding for a while. Order, always present, seems for a spate not to be present, and so the throne is empty, the court chamber turned upside-down. What other people think is forgotten. From its decidedly uncalculated angle the carnivalesque mentality perceives, critiques, softens, destabilizes the staid and unconsciously repeated moral precepts of everyday life, the rules of engagement. It twists the world into dream-shape. Standing before a travel shop vitrine and gazing at the possibilities of escape with wonder and the pleasure of anticipation, thought suddenly jumps to the side to seize an angular view, a perspective that takes in not only what the shop is advertising, that sweet hypothesis of adventure, but the fact of advertisement itself, the shop's mercantile identity, and thus the commercialism of one's "natural" encounter. Jumping this way, thought departs from quotidian rationality and dreams alternative possibilities.

But the angular view at the travel shop goes even further. Having given opportunity for a glimpse of salesmanship, it proceeds to camouflage the merchandising art of the poster layouts—adjacent to one another here—under the overriding, emotionally gripping dynamic of a sweeping view (a gallant mockery of the sweeping view of the Nice waterfront seen in that fourth poster), and it does this by implying a motion of engagement. After all, to stand pat but on the outside, with an angular view of things, is to reside in a state of perplexity, in which one desires—because it only beckons—the peculiar, tantalizing yet energetic resolution that accompanies wishful entry. One quickly projects an inward movement, one takes the angle as an entryway, a gate of a dream (whereas in the straight shot one feels as though confronted by a closed door). A further camouflage: by way of those angle shots of the hotel rooftops of Nice the proportions, balance, elevation, and mechanics of building construction (all the reasons by virtue of which ordinary citizens might conclude that climbing up to sneak into a window is beyond their capacity) are tucked away from consciousness. Again we have crept into dream space, above yet also not above; close yet also not close; supported yet also not supported. This green rooftop (a green thought in a green shade): how far could we say it is from real greenery (the hills near Vence, say, where Robie lives—a house at Gourdon was abandoned in favor of one more desirable to Hitchcock at Saint Jeannet [Erickson to Caffey, 16 May 1954])? How far from the street below, where the everyday world spins? How far from the Mediterranean, with its constantly repeating, constantly alternating, dream-inducing tides?

What is that everyday world about, the one that Carnival brazenly interrupts, that we will find at Bellini's restaurant or at the flower market, or on the beach at Cannes? Hitchcock had worked out a way to shoot close-ups (that he did not ultimately use) of an action sequence with an extravagant floral float, in such a way that they could be intercut into footage of the really-happening *bataille des fleurs*. He wanted to inhabit the everyday, and eclipse it, all at once. He understood that society, our organized routine, is what the dream of romance, the dream of elevation, the dream of spatial transformation, finally the dream of cinema all improve upon, since if it were sufficient in itself there would be no need to make films that so accurately, so cannily portrayed and eclipsed it. Society is certainly struggle rather than ease; rigid standardization of feeling and sentiment; false distinction. This film as a whole plays, in myriad variations, upon the theme of false distinction, the power and disempowerment of the gaze, so that impressions are constantly, mischievously, abysmally misleading (a theme of which Hitchcock never tires). The tedious standardization is evident here with the police, their turgid mentality, their routine, their inability to grasp the present in which they live and act: at the soirée they stand around in empty poses, looking ridiculous as the social world swirls around them. And the sense in which we are all struggling to make our lives: who in this film does not struggle, with feeling, with poverty, with shame, with mystery, with false accusation?

A marvelous moment in the flower market has Robie being beaten by an old lady with some of her splendid carnations. Finally she has him by the arm, twisted around a tree, and in a unique moment of comedic animation (and a very beautiful anticipation of what Jerry Lewis will accomplish later in *The Nutty Professor* [1963]), Robie's maillot has been pulled out of shape so that it looks very much as though she has stretched his arm double-length, a part of him, totally gobsmacked, appearing on one side of the tree and another part on the other. Is this (not) a signal of his long reach, his ability to stretch his quotidian self into the identity of the cat burglar? And also of dream embodiment? The moment is also a lovely play on the famous suaveness of Grant himself, of Robie *as* Grant, since if he can swindle, boggle, elude, and generally manipulate the various folk he meets, here is one stubborn old lady who will not be had. Also, she has an odd character, that of the wise, possibly benevolent witch, a personage we all met in the dream tales of childhood.

Regarding the carnivalesque: in Hitchcock's travel shop vitrine, angularity is itself "angled," or reflected back at the viewer, through the agency of the sunlight gleaming upon the glass, just as in the nocturnal rooftop shots the angularity is "angled" through that suffusion of emerald light that invokes, in a breath, money—American money (because francs are not green)—and moonlight. The angularity *in* the film envisions and gives premonition of the angularity *of* it, that at the soirée we are watching high society as masquerade, not as self-evident social form. The film offers us a critical "angle" on such other works as Cukor's *The Philadelphia Story* (1940; a preeminent Grant vehicle) and Charles Walters's *High Society* (filming six months later, with Grace Kelly in her final screen appearance, at MGM).

MASQUE

The narratological question at the heart of *To Catch a Thief*—"Is John Robie as innocent as he claims to be?"—is a question repeatedly posed of characters played by Cary Grant, to be sure. But beneath this question is the implication, unequivocal and irresistible as we watch, of masquerade. Is his preternaturally gracious, socially adept, always smooth presentation Robie's mask? If so, he is reinvoking a very old tradition, indeed. Welsford makes clear that although the origins of masquerade are obscure, its history from the fifteenth century and earlier was founded upon the gathering of masked persons into bands around Carnival time. But after the era of Lorenzo de' Medici (1449–1492) and Pope Leo X (1475–1521), that is to say, the late fifteenth to early sixteenth centuries, there came a significant change. For one thing, "Spectacle was developed at the expense of music" (we can note how in the soirée sequence of this film, the music is without character); but beyond that, the masquerade was adaptable in its context, and in Italy of the Renaissance "masking was a favourite form of amusement which was not confined to those taking part in a regular masquerade," that is, a festival devotion or open procession. "In the fifteenth century a custom grew up, first of all among the young men of Modena and Ferrara, of going about the streets at night masked or disguised in a particular hooded cloak or domino and of penetrating unasked into supper-parties and balls and inviting the guests to dance" (99; 100). Here we see an annotation of Shakespeare's scheme in *Romeo and Juliet* (1597) but also a distinct hint of the tonality in *To Catch a Thief*, Hitchcock's own Mediterranean romance, where the action is perpetually riddled with misidentifications and secrecies counterpoised against blunt practicalities and self-definitions. The very modern sense of the disguised figure first penetrating normative culture undetected (Mary McIntosh notes how the "relative anonymity of town life" aids in reconfiguring the social control of theft [102]), then disrupting it through a systematic professional reduction of play,[5] describes and defines the binding motive of the unseen "Cat," motor figure of our tale, and also outlines the motive for our angular view of things, the view that queries and subverts, dissects and dismantles—while also dramatizing—the vision.

Masquerade is implicit and fundamental in crime. First, Robie could well be pretending to be law-abiding when in truth he is a thief; the masquerade puts the crime out of view. But also, in thievery—even thievery openly declared as such—the professional techniques are masked, closely guarded, as much so as the worker's identity: and this not only from the eyes of the prying police but also from the eyes of competitive thieves, who could gain benefit from one's inventions. The criminal thus gains by working in the dark, which is to say, away from the illumination that facilitates a view. Dreamwork in darkness. Schivelbusch gives a full account of the role street lighting played during the seventeenth and eighteenth centuries in decreasing urban criminal activity, noting, "The newer a culture, the more it fears nightfall" (*Night* 81).

One must see that beneath the surface constructions of *To Catch a Thief* criminal action flows in many directions, a kind of system of underground rivers. What is given to the eye openly and repeatedly plays with and against a domain that is only implicit, a field of opportunity, desire, technique, impetus, and what Michel Foucault terms "acceptability," this last a vital factor in the person's unwilling participation in an identity change through being apprehended, sentenced, imprisoned, and then—as with our Robie—sent back into the everyday world. Writing about the penitentiary system, Foucault suggests that there can be

> transfer from one domain to another, from one time to another, only where there is, of course, a network of communication, but also

where there is the possibility of *extracting* the model, and of what could be called *acceptability* where it is received. How does it come about that something can in actual fact be inserted and accepted within a field? That is to say, all the problems of influence are in fact governed by the more fundamental problem of acceptability. (*Punitive Society* 101; emphasis original)

In *Thief*, even the influence of angularity on the structure of the tale and on our reception is "governed" by its "acceptability" within a matrix that involves at least two kinds of perspective in sometimes rapid fluctuation, the direct and the canted view, and our willing propensity to entertain the twin schemes these perspectives offer with a concomitantly fluctuating commitment and suspension of belief.

The matrix that has been struck in *Thief* appertains to our engagement with it quite particularly, and does not necessarily generalize: thus, what the angle shot does for us as we watch *this* film is vitally different in kind from what it may do elsewhere. The field of this story "receives," or embeds angularity of vision in a peculiar way, one associated with peculiarity itself: the peculiarity of Robie, that of his girlfriend, that of his girlfriend's mother, that of the insurance agent, and that of the Cote d'Azur and its grumbly denizens, among whom the alluring "Cat" lives.

SUSPICION

Viewers are aware that a superficial reading of the plot line of *To Catch a Thief* hangs upon a particular doubt instilled by suspicious ex-Résistance fighters (normally speaking, a noble sort) and substantiated by the local police, whom—although in film after film Hitchcock lectures us not to trust such fools—we tend to trust. This doubt concerns Robie's true self, whatever it might be thought to be in a universe of performances, plays, put-ons, alibis, and pretenses. Beyond the fact that Robie is "truly" Cary Grant, and that the star "Cary Grant" is truly a man originally named Archibald Leach whom we do not know at all, and yet whom we love to think we do know very well since he is as alive with Robie as Robie is with him, what we are intended (by Hitchcock, the maker of all this) to suspect (if not actually believe) is that by night he is a craven and abusive jewel thief, preying upon people who, rich as they are, cannot defend themselves, and committed with the panache of a dark Robin Hood to relieving the haute bourgeoisie of the excesses for which they have no practical use. By day, however, this flashy swashbuckler covers his thieving identity by living as a conventional—even tediously conventional—French citizen in a hilltop aerie; with a genteel housekeeper, an arrangement of comfortable furniture; a cute black cat; a luscious and healthy cuisine; a bird's-eye view of the countryside—all paid for in actuality by the profits of that dark nocturnal work. Even as we meet him, the man is in masquerade, and his house, his poised bearing, his gracious mien are all parts of the mask. This, I say, is a superficial reading of the plot.

Does anything in the film substantiate or further such a perspective? Yes, but of course. (Hitchcock always establishes his architecture on a solid foundation.) When he flees from the pestering police (and why would a conventional, innocent citizen need to flee from such noble types?), we find their vehicles racing across the corniche road after Robie's but then finally pulled up by a wayward band of sheep (a recollection of *The 39 Steps* [1935]). When the detectives look across at the fugitive car, whom should they see behind the wheel but Robie's housekeeper, the absolute definition of innocence and confusion. (Robie has hopped out, and is waiting for a bus where, outside the precincts of his private domain and vehicle, and tucked happily into a nook of public space [adjacent Alfred Hitchcock], he will be safe.) Why flee, though? Perhaps because innocence is not stupidity, and he knows that he will be accused if he is apprehended, regardless of the truth. Or perhaps because he is a bad man, and all his life is flight.

A further reflection of Robie's self-containment—his hiding away, his refusal to give admission of true motives—comes with his pleasant soirée with the Stevenses. Walking Francie to her hotel room he is excited but restrained. Is the decision not to let Robie's excitement show part of Hitchcock's repetitive treatment of Grant—that as a male type he is typically modest rather than honestly and directly expressive, at least until the concluding scenes of his films—or is it characteristic of a thief who is scoping out, in garrulous Mrs. Stevens, a future victim? But his reticence gains explicit dramatic focus in the context of a gesture from young Francie. At the door to her room she turns to face him, takes his face in her hands, and plants her mouth eagerly on his. Francie is a character at once attractive to the viewer's eye, central in the narrative, and unambiguously forthright—exactly in the way that Robie cannot manage to be. With her directness, Francie is the plinth upon which Robie's vacillating posture is poised. The dramaturgical "architecture" highlights the equivocation we must find intrinsic within and about Robie's character. He is a man with an angle to hide, caught by a woman who makes her angle plain. Indeed, he is a man who keeps his angle hidden by means of the "silent type" persona, thus a man who angles with his angle, an angle angler. If he is the thief, he is constantly angling for booty, and his every waking daytime moment is a secret scouting expedition for some lucrative nocturnal foray.

When we think someone false, in the way that we suspect Robie could be, we make certain presumptions about the nature of reality generally and our own involvements in it. In calculating that a person's presented surface is only *apparent*—a patently "scenic" social skin, resulting from an artfully staged dramatic presentation—we presume that behind it there lies a mobilizing, and likely contradictory, self. Taken in this perspective, the secret "producer" of the fake Robie whom we see and suspect is someone not fake merely in the way that his character is but very deeply fake, someone putting up and tightening the ropes on the deceptive surface fakery, keeping it going, and also conniving to prevent detection. Invoked here, perhaps, is Descartes' evil force. When, by contrast, we deem someone "sincere" or "authentic," that mobilizing underself is considered an exact double of the characterization openly offered. The book is like its cover. Indeed, this duplication of face and interior, implied or presumed by us, constitutes the "sincerity" and the "authenticity."

So a choice is presented. Robie appears to be charming *but is really very different*, really a businessman plying his trade. Or Robie seems charming *and he really is*. Duplicity, fakery, and falseness are forms of failed doubling, failed mirroring between surface and underself. If the underself "normally" blossoms outwardly and without contrivance into the manifestation others can see and interact with, in fakery the underself projects an inaccurate, because unmatching, shadow instead. Seen this way, if Robie is fake, his brightly daylit personality is a luminous but misleading counterimage of a darker, deeply grounded criminal self. Again, I am not arguing that this is the case in *To Catch a Thief*; merely suggesting that in order to doubt Robie's authenticity—upon which project the film decidedly sets us—we must accept a structure of presentation such as this, in which the "real" Robie, whom people do not really see, is radically turned away from, radically disharmonious with, the "unreal" one that they do. In this "turning away" is the moral culpability.

As regards the viewer (and there are numerous viewers watching Robie inside this film), one's acceptance of the radical turnaway—the dark underself disguising itself as bright—is fruit of the suspicious, angled point of view, indeed *is* that view. The film is not about Robie. It is about that point of view.

In suspicion lies deep conviction in a chthonic mine of possibilities denied to open investigation, a world of obscurity that, as I have elsewhere suggested, was born in the deepest philosophical precepts of Viennese—expressly Freudian—thought. Impulses and visions impossible to render clearly in the light of modern civilization remain unexpressed and implicit, and bring on confusion:

> If the darkness was truly light, if the greatest of truths were lurking there, then it was possible to be usefully, happily, even beatifically confounded "in the dark" and what had been esteemed as brilliant logic might be only a questionably shady, if not nefarious, dullness of mind and spirit. (Pomerance, *Eye* 68)

More: the visible figure—here, Robie as we watch him; Robie as he is watched—is understood as constantly being puppeted from within some invisible space, by a demonic version of himself, a puppeteer of such grimy spirituality that his moral dubiousness would be seen to spread outward into the figurine itself if only he could not conceal it, or if we were equipped to see (and it is the angularity of our attitude that seems to equip us):

> Barely has Gepetto started to shape his log, when he finds he has generated an entity that is "deformed, insolent, mutable," staring at him with monstrous wooden eyes ("occhiacci de legno"), mocking him, and sticking out its tongue.... At the first words of a moralistic cricket, the puppet smashes him against the wall with a mallet....

> Pinocchio can draw our sympathy, even admiration ... but most often in his career he shows himself an opportunistic and often cruel creature, willful, self-pitying, and sly. (Gross 101–2)

This is the dark dream that is implicit in the suspicious attitude, the constantly besmirched dream, the nightmare.

But:

If, in the film's finale, we should discover Robie as a genuine innocent, even a savior who worked all along to protect Mrs. Stevens and the other old women of the Riviera; if, that is, it should become clear that Hitchcock were to have arranged his film in such a way that unequivocal opportunity for a vision of Robie's innocence might be presented to us only at the end, then we would be forced to undertake a new, redeeming construction of this (previously suspected) character, and the challenge of doing so would be met along a forked path. One possibility is, that we might imagine Robie's "backstage" having been flooded, miraculously, with a kind of moral bleach. He was in truth as dirty as we thought, *at one point*, early in the film or early in his life, but through some startling sanctification, call it a miracle, the dark deep burrows of his self, where we had suspected an evil manipulator twisting our puppet to (only) appear sweet and clean, are now, suddenly, cleansed utterly, and cleansed for real. In a scrubbing like this, no creature habituated to the fetid darkness would survive, the germs of malfeasance and misbehavior would be exterminated, and, in this way, Evil itself, in all its gargantuan form and subtle ramification, would be extirpated. A bath in the spring of Rebirth. In even seeing Robie from this kindly point of view, we would ourselves be performing a true moral policing, in the oldest sense of the idea, making (by imagining to make) a polluted underspace finally safe, safe for the habitation of innocents such as the now freshly recuperated Robie and such as we take ourselves to be in watching film. Robie's principles, as, in our present enlightenment, we choose to understand them, would seem high and sacred now, impossible to stain, unable to tumble into the mud. An Adam whose memory of the apple has been quite lost.

If such a cleansing of the underself and underspace constitutes one concluding option open to us if finally, in a signal finality, we were to find Robie redeemed, the alternative is complete erasure. Robie may be converted, with the film's conclusion a happy one, to a man who does not now—nor ever did—have a malevolent doppelgänger at all. There is no filthy underself, never was; no mobilizer of performance from behind the curtain, with him or with any of us; because there is no curtain and no performance. Robie is finally, Robie always was, only himself, and himself as we would easily have perceived him to be, as he would naturally have been for us, had we but eschewed our blackening doubt, pushed the clouds away. The angling doubt (that may linger for some viewers as a kind of bittersweet aftertaste) was, in this calculation, only a manifestation and projection of our own uninformed way of understanding, our own limited field of visibility, our own warped dream sight, or, more profoundly and expansively, I think, our own utter refusal to enter the truly civil dream. As we cannot see everything there is to see of people (Robie or anyone else); as there are aspects and details blocked from our perception, we create a projection of what people are or may turn out to be, and that we ought not distrust.

The mere projection of his enshadowed interior, this confusing imagination, a product of our fallibility, was the problematic Robie "underworld" we thought we found. It was drawn up out of the confounding darkness of our own felt but undetected—and undetectable—interiors. Robie, as it could turn out, has never been other than exactly the presentation given on the screen—given straight, even through the persistent angularity that teased us; and if in recollection we were to find expressions and situations open to darker interpretation, still no clear-cut and definitive reason was given that should have led us to jump in that direction. Here is one of Hitchcock's brilliant secrets: that he can make us believe we are seeing something that is not actually there at all.

If the ending of *To Catch a Thief* were to be such as I have just suggested, both positive and redeeming, Robie might well come to be taken as a man with no angle, a man, indeed, who, inhabitant of a world full of angles, anglings, and angularities, persists in being straight. Back to that maillot he wears early on, when first we meet him. Straight lines and nothing but straight lines. But a garment woven in such a way that as we stare at it, a kind of hallucinatory flicker appears whenever he moves. It distracts the moral eye, which is to say, it makes open war on the one organ indispensably important for understanding Hitchcock's work and human life as he shows it.

CHAPTER SIX

FAMILY PLOT
The Spirit Is Never at Home

The hollow of the future is always filled by a new present.
—Maurice Merleau-Ponty

There is a gradually expanding, almost terrifying hint in *Family Plot* (1976) that we are watching, at once, through some barely conceivable diopter, two films, two stories, held in proximity by a very slender thread of morality and mortality. Finally swims into view a wholly modernist and very glorious architecture: the two shards, the two threads actually compose one unity, each having ramified itself and stretched outward to seduce and incorporate the Other that we thought it was not. One could be observing the development of a brain, the left and the right hemispheres initially unconscious of one another but the corpus callosum diligently extending connective fibers in two directions, one way into a mystery and the other way into a crime, so that finally there is generated a startling consciousness of wholeness and dreamlike contradiction. This was Hitchcock's final film.

In a sense, the film presents us with an essay on sincerity, but while with *To Catch a Thief* credibility rested and jiggled in an uncertain appearance, here the problem is the limit of rationality itself. The challenge is no

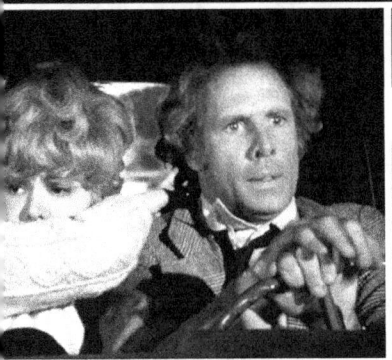

longer falseness or mere duplicity; it is the magnitude of our faith, our susceptibility to what we cannot know and what cannot be known.

We begin by meeting Julia Rainbird (Cathleen Nesbitt; eighty-seven years old, a regal presence of stage and screen with almost four hundred appearances, including *The French Connection II* [1975], *Three Coins in the Fountain* [1954], and *Pygmalion* [1938]). Julia is one of the "little old ladies from Pasadena" of whom the Beach Boys fondly sang (and as rich as can be), a personage of the purest innocence in her dotage, so eager to "contact" a deceased sister she is availing herself of the services of Blanche Tyler (Barbara Harris), a cheery young medium. Blanche has an intimate, if sweetly ditzy, chum (with whom, we cannot help but learn, she adores to make love), George Lumley (Bruce Dern), an unemployed actor currently driving a cab (in yet one more twist of the repeated trope that Southern California is populated by actors in service jobs). It will become significant to note not only Blanche's spiritualist routine (as executed with Julia Rainbird, while we watch from the side) but also the fact that Lumley treats her, rather matter-of-factly, as a charlatan, one of those commonplace tricksters whose trade it is to bilk desperate innocents, and busy at present working Julia Rainbird for all she can get.

In a second—dissociated—line of action we find Anthony Adamson (William Devane) and his help-meet Fran (Karen Black), a pair of definitively slick shysters who have been undertaking a spree of serial high-level kidnappings, to very great profit. In the basement of their house—a tidy, broadloomed, middle-class retreat (the exteriors of which were photographed at 2230 Sacramento Street, San Francisco)—they have fashioned a soundproofed cell and tucked it invisibly behind a faux-brick wall. On her head during their capers Fran wears disguise: a wig and sunglasses, sometimes latex jowls; her husband has his jewelry store as mask in everyday life. As ransom, they demand diamonds, not cash: giant diamonds, diamonds as big and as glimmering as hungry eyes.

Perhaps the presumptions we are given to entertain in Ernest Lehman's script—that on one side Blanche is unmistakably a fraud and that on the other Adamson is nothing but a crude thug—will be deftly undermined. The film will elevate us above their humdrum realities into something on quite another plane, perhaps something sacred, certainly something that troubles our sense of the real.

SARCOPHAGI

In order to ground a discussion of realism in the contemporary plastic arts, André Bazin famously postulated a link between the aesthetic tendency toward representation of the body—a regular practice, as he makes a point of noting, even among the ancient Egyptians—and a certain backward movement, the struggle to defeat death which is "but the victory of time" (9). Bazin adduces the ancient habit of placing next to the sarcophagus a tiny statue of the regal body, "substitute mummies which might replace the bodies if they were destroyed." The body and the presence live on, then. This religious use, he concludes, "lays bare the primordial function of statuary, namely, the preservation of life by a representation of life" (9–10). One need not struggle to see in Bazin's dictum a possible origin of the photograph as record of presence, of the cinematic image as record of arrangement and movement, records that may well promise immortality since at each moment, alas, the complexly alive flesh of the real passes toward its own decay, its own submission to the lordship of time, while the image, in per-during, replaces that vitiating transience with something at least relatively long-lived, something whose metamorphosis proceeds so sluggishly with respect to that of human life that it can appear to be permanent and real.

Yet there is to be found in Bazin's "Ontology of the Photographic Image," notwithstanding its deep significance for thinkers about cinema, and its clarity, and its historical power, and its charm, something, still, of the hermeneutic imagination. He is working to unpin and explain a phenomenon he detects in his own (mid-twentieth-century) time, the penchant for gazing at imagery with a psychological bent toward interpreting it as springing from the everyday, yet in his work he perhaps does a little conjuring: the idea of the statue accompanying the sarcophagus is well known to Egyptologists, for example, yet the ancient cultural practice, it is now widely believed, was to include numerous such facsimiles, so that they would function not as representations of the dead monarch—"Louis XIV did not have himself embalmed. He was content to survive in his portrait by Le Brun" (10)—but as servants, *ushabtis,* to make passage to the Underworld possible and continuation of existence there untroubled, much as in the monarch's earthly life.[1] The exact idea of the statue as originally preserving life through its presence, through its existence as a representation, is likely to be Bazin's invention, yet an invention that serves its purpose neatly. Beyond Bazin, we may be looking at a ritual regarding servitude.

Undeniable about the "Ontology" essay is the fact that many cinema scholars have found it compelling, have at least wished to believe in representational power both situating itself in that ethereal zone outside practical concerns, bordering the metaphysical, and also traveling back to a distant time, all the way to Egypt (and even, if we might imagine, beyond). Death, in short, has become fashionable as a deep subject of cinema. Cinematic imagery can be understood as an address to mortality. Daniel Herman, indeed, goes so far as to think of cinema, along with photography, radio, and television, as a modern method for animating spirits, for "spirit materialization," which is to say, either communicating with the dead or bringing them back to life. How vitally can we be stunned by cinema's ability to rematerialize, indeed, when we watch classic films with performers who are no longer alive yet seem fully vivacious in our watching, a phenomenon guyed up in computer-animated productions where now-deceased actors are mixed onscreen with currently living ones, in scenes the temporal placement of which is thereby confused.

Cinema and death: as we are all in the human family, and as mortality is omnipresent one way or another, we are all living in a family plot.

Family Plot immediately invokes the specter of mortality, commencing with a spiritualist's crystal ball, within the greenish milky depths of which the credits are displayed to the tune of an eerie, chorally enhanced, chromatic melody (reminiscent of Ravel's *Daphnis et Chloë*) by John Williams.

The séance as a vehicle, "part of a larger, American carnival of vision" (Weinstein 127), could function in part because still, during the earliest days of table-rapping, as John Kucich sagely notes, "in most Christian denominations heaven remained a thinly sketched promise. With the advent of Spiritualism at mid-[nineteenth]-century, however, heaven became a more central category of religious experience. Once spirits had established their otherworldly credentials at a typical séance, they were peppered with questions about their surroundings" (109).

Here, the question-peppering takes the shape of a conversation between a group of personae all (strangely) embodied in one tiny female figure, Blanche: first we hear her own, occasional, interruptive, and hesitant voice; then her spiritual voice, melodious and proper, interrogating her dead chum "Henry"—this is very high pitched, even piccolo-esque, and notably breathy; then "Henry himself" in reply, gravelly, gruff, staccato, relentlessly urgent; and lastly, for but the vaguest of moments, the visiting spirit, Harriet Rainbird (identified, we might note, not by Blanche but by the eagerly recognizing sister), melodious, curtailed, definitely and irredeemably lost. "Henry," it seems, has been willing to permit conversation with Blanche on some regular basis, and he typically has on hand—nearby, we are to understand—whatever figures Blanche's clients might wish to contact "over there." If it is out of Blanche's deep chest that "Henry" emerges to address her questions, the client of the moment, Julia Rainbird, is intended to think of him floating invisibly in the heights of her lavish room; and Blanche's rather talented ventriloquism helps us share Julia's wonder. With Blanche and "Henry" we instantly seem to meet a pair of twins, one gruffer and more masculine and the other emotional, desperate even in her swooning.

This modest introduction is merely to give us occasion to hear the confession Julia Rainbird wishes to send across the Great Boundary. She yearns, as her life winds down, to make amends for a great infraction she believes she committed against her sister long ago, by coldly disinheriting the sister's child, who was born (too embarrassingly for the family) out of wedlock. She now directs Blanche to find this child, what does he look like? where might he be? and makes an offer of ten thousand dollars as prepayment of costs. Blanche is to locate the missing Rainbird heir and bring him back into the family, thus making it possible for him to secure his legitimate—now expressly relegitimated—rights. As to that ultimate inheritance: we are to presume a great deal of money is involved, an amount beyond calculation.

Immediately in the first scene, then, all of the following come bounding to the fore: duplicity, duality, death. And wealth of immense magnitude. Money because of death; money in spite of death; money addressed to death; money to make Julia Rainbird's mortality bearable because through producing an heir to the Rainbird fortune she will presumably achieve a kind of endurance (being photographed in this process only now, so that we can watch). While the deceased Harriet gave birth to him, Julia will be producing that heir in effect, through a kind of immaculate conception. "It is I, Julia Rainbird, who has made the decision.... If he's still alive, I'll find your son, and take him in my arms, and love him as if I were you, my poor Harriet. I'll make him one of us, and give him everything. Everything!" Blanche's friend "Henry" intones his heartfelt reaction: "In the ennnnddd, there will be happinessss, and in the tears of the past the desert of the heart will bloom." (Here in Pasadena, Julia is not so very far from the desert.)

The Rainbird fortune: yet again the theme that winked in *Shadow of a Doubt* (1943), an old woman whose dead husband's great substance has come into her control, the surviving widow, the widow of great means—yet in our present case, also the impotent widow, because she needs to discover her dead sister's secret if she is to find the child, needs Blanche to scout for the hiding place of the missing Rainbird, and through this need accommodates herself to the system that Blanche represents. Julia is unmistakably lowering herself in sharing her privacy with a bourgeoise like Blanche.

"Elites created spiritualism, after all," writes Herman (418), by which we may infer that the higher classes were the customers. Blanche's system gained its power by "offering the public a social product that it greatly valued and was unable to obtain elsewhere." San Francisco in particular, Herman notes, became a "spiritualist hub" for both California and Nevada in the latter half of the nineteenth century (the time zone in which *Vertigo*'s McKittrick Hotel was born; in which the Bates home in *Psycho* was built). "By offering patrons the comfort and counsel of the dead ... spiritualism prefigured a therapeutic movement" (418), the very sort of movement, I would add, that we see elaborated in *Spellbound* (1945) (see Pomerance,

Eye 58–68). That is, psychoanalysis as a talking cure can be thought to emerge from a late nineteenth-century fascination with the talking therapy of spiritualism: Freud's magic was to discover the spirits inside the body, embedded in the hidden tissue of the patient's consciousness. Herman significantly notes that whether spiritualist *séances* were fake or not is less important to resolve as an issue than the population's seduction by that question into a kind of "detective" mode, involving perceptual work that "helped Americans negotiate, and to enjoy negotiating, the facts and fictions of nineteenth-century society, which increasingly required individuals to judge the character of strangers, to distinguish confidence men from respectable sorts, and to make their own 'true' and 'false' representations in the public sphere" (418–19).

As to detection as a means of distinguishing the true from the false, not to say a way of offering rectification to a social order gone awry, one may also regard the modern tendency toward illuminating and uncovering that is discussed by Tom Gunning when he points to the detective figure, "whose intelligence, knowledge, and perspicacity allow him to discover the dark corners of the circulatory system, uncover crime, and restore order" (20). A great deal of the "detective work" in *Family Plot* is undertaken by the film viewer, whose grasp of Blanche's technique and authenticity is stretched almost to the breaking point and whose search for order, through the spaces of Hitchcock's narrative picture, becomes gradually confounded between the "other world," what the French call *l'au-delà*, and the everyday.

CALIFORNIAN SPIRIT

A word about the Californian base of spiritualism, the home of the spirit, as shown here, since the object of transposing a certain "California" to the screen, a repeating fascination of Hitchcock's, gains in *Family Plot* a powerful, oneiric, mysterious quality. In *Family Plot* we travel through a wholly *indeterminate* California. At no point in the film is any location definitively specified, either through dialogue or by means of authentic signposting on the screen. We find ourselves in some fabular space, one that incorporates—indeed adjoins—the contradictory zones of north and south, which, separated in geography by the Tehachapi range, have provoked historical tension and cultural detachment. At one end of the state is the free-floating utopian south, "a land of exaggerated religiosity and also of careless skepticism, where old faiths die and new cults are born" (McWilliams 270). Southern California is magically irrigated by waters "stolen" from the Owens Valley in the north and shunted down by means of a politically fractious aqueduct—"Turn off the flow of water that now reaches the region ... and the whole region would be bankrupt" (183). The area underwent radical transformation as the orange groves were sold off and replaced by real-estate developments and movie studios—"vast citrus forests that once surrounded Los Angeles ... transformed into pink stucco death valleys full of bored teenagers and desperate housewives" (Davis, qtd. in Pomerance, *Red* 159).

Southern California harbors a deeply migratory fatalism, contrasting markedly with the staid nobility of the mission-dotted north, with its self-conscious coterie of controlling, cloistered, and vastly influential wealth. The Bohemian Club of San Francisco was founded in 1872, Joan Didion tells us, by journalists who "appear to have remained resolute in their determination not to admit the merely rich" but whose "over-ambitious spending, both on the club in town and on its periodic encampments" in the redwoods of Marin County "quite soon overwhelmed this intention" (83). She quotes a late nineteenth-century memoir by charter member Edward Bosqui, reflecting that it was decided to "invite an element to join the club which the majority of the members held in contempt, namely men who had money as well as brains, but who were not, strictly speaking, Bohemians" (84). Didion proceeds to notify us that "among those attending the summer encampment at Bohemian Grove in 1970 ... at least one officer or director from forty of the fifty largest industrial corporations in America was present" (84).

But in *Family Plot*, are we in the south or are we in the north? The residence of Adamson and his wife, where they keep their kidnap victims well fed in that basement sound-proofed cell; Adamson's jewelry store; and the great cathedral into which Adamson enters to swiftly debilitate the bishop and whisk him through a side door to a waiting town car, are all clearly—if without diegetic announcement—in San Francisco (the residence garage and interiors and jewelry store were built at Universal but the streets are shot on location; the cathedral is Grace Cathedral). However,

Blanche's tiny bungalow and the quiet streets on which Lumley cruises in his taxi are to be found in Los Angeles, equally unstipulated (the residence interior and exterior were on Lexington Avenue, Silver Lake). Julia Rainbird's mansion—and, we must imagine, the heart of her estate—is in Pasadena (the interiors shot on location, and two different addresses shot for the outside, but only one used, with a long ruler of trees margining an iron gate). Adamson's old chum and henchman Joseph Maloney (Ed Lauter) lives with his wife (Katharine Helmond) in the hills north of Los Angeles, where, on a deliciously steep road near Mt. Wilson, he stages the attempted murder of Lumley and Blanche by draining the brake fluid from their car so that sweeping down between the abyss and the picturesque pines, at uncontrollable and increasing speed, they are soon out of control (this being one of the truly memorable set pieces in all of Hitchcock, reminiscent in some ways of the drunken drive of Roger Thornhill near the beginning of *North by Northwest*). The Shoebridge grave sites are in Sierra Madre, but the stonecutter's work hut was on the back lot. Between these locations (in the actual north and south of the state) there are no demarcated diegetic transitions, but instead Lumley and Blanche navigate around as though in a single smoothly connected meta-Californian space. Julia Rainbird lives in a different cultural zone than Blanche does, but not so far away; the same is to be said for Adamson, and for Maloney.

In his unique fashion, then, Hitchcock takes a real, but culturally divided, geographical zone and transforms it by way of the designed screen, in order to create a story world in which marked difference can attach, if not to locations then to characters, by way of their variant, even incompatible psychologies. D. H. Lawrence's celebrated "spirit of place" is thus first doubled and then melded here, creating a narrative territory made up of patches, a kind of spatial freak. In this strange sense, *Family Plot* is not only a comedy but a monster movie. By way of his generalization, Hitchcock clearly evokes something that realist depiction cannot, the spiritualist's California, a haven for those who have come to the limit of their need and imagination, urgently, even desperately, wanting to cross a border. Davis suggests "nervous eastern imaginations" (*Ecology* 11). And the attempt to cross over, though the border be of the purest imagination, will have real consequences. For example, Blanche and Lumley get caught up with Adamson and Fran only because they are on the hunt for the Rainbird heir, a pure figment except that he has been invoked in a séance situation by a rich old lady whose world is fragmented. Because Julia Rainbird has a family problem, the winding story of the hunt for her heir becomes a "family plot" (one among many family plots in a film that is effectively a cemetery for such plots).

A perfume, echo, and dream resonance of Los Angeles permeate the action (we can recall that even though Adamson's abode is distinctively in San Francisco, the streets on which he drives to and from the kidnappings are distinctively in L.A.). "There is something about Los Angeles," wrote Carey McWilliams, "its proximity to the desert, its geographical position (facing east and west), its history of rapid social change through migration—that leads me to believe that some new religious movement is brewing here" (270–71). William Butler Yeats's wife "had a series of occult experiences" (271) or, as William York Tindall notes in *The Asian Legacy and American Life*, "received the demons" (175); and described the "Catholic churches like Canterbury Cathedral, synagogues disguised as Hagi Sophia, and Christian Science churches with pillars and pediments, like banks" (270). McWilliams, *the* historian-chronicler of life and social conditions in early twentieth-century Los Angeles, along with Mayo Methot, concludes, "The attraction of this place for spiritual men and even for spirits is plain. But I am not sure that I know what it means" (271–22). But Emma Harding, McWilliams tells us, wrote in her history of spiritualism that cults thrived on the West Coast "because of the wonderful transparency of the atmosphere, the heavy charges of mineral magnetism from the gold mines which set up favorable vibrations, and the notably strong passions of the forty-niners which had created 'unusual magnetic emanations'!" (272). It was, and is, as places go, a magical place, a zone beyond the practical and the contingent, the frowsily plain and the normatively causative. In his wondrous play *Angel City*, Sam Shepard said the west—he meant Los Angeles—was the Looks-Within place.

The mansions of Pasadena, notably South Pasadena, shying back behind high iron gates and stupefying hedges, gilded with belts of exotic roses, silent and dark and brooding in the bath of sunlight, offer the perfect atmosphere for a film like this to begin, and it does, indeed, begin there. "Pasadena," says McWilliams, ranks first among the 295 American cities ... in the ratio of radios, telephones, bathtubs, and dentists to population.... Tax assessors have estimated that fully 75% of the wealth of Pasadena is owned by women. In 1930 Pasadena had the highest percentage of widows of any city in America.... Compelled to remain single by the prevalence of non-remarriage clauses in trusts and wills, the widows of Pasadena have attracted scores of playboys, amateur actors, amateur playwrights, amateur musicians, and amateur writers.... Practically every other house in the scenic ... sections of the town ... is occupied by a lonesome widow who still entertains the notion that life has cheated her. (327)

A widow cheated by life, that is, by *her way of living* life, in which she cheated a sister and nephew: Julia Rainbird, now seeking forgiveness, salvation, divine sanction. The amateur playwright/writer: Blanche, making it up as she goes; an inventive, spontaneous, a perfectly adapted improvisatory performer. The amateur actor: Lumley, scheming to decode situations, scheming to play along, always on the lookout for the next opportunity to give a show, and with a pipe that never seems to leave his mouth.[2]

KIDNAPPED

Bazin's sarcophagus originated far back and far away, sourced near the Nile, with the statue companion bravely offering "the last word in the argument with death by means of [a] form that endures" (10). I have suggested that the substantive material upon which this great critic's powerful imagination flowed and played was the practice of placing *ushabtis* adjacent the dead monarch: servants for his Great Voyage. In short, the issue of servitude is at least melded with the issue of—as Bazin saw it—representation. The representative figuration is a servant to the master being represented, the photographic portrait a servant of the poser, the cinematographic image a servant of the actors who lived before the lens. Shall we say the *ushabti* manages to snatch the spirit from the clutches of Death? We may note how Blanche serves Julia Rainbird; how in his jewelry store Adamson obsequiously serves his wealthy clients; how Adamson and Fran serve the victims of their kidnappings with gracious gentility; how Lumley serves (and services) Blanche. In America, servitude occupies an equivocal position, openly belying the equality of all while continuously providing exceptional value to those who have climbed above. Since he was versed from childhood in the British class system, and was now a longtime citizen and resident of the United States, Hitchcock's eye would have been attuned to the hierarchical motif a servant class implied.

Of *Family Plot*'s multiple kidnappings we may recall that of all crimes, this particular one originated in the last twenty or thirty years of the seventeenth century, in the oft-repeated tactic of stealing English children in order that they might be transported across the sea to act as *servants* or laborers in the American colonies. Kidnapping is at its root an American crime, then, or a crime upon which American structure depended in its earliest days, and it is linked to class issues, to the provision of not just bodies but servants. Evidently many who had fled the Kingdom for liberty in the New World wanted to bring their habitual class position along, much in the way that, as William Carlos Williams explained, they had brought their language, too:

> They saw birds with rusty breasts and called them robins. Thus, from the start, an America of which they could have had no inkling drove the first settlers upon their past. They retreated for warmth and reassurance to something previously familiar. But at a cost. For what they saw were not robins. They were thrushes only vaguely resembling the rosy, daintier English bird. (134)

Such misguided settlers bore the families out of which the Rainbirds sprang (as embodied by the impeccable Nesbitt, Julia Rainbird retains an English tonality in her speech).

Here is to be found a line of story development involving kidnapping and the two nefarious kidnappers interwoven with a line of story development involving spiritualism, the hunt to speak with or reconstitute the dead. Blanche and her chum George are searching for a connection between the dead and the living, in short, per Bazin, trying to represent—*re-present, present again*—the Rainbird heir. This search, because it crosses the border of Death, is aimed to arrive at the origin of representation (re-presentation).

At the same time, Adamson and Fran are coming at this process from the other end, capturing "servants" in plain fact. In their case, the victims are not to be exchanged for employment elsewhere but ransomed in the service of Adamson's cupidinous quest for wealth. They will *serve* as a means of exchange for Adamson, the whispering jeweler, who wants servants for a particular utility and kidnaps in order to have them and sell them off for diamond wealth. In the seventeenth and ensuing centuries, one signal function of servants for their masters was to adumbrate status and privilege; the more *ushabtis* one could cram into one's lower quarters at home, the higher one was presumed to stand in the architecture of society. Adamson is fashioning himself into a high-class jeweler, a jeweler to the aristocracy.

Who is Anthony Adamson, that he might be accustomed to the pleasures of servitude and willing to go to such lengths to secure them? Is he a seer? No stranger to spiritual thought, although he has turned himself to craven desires, this strange, repressed, meticulous, coldly calculating man, an angry murderer (as we will discover), a man who visualizes his future in terms of the sharp beams of light that transit the magical space of a diamond, knows something about spirits, knows what the merely zealous and merely groveling of this earth do not know. In an important scene he is in his dark car parked outside Blanche's house. This address was confided in him, since the resident owns a vehicle that was used by a tall pipe smoker to query Adamson's old pal and current flunkey, Maloney, at his mountaintop garage. Adamson sits in reposeful silence, his lips drawn, a kind of mummy, waiting to catch a glimpse. Fran has been scouting around and comes back to the car with the information that the woman who lives here is a spiritualist, and she's not home.

"The spirit," says Adamson, very casually—much too casually, "is never at home."

By this, a speaker may mean many things. "I make my own moves and don't need any spiritualist to guide me, I'm a practical businessman, because everything in life is business (a sentiment articulated only moments before to Lumley by Wheeler the stonecutter [Charles Tyner], who took cash payment from a stranger picking up a stone marked Eddie Shoebridge, a person who could show no death certificate: "I wouldn't know about that—and I don't need to know—I'm just a businessman"). The spirit is never at home *in me*, then, Adamson might be claiming; "I don't get confused by the spirit."

But something about his intonation, his tranquility, his sense of awareness suggests he is speaking more deeply and more broadly of Spirits and their abode, their tendency to have no fixation but to wander endlessly through the corridors of time (an idea Hitchcock could have seen expressed by Jean Cocteau in *Orphée* or *La Belle et la bête* and certainly expressed himself in *Vertigo* and planned to treat further in *Mary Rose*). If the spirit is never at home, it is always everywhere, or at least potentially everywhere. Spirits are nearby, spirits are unlocatable. Adamson is himself—we will learn later—the abode of a hitherto unlocatable spirit. And you cannot kidnap a spirit. In her séance conversations with "Henry," ephemeral as he may seem and of whatever questionable reality, Blanche is continually addressing him as though he wishes to be gone, wishes to fly, wishes to move to other business, as though he won't be possessed, notwithstanding that she wishes, fruitlessly, to hold him just a little longer.

And more pungently still, if the spirit is never at home it has a home that remains vacant, thus our ability to ascertain the spirit's spatial and temporal properties is confounded by our having an address. In this way the spirit becomes a creature of the dream and the spirit's empty home a dreamscape. So it is that when she encounters "Henry," Blanche must seem (at least to her gulled customers) to be not in rational control of space, physical or mental, but in a "trance," a state of non-awakeness to everyday reality. "Henry" is part of her trance-dream, but because she is part of ours, he infects us as well with his indeterminate presence. The spirit is never at home.

The spirit, in other words, is lost.

Adamson and Fran execute a significant amount of clandestine movement themselves—silent, masqueraded, unmapped. They move with consummate skill and grace—a silent ballet, very like Hitchcock's camera and directorial self. That camera is another spirit never at home. When he made this film, Hitchcock was not at home, which is to say fixed, placed, defined, and unsearching; and he was something of a kidnapper, too, in the simplest sense that he drew to him, encaged within a story, and mobilized through a script, a number of otherwise free-spirited performers whose motions in life had less guidance, less choreography. Lumley and Blanche are having a little spat in his cab. "Listen, fatso," he says to her, "I'm an *actor*, not a cabdriver. I can *play* cabdrivers, but that doesn't mean I have to *be* one." This, of course, is Dern speaking through the agency of Lumley, and with an ironic edge, since at the moment of speaking he (Dern) is actually sitting behind the wheel on which we see Lumley's hands (but not actually guiding the car). It is through Hitchcock's agency that Dern has become trapped (however momentarily) in Lumley, Harris in Blanche, Black in Fran, Devane in Adamson.

Adamson and his partner kidnap people by injecting them with a narcotic that induces sleep. Unaware of being moved, then, the victims are shifted to the Adamson garage, and thence into the basement cell. Wakened there, they are treated with respectful, considerate hospitality (we may think of the delicious little moment in Jules Dassin's *Du rififi chez les hommes* [1955] when the robbers infiltrate the apartment above the jewelry store and tie up the concièrge and his wife, being delicate in lacing them to their chairs to gently put pillows behind their backs); their veal parmesan is served with parsley on top, their wine is tasty. How progressive an arrangement, when we think back to conditions typical of prisons in the age when kidnapping was born. "You would be shut up day and night, often with little ventilation, for the window tax, paid by the jailers, tempted them, in [John] Howard's words, 'to stop the windows and stifle their prisoners'"; further, and notably contradictory to the practices of Anthony and Frances Adamson, "very seldom was any attempt made to clean the premises, or any apparatus provided for the purpose" (Hammond and Hammond 318; 319). We even catch a tiny marital squabble about whether Adamson will clean the porta-toilet immediately after releasing the first victim, Constantine, or later on; Fran enjoins, "Never put off till tomorrow." When ransom has been paid and victims are to be returned to their everyday lives they are asked courteously, through a wall intercom, to sit facing away from the door, at which point Adamson and Fran enter as shadows and inject them from behind. The victims never see their kidnappers face to face; never have a clue where they were imprisoned, nor, indeed, that it is precisely a prison that held them, so gracious were their new hosts, so considerate and generally kind. One must imagine the experience of this victimhood: that in everyday life one's world would quickly and simply disappear (the injection from behind); and one would open one's eyes in a strange new space, where voices came over a speaker, food was miraculously delivered, and one was left quietly to meditate. Then poof, a transition again to everyday life. It would be like walking through the gates of a dream into another world, yet with a perfectly ordinary step. Spirits never at home.

In passing into a dream we traverse something of a gate, though it does not appear to be one, in a way quite like the actor in role, who appears to be—without actually being—the character (as George lectures Blanche). Central to the dream world is its distinct sense of presence without boundary, that it is clear in the moment yet not margined. It is Einstein's universe, finite but unbounded. That doorway to the Adamson cell, coated by a brick façade and undiscernible as a doorway, matches in form the meticulously designed movement of victims' bodies into and out of the secret room behind it: that they are unconscious during the repositioning itself, thus open to finding their new environment dense and real, yet discontinuous from memory of the "other" life outside, much as dream space seems discontinuous from the everyday, no matter how much it might seem to reflect it. The quality of experience in that cell, the inhabitant's inability to calculate how he got there or where he is going, mirrors our life more generally, of course, and draws up the microcosmic re-presentation of daily life in the dream, since we do not know where we came from, except through the conventions of arbitrary, socially constructed biography, nor can we fathom what's next. The repeated dramatizations—tiny plays-within-the-play—inside this cozy cell bring up the link between dream consciousness, displacement, arbitrary curtailment of memory, and the unremembered (spiritual) zone out of which we came.

The "other world" of the kidnappings—the quotidian reality from which victims were taken, or what lies outside the confines of the little cell—is cued metonymically by the Adamson residence, shown to us as a perfectly conventional bourgeois interior. It is well furnished, softly carpeted, lit by chandelier, and sedately situated on an urban street (the garage and home sets, including the sound-proofed room and the Adamson house doorway exterior, were built on Universal's Stage 24; shots inside the Adamson car were done on the blue-screen Stage 27; and Stage 12 was used for some garage exterior shots). Adamson even possesses one of those new-fangled devices, exotic at the time, for opening the garage door from the moving vehicle half a block away. Hitchcock loved that gizmo, commenting to Lehman:

We have the same arrangement at our house up at Santa Cruz. We have big gates and you carry this little instrument inside the car. You press the button and the gates open. If, however, you have no such instrument in the car and you are a stranger, you must go up to the side of the gates and press a button. This will *not* open the gates, but will ring a bell up at the house, which, in our case, was just under a quarter of a mile up the driveway. In the house a bell is rung and then you go and press down a little lever and speak into a microphone. At the gate, the voice from the house is heard asking the stranger who they are. (*Family* First Draft Screenplay)

Hitchcock the kidnapper had his own remote control, his own little "speaker system."

For Adamson, communication by speaker made possible a kind of interpersonal relation freed from movement. Nor did he and his partner use navigational space in an overt, dialogic way. To pick up a ransom that has been hidden at a predetermined spot in a forest, she goes in disguise to a police department, silently enters an official helicopter, and silently directs the pilot's movements by pointing with a pencil to the compass on the control panel. This was Lehman's idea: "When the PILOT says: 'Where to?', I think she should point her pencil to his compass and indicate a certain direction (not North by Northwest)" (First Draft Screenplay). Fran acting in disguise, her refusal to speak, even the agency of a pencil to disguise the shape of the finger: all of the pre-planned movement is fluid, slick, polished, thought-out, untraceable, even invisible—that of a spirit not at home. Adamson himself guards his emotions when he speaks, articulates as crisply—and with as little true personality—as a radio announcer. He is present to the lens and yet he gives us nothing to look at but his shifting eyes and marginal white-toothed smile.

THROUGH THE GATE

I want to reprise that peculiar, pointed aspect of the kidnap victims' experience in *Family Plot*—an aspect alluded to onscreen, even if it is not developed in the storyline—namely, the untraced passage out of everyday life and into the dream of captivity. A confused Constantine (Nicholas Colasanto) makes reference to this transition in his office, attempting to convince police officers that he really doesn't know anything about what happened to him. A prick in my arm and I wake up somewhere else, and so on. Dream consciousness is built in such a way that our movement into its space is unrecorded (the moral weight lies in the dream content itself, not in the arrival in dream space). Speaking filmically, motion away from one—realistic—zone into a separated space is handled discontinuously; and in *Family Plot* Hitchcock eschews the idea of following the victim and handles transitions by cutting sharply. For instance, when the bishop (William Prince) is taken from the cathedral we see his body being carried or dragged across the stones (a labyrinth is inlaid on the floor) and toward a doorway; there follows a shot of the town car speeding away as a few members of the congregation and the verger stand outside gaping; then we are inside the car with Fran and Adamson stripping off their disguises as he drives. We do not see the bishop again until the moment when Fran and Adamson enter the cell to tranquilize him for departure, and our only close look at him comes in the garage when Fran notices some of the scarlet cape caught in the car door and, opening it to make the fix, permits the bishop's head to drop out (and Blanche to recognize him with a gasp). But in all of this, there is no depiction or consideration of the bishop's experience leaving the real world of the cathedral and awakening in the padded dream cell.

The kidnapping of a body involves the kidnapping of a consciousness. And what Hitchcock accomplishes in this film, through his use of repeated kidnapping as a plot contrivance, is an open play with the viewer's awareness in being "kidnapped" by the filmmaker and shuffled through experience scene by scene, anticipating nothing, and typically, as the film rolls on, recalling nothing of how she came to be here. The continuity of cinema is analogized by the continuity of the kidnap-dream sequences in the film. Another way to come to this: film is always dreamlike, in part because we move into spaces without discerning ourselves moving.

We may recollect something Julia Rainbird told Blanche at their first meeting. That the boy, who was sent away forty years before, is someone she has been thinking about *for a year*. In short, for almost forty years she paid him no heed at all. Now, suddenly, he is on her mind; she is seventy-eight;

she wants to leave this world with a clear mind. And in her mind he remains the entity he always was, the little boy born out of wedlock to a sister she felt she had to shepherd. Since the film ends without resolving on Julia at all—Adamson is trapped in his own cell; Lumley is calling the police; Adamson will go to prison for kidnapping and possibly for attempted murder (of the Shoebridges, whose death he engineered)—Adamson as the Rainbird heir may never actually come to this old lady's attention, since now Blanche and Lumley will get the far greater reward for finding the kidnappers and returning the diamonds. Julia may well leave this world still believing that little boy, merely grown older, is out there to be found. For her, Adamson never actually *becomes* the Rainbird heir. And if, for Julia at least, the little boy is still out there to be found, then time has not really passed. Or: the spirit of the little boy, as a little boy, remains intact and in eternal passage, a passage, to be sure, through conversions and darkenings. Then, our Adamson is not really himself, but only a grown man who appears to be himself. In fact he is little Eddie Shoebridge; and even that only arbitrarily, since Max and Sadie Shoebridge named him Eddie when they had him in their arms. Before that he was—the person with no name, Harriet Rainbird's secret child. And who is Harriet Rainbird, except Julia Rainbird's guilty memory, whose voice comes to us by way of "Henry," whose voice comes to us by way of Blanche, Blanche whom Lumley calls a charlatan, Lumley who is, when all is said and done, an actor.

TWO STRANDS LINK

The two genetic strands of information that constitute the parallel plots of the film, Rainbird-Shoebridge-Adamson-clairvoyance and Adamson-diamonds-kidnapping, come together at one single startling point, after a brief introductory preparation when we are clearly shown that nothing else can reasonably happen. There is an *almost coming together*, when Lumley and Blanche, squabbling as they drive, almost run into a woman crossing the road in front of them, a woman we veer off and follow, and who turns out to be Fran. But for the actual intersection: we are in the air, looking down at the unweeded little paths between the graves of the Barlow Creek Cemetery, as during the interment of her husband Mrs. Maloney tries to flee from Lumley and Lumley tries to catch up with her. This is both a stony and a green place, as though landscape and verdure, once in domination, had fallen back beneath the prevailing geology. "The [nineteenth-century] effort to domesticate heaven," writes John Kucich, "to chart its pleasures in terms immediately recognizable to a still-rural nation, increased and indeed still persists in the form of lush garden cemeteries that began appearing across the country in the years before the Civil War" (110). Barlow Creek is a rural backwater, and our aerial perspective turns even this tiny plot of ground, and all the family plots it contains, into a "charted" zone. Lumley, pipe clenched in his teeth, thinks Mrs. Maloney possesses the great secret of Eddie Shoebridge's death, handed over from her dead husband. Mrs. Maloney thinks Lumley is badgering her about her husband because Maloney made an attempt on his life. The pathways lead onward, delicately onward, between the gravestones, effecting tidy ninety-degree turns, all this mapped against the green grass and bare earth. Finally, as in a diabolical board game, she has taken a turn that can lead only to a collision with Lumley. We cut into a medium close shot at the confrontation.

And stammering, she finally releases the one piece of information that brings the two stories together: that Eddie Shoebridge went up in smoke twenty-five years ago and came back in the city as Arthur Adamson. The viewer knows this already (as in *Vertigo*, Hitchcock revealed a key plot point somewhat early in the development), because we were in Adamson's back room when Maloney strode in and addressed him as "Eddie." But the key to grasping *Family Plot* is Lumley, charming, goofy Lumley, Lumley the eager "detective," the man who is putting pieces together to make a picture. Lumley doesn't know what we know, until Mrs. Maloney gives it away. And since we want him to know—out of affection, out of dramatic loyalty—we abjure our own knowledge until dear Lumley shares it (a spectatorial formula in which Hitchcock was expert).

To make matters stranger, Adamson himself doesn't know what Lumley and Blanche know (that they are seeking a reward), and thinks they know what they do not know (that he is a criminal). He thinks, when Blanche comes upon him, finally, in his garage, that she has cannily caught The Kidnapper, or has unearthed his older, blacker form, Eddie Shoebridge, killer of his parents. Being completely unaware of Julia Rainbird, Adamson cannot fathom that as her employees Blanche and her boyfriend are hunting Eddie Shoebridge only because they believe he might be able to put them in contact with the Rainbird heir, for whom they want to arrange the transfer of a fortune. When Blanche finally finds Adamson—and with the greatest glee—he is therefore frozen dumbstruck to hear the magical word "Rainbird." (Magical: birds tend not to fly in the rain.)

Indeed, the portrait shot of William Devane with a face of utterly uncomprehending blankness reflects a tour de force of screen performance. At this rapid instant, we must grasp how an entire puzzle that has been captivating us through the film so far has been entirely nonexistent to him. He has had his mind on diamonds, and only diamonds (diamonds are a churl's best friend). Yet one may wonder as to the comparative value of the diamonds he has thieved and the possible Rainbird inheritance. But of course this never comes up: it would sink the film in a morass of calculation.

It is Fran who quickly surmises what is happening, that the kidnapped bishop hidden in the back of the car has no bearing for Blanche at all. But seeing that a small scrap of the scarlet cape has been caught in the door and is showing, she moves to make a fix. It's too late. The weight of the bishop's head forces the door all the way open and he drops partially out. Blanche sees. Now she must be silenced, but first we must grasp her moment of seeing the tables turn as the second—the kidnapping—part of the plot becomes ostensible *to her*, because as she walked into the garage there was no thought at all of finding anything but the Arthur Adamson who might lead her to the Rainbird heir. Now she has discovered an unanticipated treasure.

Standing back from this moment, we may find it easy to see how everyone in this film is someone other than he or she seems to be, more than one person, some of the doubling coming at us in dramatic surprise, some of it being displayed rather casually, as though no other circumstance were possible. Blanche the conniving, clever, money-hungry charlatan is Blanche the sympathetic visionary; Lumley the cab driver and detective is Lumley the out-of-work actor; Adamson is Shoebridge, and also Rainbird; Fran is tall, short, brunette, blonde, dictatorial, chummy, talkative, chillingly silent; Julia Rainbird the well-meaning old lady was Julia Rainbird the censorious sister; the bishop was once a hated, unkind parson; Maloney the henchman was Joe, the childhood friend; Mrs. Maloney the secretive recluse is Mrs. Maloney the bearer of clarity; Mrs. Hannagan (Marge Redmond), in the bra department at Bullock's, is both dutiful saleslady and illuminating family gossip.

SMILE AND SMILE AND BE A VILLAIN

William Devane came into the production as of Monday, 16 June 1975, after the actor originally cast as Adamson, Roy Thinnes, was dismissed the previous Friday. As to Thinnes's unsuitability, facts are thin, and the daily production reports—rather understandably—give no clue. Hitchcock's assistant Peggy Robertson told Barbara Hall a somewhat vague story:

> We were on location shooting in the street [this must have been at Lexington Avenue, Los Angeles, where Blanche's house, interior and exterior, was set (Wehmeyer, March 19, 1975)], and someone said to Hitch *something* to the effect of, "He doesn't look like a heavy to me." Or *something* that got Hitch upset, that the character would have this effect. I can't remember *who* it was or what the thing was. So at any rate, as far as I knew, when he came back to the studios—that had been said to him like a week before—he said, "I just can't work this way." (Oral history; emphasis original)

and we are also free to presume that a letter sent by Thinnes to Hitchcock some two and a half weeks before the replacement, offering the inspiration of a bit of stage business for Adamson (in which he cuts himself shaving, then wears "a small, bloodied piece of tissue" that Fran notices and removes [Thinnes]), may have soured the filmmaker to some degree. At any rate, Devane was in—a fact requiring retakes of several days' shooting: the 20 and 21 May exterior sequence of Adamson and Fran keeping watch at Blanche's house ("Will work at night dress warmly—Report having had dinner" [Call sheets]); the 2 June cathedral kidnapping; and the 10 June interior car shots, garage shots, stairwell shots, and soundproofed room shots. Devane brought to the part a twangy eastern elocution and teeth to match, enormous, pearly teeth, one might go so far as to say diamond teeth, that twinkled whenever he produced one of his acidly sarcastic smiles (bringing Mack the Knife to life).

Adamson, as played by Devane, is a creature devoted to glitter—a swank jewelry store is in his possession, and he is illegally collecting massive diamonds, eager always to think of them in terms of heft and monetary return. The ransom for the bishop is cited by Fran as a huge stone being sent westward from Harry Winston in New York, all this possibly flowing from a 23 May 1975 research report put into Hitchcock's hands:

> THE STAR OF SIERRA LEONE is the third largest uncut diamond ever found. Its weight 969 CARATS, UNCUT. Harry Winston bought it for between 5 and 6 million dollars.... Two small stones have now been cut out of it, but it is still the largest mined in recent years. (Research report)

But he is also glittering himself, in appearance, "those stimuli which function at the time to tell us of the performer's social statuses," and manner, "those stimuli which function at the time to warn us of the interaction role the performer will expect to play in the oncoming situation" (Goffman, *Presentation* 24). He is a master of diction and he phrases with eloquence. The spirit is never at home. His attitude toward those from whom he robs (through both the sanguine conventions of everyday commerce and the darker passages of high criminality) is snide, superior, and—perhaps most notable—mechanical, as though for him the world is an elaborate machine that will tinker away regardless of anyone's well-planned interventions. Because he comprehends the police with such finesse, he can prepare Fran to encounter them painlessly. Because he knows all the ins and outs of the jewelry business—his conversation with Maloney is interrupted by a pair of police inspectors, to whom he offers an impromptu lecture on how and where a giant diamond would be cut and transacted—he can predict with accuracy his chances of obtaining the most precious stones, and only those, in ransom. Adamson's only nemesis is the dream-obsessed Blanche, who floats into his presence when he does not expect her, utters a dream invocation he at first cannot fathom, and sees what he has artfully staged in order that no human being should see it.

One may well imagine that Adamson's cupidity is a metonym for a broader stream of allusions in the film, that this evil grabber bespeaks a general crass materialism, an objective concentration upon amassing wealth that we can find diffused through Hitchcock's fictional California. The wealth itself can be conceived—cannot easily *not* be conceived—as practical, hard, measurable, and thus, in the sense that it finally offers resistance to our hands, "real": "An age-old habit, founded in vital necessity," writes Ortega, "causes men to consider as 'things,' in the strict sense, only such objects solid enough to offer resistance to their hands" (111). Thus, the various instantiations of Adamson's greed (founded in a history he does not appear to remember) and of its reflections in the eager cravings of others: Blanche, eager to make Julia Rainbird's ten thousand dollars by finding the heir; Lumley in the conclusion, ecstatic to think of the reward; the desperate stonecutter, who eagerly takes money he cannot truly account for; even Julia Rainbird herself, looking with hunger toward a momentous release (a form of wealth as she would see it) in which she can rid herself of a longstanding burden of guilt. All these can be understood as cumulating an obsessive fixation with the "things" of life.

Historically in terms of art, the *things of life* were a fixation of the Quattrocento, when painters, claims Ortega, worked with particular concern to render the things of the world. "The guiding law of the great variations in painting [from the Quattrocento forward to the modern era] is one of disturbing simplicity. *First things are painted; then, sensations; finally, ideas*" (127; my emphasis). Ideas are relatively immaterial, indeed, stand away from materiality. Toward Hitchcock's ideas we will shortly travel. But first, given the need to establish materiality onscreen, it makes sense for him to fixate on the collection of diamonds (amassed by means however questionable), since if they "stand for" cash yet, by glimmering in light and thereby holding themselves away from complete appropriation, they seem to float above it. The diamonds tease us, they must be clutched. They must be gazed at. Adamson uses some cellophane tape to affix the Constantine ransom to his chandelier, which is another glittering object but composed of a myriad shiny translucent drops of glass, each so exquisitely similar to a diamond that our principal Figure, our Heroic diamond, can "hide" among them.[3] There is nothing notable about the chandelier, and once the stolen diamond is placed inside it, the special thing loses its speciality.

The search for wealth in *Family Plot*—the entire Adamson-Shoebridge portion of the story—points to the family as a site of inheritance and money transfer. This invokes the Freudian idea of money in association with decay. One actual "family plot" in the film is a grave in which Max and

Sadie Shoebridge are buried together, since they died at once in a fire. Lumley pregnantly questions the gravedigger (Hitchcock's direct allusion to Shakespeare) why, if they all died together, Eddie isn't buried in the same plot; and subsequently follows up with the stonecutter:

> STONECUTTER: Sure! I remember that kid, he wasn't too popular around here. Some say he set that fire himself. In order to get rid of his family. And then disappeared to make it look like he died in the fire, too. They never did find the body.
> LUMLEY *(wide-eyed)*: You mean there's no body in that grave?
> STONECUTTER: That's why the local parson wouldn't say any services for Eddie.

With Lumley we are now drawn to concentrate on the details of the Eddie Shoebridge stone and what those details lead to: money, the organicism of family relations, expansion of mystery over time (even Julia Rainbird's great fortune, held back for so many years, now aggrandized because of inflation), and, more chthonically, the reason and "grounding" of the earth itself, since the stone is planted and diamonds are dug up, excrescences of geological time, treasures composed of materials found by unearthing—unearthing, perhaps, graves. Unearthing a diamond, the activity obsessing Adamson, is related to digging up a corpse, the activity engaging Lumley and Blanche. All our major characters thus share a fascination with and commitment to unearthing. They are digging up the past. They are digging for things.

And as to digging up the past, Hitchcock makes some entirely playful references in the most blatant of ways, by digging up his own past onscreen. At the department store (shot at Bullock's, on Wilshire Boulevard), where Lumley interrogates Mrs. Hannagan, he is in—of all places—the bra department, a subtle reference to Midge in *Vertigo*, whom we meet as she designs a bra ad (that we are given to think is rousing, in her chum Scottie, exciting dreams); here, there are bras on display behind the saleslady as she answers Lumley's questions. In the Adamson garage, as Blanche struggles with Adamson, he is clumsy injecting her with sedative, with the result that her white silk blouse is stained with red drops of blood—a direct allusion to the telltale office scene in *Marnie* when a white blouse is stained red, too, the signal that triggers her nightmare. The bishop in his cell, like the McKennas and Draytons in *The Man Who Knew Too Much*, dines on fowl, even compliments Adamson on its quality, invoking a dream of etiquette that contradicts his real situation. When Adamson and Fran keep watch outside Blanche's house (for the spirit who is never at home), we see by a corner sign that they are at (the entirely fictional) Bates Street, a soft allusion to *Psycho* where another brand of spiritual endeavor is in play, and where a young man is keeping a long cherished dream alive. At Maloney's gas station, Lumley is warned not to strike that match to light his pipe, calling up the catastrophic gas station faux pas in *The Birds*. In that elaborately staged moment we see how the destruction of Bodega Bay is the birds' great dream. Gathering up Blanche's purse in Adamson's garage Lumley may call to mind the police sergeant in *Dial M for Murder*, walking away from his superior with Grace Kelly's little Hermès bag over his wrist: "Not like that, you clot!": a comical daydream blotting out the seriousness of the moment. The purported moral culpability of the priest sitting at Abe and Mabel's diner reflects the purported moral culpability of Father Logan in *I Confess*. Logan's troubles flow from his being caught up in dream memories of a younger day. Julia Rainbird, Blanche's other client Ida Cookson, and the unnamed elderly widow shopping for jewelry at Adamson's all call up the hidden widow figures in *Shadow of a Doubt*, who make their dreams come true on the money of deceased men. Adamson's diamonds used to belong to matrons on the Riviera, discovered in *To Catch a Thief*. While we are of course free to speculate on meaningful connections in this "referencing," still, Hitchcock's primary accomplishment in his digging is to display to us the act of digging itself, that one digs into one's past, that one moves forward by remembering. All of what he produces through his memory is concrete, transactable: shots for the present film that can be incorporated logically into the edit, an edit that will make a finished work, a work that can be traded at the box office for money.

A developing strand in the film thus points to materiality and the economy: this, at least, is a material way of understanding *Family Plot*, and legion are the filmgoers whose logic is material. One delightful side effect of the depiction of Adamson's *modus operandi* is his banal organization, and our ability to see it; that, as he devotes himself to work, kidnapping and ransoming are as mundanely structured and tidily arranged affairs as running a little shop, giving his manager instructions to close up early, and so on. It's all a matter of doing this and doing that, with care and attention. It's profit and loss. It is true that, working in the studio system, Hitchcock and his team make films this way. Enormous care. Enormous attention. Even a minor character like the jewelry store manager Mrs. Clay (Edith Atwater), who appears onscreen only three times, and only once away from the background, merits her own costume drawings from Edith Head, showing a shirt in grey-green and black paisley and, elsewhere, a skirt in dark rust jersey.

All of action, all of what is given to be seen, registers on a balance sheet somewhere.

WANDERING

But the tone, the wandering lyricism, of *Family Plot* does not come to attention if we take the film to be principally about economic matters. The wandering, curious, unknowing quality of many scenes, as though the camera is seeking for a truth it cannot quite see. The oddly perturbing, chromatically structured musical cue composed by John Williams to accompany scenes of Blanche's spiritualism and apparent voyage toward truth. The nocturnal stress of the setting. The doubting expressions we keep finding on faces: Julia Rainbird's, Blanche's, Lumley's, Adamson's, Fran's, the bishop's, Constantine's. And the film is riddled with curiosity, as in the winding staircase, the silently moving automobile, the simultaneous voyage forward to outcomes and backward to origins in a dream locomotion. On one side Blanche, on the other Lumley, convey a quality of curiosity, a precariously poised conversation between doubt and belief. Blanche's swooning as she speaks with "Henry," for example—exceptionally demonstrative, to be sure, and thus possibly part of a performance, but also musical and deeply felt. Her ravenous appetite for hamburgers, as though some deeply buried inner self is being starved. Her clearly enunciated sexual appetite (as she rides in Lumley's cab she is explicit with him about what she wants and expects tonight), indication of a characterological zone Hitchcock does not frequently address so openly but also evidence of a mystery, since sexual desire is outside the realm of comprehension. Her evident capacity for genuineness, as when, confronting Adamson and Fran in the garage, she is quite bluntly elated to finally meet him, and overjoyed to convey to him the rich possibilities of his immediate future; this is no performance from Blanche, nor is she performing the frigid shock when she sees the bishop's head and realizes where she is, whom she is with. Yet, at the same time, *why* would we find this well-meaning innocent trapped in a bourgeois garage with a slick jeweler and an unconscious cleric!—that is, outside the constraining brace of the story, how does the image sustain itself except as something fantastic, a dream space in which forms collide?

As to the sweetly incomprehensible Lumley, he has a kind of curt and playful mind, as we hear listening to him banter with Blanche; but his physical movements are lazily relaxed if unceasing in their forward progress. (He doesn't know what he's doing as much as an observer might think.) The cab-driving, with the head repeatedly turning to the back seat and the car always gliding forward; the meandering through the cemetery and chatting casually (but intentfully) with the gravedigger, who muses coldly, "Never liked them multiple funerals. Too much work involved all at one time"; the conversations with Mrs. Hannagan (using circumlocution to hide the real truth about his motive), and with the stonecutter, and with Maloney. We can see in each of these conversational moments how Lumley the under-employed actor uses his skills (gets free exercise) by trying out voices, attitudes, angles. The delicious car-catastrophe scene where the editing cuts back and forth between two perilous threats, never allowing us to rest with the knowing determination of which is the greater: the road fast approaching, with its oncoming traffic and hairpin turns, at the edge of a distinct precipice, or Blanche in nervous-wreck mode, crawling all over Lumley, blocking not only his view forward but also his ability to control the vehicle (to whatever extent he still has some ability, given what Maloney has done to it already). As always with Lumley, here we have a sense of forward progress, even relentless forward progress, and at the same time panicking incapacity, intensively magnified self-doubt, paralysis.

Lumley with his pipe, long and curled, in the Sherlock fashion made popular by Basil Rathbone—except that this one is no Sherlock. He doesn't rationally insinuate himself into appropriate but dangerous situations; he stumbles and falls into them. He is a bumbler, but an entirely well-meaning one. The pipe dangling as he strides through the cemetery. The pipe coming out of the mouth and going into his pocket, in the cathedral. The pipe is his Blanche, of course, since he doesn't chew it when he is with her, and he will not let go of it when he is not. In the finale, having discovered

Blanche's note at Adamson's door and gone probing around so that he can sneak into the house, Lumley enters the Adamson garage and finds Blanche's purse there, spotted with her blood. We see in unanticipated close-up that he is far more than horrified: she is his soul-mate, not just his chum, and the thought that she has been assaulted, perhaps killed, momentarily destroys him.

None of the film's play with Blanche and Lumley works to emphasize their link to materiality, and much in fact works to suggest they inhabit some other kind of zone, something less definitive, evoked in its way by that haunting chromatic musical theme. They are dream-walking through an adventure, rather like characters in a movie. The musical theme invokes aestheticism more generally: tones, colors, forms, incalculable effects. The Adamsons and their business are shown either at night, with them surrounded by darkness and dressed in dark clothing, or in flat daylight, with a neutral or pallid color scheme. At work Adamson is tweedy, his establishment pale green. The sunlight outside is strong, bleaching the colors. By sharp contrast, the mystery invoked by Julia Rainbird at the film's outset is constantly articulated and rearticulated in areas of deep, evocative, saturated color. Her house and salon are red, the color of blood and kinship, the furniture Mission style, the tonality invoking a lost past. While Julia resides with us by implication throughout the film, we never meet her except in this place. Blanche's living room, much less opulent, is quaint and old-fashioned, colorful. Two diversions from the color scheme work to bolster, not destabilize, the story. The golf course is a vivid nocturnal green, the darkest of greens; and the bishop of necessity wears the scarlet of his calling. But this scarlet and green, connected both to kidnappings, subtly invoke a link between Adamson (who is engineering the action) and the Rainbird fortune; so that even early in the film, and merely because of the color used to suggest it, there is a hint offered as to Julia's heir. It is a hint offered to us, not to any of the characters, because its language is color, and film characters—save in exceptional situations—act as though color (their own color; the color of their own world) does not exist.

Adamson and the plot skein he invokes are cold and cashable. Blanche and the skein she invokes are warm and wondering. And this contradiction brings me to what I believe is the heart of the film, and also the heart of Hitchcock's oeuvre.

A DREAM OF HITCHCOCK

> Life is a comedy for those who think—
> and a tragedy for those who feel.
> —Len Deighton

Back, back, back, into Blanche's séances and Lumley's scouting. We must never forget that in trying to glean information he is aggregating confusions, following a winding path without clear destination (which is why the aerial cemetery shot and the downward race on the mountain road are so iconic of his condition), and that she is lost in a dream zone of another kind, a zone filled with voices. It matters little whether Blanche's dream is a ride toward the spirits, or a ride into theatricality: in either case, it is feeling, it is sadness, and it is desperation that she courts, and all because of Julia Rainbird. Julia Rainbird is in a great deal of pain, and is nearing the end of her life while inhabiting the past.

A riddle is posed that leaks into the film as a whole, fills every nook: is Blanche Tyler faking it?

Her one eye opening briefly to glimpse Julia Rainbird, who has walked a few steps away and is anxiously thinking to herself. Lumley's chiding and doubting comments to her, and hers to him—that they have caught a big one this time ... ten big ones. A little escapade as Lumley enters her kitchen and uses her charming little wind chime to simulate an "other-worldly" sound (the sort we hear in Williams's theme) while she is in conference with Ida Cookson—he wants to get her car keys. She quickly puts on a notably ostensible act to cover his quest: "Henry" keeps splattering and moaning (as is his wont), and she loudly cajoles and coos to "Henry," all part of a show-within-the show, mounted in the backstage (as Lumley thinks) that is really, one may see, a stage and designed for an audience of one never to be admitted to the secret. Lumley (innocently) taking credit for "Henry's" genius knowledge, by telling Blanche she should thank him more for having found out from Julia Rainbird's favorite druggist that she needed sleeping pills, and so on—he's done all the real work, detective work, spade work; he's a real Sam Spade, the research department behind the presentation, the script under Blanche's surface. Is Blanche Tyler no less an actor, then—a moonlighting actor—than her friend George, because George surely sees it that way. Are the two of them just a pair of kids who met one afternoon in an acting class, became chums, eventually lovers, then dreamed up the preposterous charade that she now practices as a profession with his uncredited help?

For Hitchcock, this equivocal portrait of Blanche, meticulously set forth for us, is a mere surface, nothing but a way of stimulating a far more important and far larger conundrum: Is the spiritual realm itself real? Is the spirit who is never at home *really* never at home?

He means us to wonder seriously whether material social conditions, as given from age to age and as measurable through science, are all that we have. Are we capable only of knowing the world, of working to know it? Or do we know too much? Could there, indeed, be something else, beyond the image of ourselves that is reflected in our claims to understanding? I think perhaps Blanche's waltzing with the spirits is a demonstration that doubt and uncertainty are important in life, that figuring things out isn't so very satisfactory an answer to the riddle of experience. Thus, to pose a question tied practically to the film's script, has Blanche invented her "Henry" or has she not? (Is he speaking through her? Or is she speaking him "speaking"?) Who, for that matter, then, is *really* speaking by way of these characters? If Blanche is not speaking for herself but is merely being puppeted by Barbara Harris, why is Harris doing this? In the name of whom is she at work? (The landlady, once a month?) For many watchers of this film, of Hitchcock films more generally, and of cinema itself, the question of spirit will seem blasé, because they formed an answer long ago, an answer smugly material, blithely worldly, and one in the light of which Blanche is only a talented fake. She is a fake spiritualist, and she is a fake being, and Harris was faking it in pretending to be Blanche. Our pleasure in watching *Family Plot* derives simply from watching the production of all this fakery, as though, from the wings, we might observe how some great magician mechanically plays out the tricks that the dupes in his audience take, with such eagerness, to be real. It is easy to see how this question bears on the appreciation of cinema—another trickery: on how one may think to gain great pleasure from seeing how the army of manipulative offscreen agents worked together to deceive the credulous many. Yet if there is no Blanche, if there is no Blanche *really*, what is a story?

It seems to me that if Blanche is not there, if none of the persons we are watching in this film is *really* there, the story—like all film stories: like all stories!—is but a trap for consciousness, a way of distracting populations from the violence of existence. The only reality lies in that violence (essentially, class violence; or personal violence; or national violence), and then, as is perhaps offered to us as warning in *Un chien andalou* (1929), the film is just a slash of the eye. Seeing is a lie, art is a deception. This undercuts everything of experience, however, especially of our experience of art, which is rich and meaningful. It undercuts vision, art, memory, aspiration, and thus breath, movement, life itself. What film shows, ultimately, is life itself.

Debunking the trickster has long been a project on offer. In the early years of the twentieth century, Harry Houdini, while having spiritual beliefs of his own—*The Man from Beyond*, his first produced and partly written film, dealt "in a rather stumbling way with the problem of the hereafter" (*Variety*, qtd. in Solomon 103)—was one of those advocates who took adamantly to the task of debunking spiritualists and their chicanery, this partly in order to make plain to his public that he did not utilize spiritual tactics for accomplishing his own performances (though the performances were "occult ... since the audience was kept on the other side of the veil" [Pomerance, "Empty Words" 44]). The veil was essential, was elemental, for Houdini, and worked most effectively if it were not pointed to as such.

But to dig further back in time: Michel de Montaigne writes at the end of the sixteenth century:

> There is a silly arrogance in continuing to disdain something and to condemn it as false just because it seems unlikely to us. That is a common vice among those who think their capacities are above the ordinary.
>
> I used to do that once: if I heard tell of ghosts walking or of prophecies, enchantments, sorcery, or some other tale which I could not get my teeth into ... I used to feel sorry for the wretched folk who were taken in by such madness. Now I find that I was at least as much to be pitied as they were.... If you condemn ... anything whatever as definitely false and quite impossible, you are claiming to know the frontiers and bounds of the will of God and the power of Nature our Mother; ... there is nothing in the whole world madder than bringing matters down to the measure of our own capacities and potentialities. (74–75)

And he concludes, "There is a dangerous boldness of great consequence in despising whatever we cannot understand" (78). As though ennobling factuality in the denial of fiction—the spiritual world is surely only a fiction!—were a notable case of such despising, and as though a monumental elevation of our own knowing were a narcissistic rite. Surely, Blanche Tyler is a character we do not understand, and Hitchcock has worked assiduously to offer her as such. She often seems half asleep, both as though too self-indulgent and indolent to rouse herself fully to the everyday and as though caught up in a dream of some otherwhere. In the spectacular falling-car sequence, with Lumley bravely working to navigate the vehicle in a rational fashion, clinging to the road, always looking to the onrushing future, Blanche entirely abandons rationality, throwing herself over him, impeding his actions, quite as though caught in some maelstrom of indiscernible and undefinable feeling and impetus. She is always marginal. Thus, the riddle of Blanche's séances is finally part of the Hitchcockian construction, down to the very precise camera angles from which we watch her "at work." She connives, perhaps; but she also floats. Is the flotation real?

In the film's final moment—in Hitchcock's final moment as filmmaker—we experience a colossal ambiguity, something radiant and splendid and, ultimately, incomprehensible in everyday terms. It is a darkness into which knowledge will bring no light. Lumley, the hunter, has hidden himself behind a heating unit outside the basement cell, listening as Adamson goes in to check on the sleeping Blanche and watching carefully as, with the door left ajar, the crook goes upstairs to plan Blanche's "suicide" with his hesitant mate. Lumley creeps in and finds Blanche playing possum. She is awake! She is mentally at work! When the two kidnappers come down to get their victim, Blanche jumps up, startles them, and races out of the chamber screaming "George!!!" at which point Lumley slams the door shut and locks the Adamsons in. All perfectly sensible, organized, mechanical. But:

We now see Blanche stumble upstairs into the house "in a trance"—or, in a trance. She somehow arrives at the carpeted staircase, slowly ascends it, and suddenly, in a gesture out of the air, points to the hidden diamond. George is more than taken aback. A glow of pleasure suffuses his face, but then a wide-eyed astonishment—not at the diamond but at his own diamond, Blanche. "You really are psychic!"

Should we take it that she knew all along? Hitchcock suggests no way she could have. We can invent a way, and thus conjure her knowledge out of the narcissism of our own.

Should we conclude that in her scathing intelligence and practicality she intuited that this was the obvious hiding place? From a rational, navigational point of view, there is nothing obvious about the chandelier—nothing that would meet the eye. Nothing in the film that attracts her.

Lumley leaves the screen to call the police from the next room, at which point, and just for us, wholly and deliriously for us, for us alone, Blanche gazes into the camera as the credits roll and gives a telling wink.

What, however, is Blanche telling with that telling wink?

It would be easy enough—but, as Montaigne teaches, arrogant—to assume her delivering a skeptical message: "Of course I'm not psychic. Nobody's psychic! I've pulled the wool over George's eyes, and so I win the game (the game of boys and girls)!" Such a claim, making us arrogant in our "definitive knowledge," would also make Blanche arrogant in her cunning and manipulation. It would bring the tone of this finale note down very low, as though to say, "All of the film has been a put-on, and nothing but." It would suggest, far too bluntly for doubt, that Hitchcock viewed the entire construction of his film—of any of his films—as a trifling game board, the players as trifling games pieces, the action as a trifling diversion for the mind. Life is a comedy for those who think.

Yet Blanche could mean something else. "Of course I am psychic, just as psychic as you secretly hoped. And my problem has been to hide this fact from a world that would too eagerly dispute it, including even you, my dear George, since nobody credits psychics in this spiritually bankrupt world, not even lovers, and surely not actors. So it is that I've pretended outwardly to be putting on a show, while all along I have been reaching into a space no one else could fathom."

Before the moment when we saw her wake for George, where exactly, on the map of consciousness, was our Blanche, or how could it be possible for us to know? What could she have been calculating or surmising? And most importantly, of course, how can we resolve the debate about Blanche's spiritualism before the story ends? Blanche always seems to be reaching, but toward what? Toward acoustic or luminous vibrations that hit the eardrum or the eye, vibrations she can decode—in short, science? Or toward sensations for which neither Blanche nor anyone else can fully account, call it intuition or dream life. In the latter case, the vibrations she picks up are indeterminate and inexplicable, beyond knowledge.

In the late nineteenth century William Crookes posed a horrifying riddle when he reflected that the spiritualist séance produced "an antagonism in my mind between *reason,* which pronounces it to be scientifically impossible, and the consciousness that my senses, both of touch and sight,—and these corroborated, as they were, by the senses of all who were present,—are not lying witnesses when they testify against my preconceptions" (82). Crookes was caught in a bind, as we are, but it is a delicious bind, one we would not wish to escape. "Once the performance has come to an end," wrote Merleau-Ponty, "we cannot do anything in our intellectual analyses . . . but refer back to the moment of the experience" (188).

And this referring back, the throb of memory, with its wavering light and snippets of sound, is a dream, what else? Constructed, warped, swollen here and shrunken there, colored where there was little color—it is a vision of our dream world. Ergo the pronounced chromaticism—the irrationality—of Williams's music. And shall we take dreams less seriously than astute perceptions? Hitchcock most surely does not lead us to believe we should. Does he not show again and again in *Family Plot* that our moments of experience are finally voiced through a veil, from across a border, originating in some source within "the frontiers and bounds of the will of God and the power of Nature our Mother" that science will never clearly see?

I prefer to think Blanche's wink is an ambiguity with many facets, very like a diamond perched in a chandelier. There is so much one could say to read or fathom Blanche, before the credits roll, that choice is out of the question. What is unmistakable is that she is winking. Winking at us. Which is to say winking to the camera, the Hitchcockian presence, since in his films the camera is Hitchcock's, and the camera's eye always belongs to him. In this closing moment that we yearn—but fail—to understand, is the riddle itself not the hero? And does not the camera also wink?

NOTES

CHAPTER 1. ALL IN THE GAME

1. I write this the morning after a horrendous calamity in Hoboken, NJ, where, as has happened before on the railway, a train spectacularly failed to fit its station. A key historical example (played up by Martin Scorsese in *Hugo* [2011]) was the Granville-Paris Express smashing through the wall of the Gare Montparnasse on 22 October 1895.

2. The takeoff of American jet air transportation did not come until 1958.

3. Whom I took—unfamiliar as I was with any Hitchcock work beyond *The Man Who Knew Too Much*, which I had seen shortly before—as Topper come alive to say a shy hello to me.

4. Hitchcock had adored trains from his childhood. In his biography, Donald Spoto observes, "At home he continued to study [railway] timetables, and astonished his family by reciting from memory the schedules of most of England's train lines" (20). Whether the filmmaker-to-be ever visited a local library to peruse the engravings in *Bourne's London and Birmingham Railway* is unknown, yet he could well have done, and other volumes, filled with similarly tantalizing illustrations, would have been available to any curious child. One particular picture, "Locomotive Energy House," gives a depiction of railway tracks criss-crossing that is a startling precursor to the shot (taken from the engine) in which we see the criss-cross in the film.

5. Metcalf, it would seem, is in Connecticut; but oddly, voyagers heading there from DC do not appear to pass through New York. As we will see elsewhere in these pages, Hitchcock was fond of making dream topographies.

6. In the carbon-arc lamps used by the studios for lighting scenes like this one, an electrical spark jumped between two carbon filaments brought into proximity.

7. A case I would not press for the earlier *Rope* (1948), in which Granger works with John Dall, with or without the clearly evident mutual erotic kick, to portray what can only be sensibly read as an acknowledged homosexual marriage. In some ways with *Rope,* it seems Hitchcock may have been reflecting not so much on homosexuality itself as on a salient aspect of Manhattan lifestyle at the time.

8. I recall Aaron Copland's ingenuous surprise when, as he stood ahead of me in line one day at La Guardia and I tapped him gently on the elbow to say hello, he smiled, "You made me!"

CHAPTER 2. DON'T LOOK NOW

1. Jeff makes his money keeping at a distance and regarding things through his viewfinder; Lisa works now and then, we are given to imagine, as a sales assistant at a very posh department store (one might imagine Bonwit Teller) and has learned, there and in society, to "listen" to other people's thoughts by thinking past what she sees them do.

2. For a notable example, see Allen, esp. 164–69.

3. It might be illuminating to think of Jeff being entertained by tiny simulacra of people, little dolls, such as we see expressly demonstrated in the royal toy scene of *The Thief of Bagdad* (1940).

4. There were no digital photographic devices available in the 1950s.

5. The development of the variable shutter initiated a revolution in our way of assimilating and thinking about time and space. The human beings and their artifacts that Jeff typically photographs move relatively slowly, so that shutter speeds up to, say, 1/100 second were more than sufficient to catch action without blur. In cinematography's conventional frame rate, the exposure of any single frame is at 1/24 second. In 1932, however, Harold Edgerton showed with his photography of liquids in motion that it was necessary to use a speed approaching 1/2000 second in order to achieve the look of stillness. The human eye does not normally see what Edgerton's lens captured because in life the temporal fragment of his photograph is beyond the scope of unaided vision. This problem—the relation of proportion to experience—is examined by Jack Arnold three years after *Rear Window,* with another version of the dollhouse miniature and the tiny observed

protagonist, and a stunning philosophical observation, in *The Incredible Shrinking Man* (1957).

6. A wonderful discussion of historical awakening through gazing at a photograph is offered by Roland Barthes in *Camera Lucida*.

7. What is not there, but what we conclude must be there. On the issue of the constancy of physical laws and their eventuations, which underpins our conjectures about reality, see Meillassoux 83ff.

8. With a gender flip, the constant importuning was reprised by Richard Benjamin's whining to Carrie Snodgress in Frank Perry's *Diary of a Mad Housewife* (1970).

9. The inclusion of this little tale-within-the-tale makes plain that already in the early 1950s—that is, well in advance of city dwellers' loudly reported civic irresponsibility (after the 13 March 1964 slaying of Kitty Genovese in Kew Gardens, Queens, while residents coldly watched)—the alienated neighbor was a regular citizen of apartment-building life.

10. Like John Ballantine, at a critical childhood moment that keeps being revived in his adult amnesia, in *Spellbound* (1945).

11. A lengthy discussion of Jeff and recuperation is in my essay "Recuperation and *Rear Window*." Further comment is at Celluloid Junkies, online at celluloidjunkies.com/.../episode-9-alfred-hitchcocks-rear-window-1954/.

12. On 8 October 1953, it was decided to go not with the Technicolor shooting process but with Eastmancolor negative. "Hitchcock feels that due to the fact he will be jumping around in the various apartments so much that color of background walls within the apartments, as well as color of wardrobe, will help orient the audience quicker than any other thing," read a letter from Paramount Production Manager Frank Caffey to Paramount Assistant Secretary Jacob Karp. The negative would head to the Technicolor labs for imbibition printing, thus the telltale Technicolor reds and deep blacks we see.

13. "I know, however, more than I see," Kenneth Boulding writes; "I know that beyond the mountains that close my present horizon, there is a broad valley; beyond that a still higher range of mountains; beyond that other mountains, range upon range, until we come to the Rockies; beyond that the Great Plains and the Mississippi; beyond that the Alleghenies; beyond

that the eastern seaboard; beyond that the Atlantic Ocean; beyond that is Europe; beyond that is Asia" (3).

14. Readers interested in the care with which personnel at Paramount would have addressed the technical needs for a film like *Rear Window* can learn from some of Johnson's other requirements as stipulated to Erickson:

> Take courtyard and vista in all its moods, dawn, morning, noon, afternoon, last rays of sunlite on B.G. [background] buildings, dusk and nite.
>
> Shoot north, northeast and northwest, showing all sides of court in color only.
>
> Shoot at least three different courts. Also shoot random color shots of rear courtyards in the Village, for detail of color of buildings, any time of day. I will use these in painting the set.

15. And where, as Norman Ohler demonstrates thoroughly, a culture of pain and escapist medication developed during the rise of the National Socialists.

CHAPTER 3. HIS OWN SENSE OF LIFE

1. Readers can find considerably elaborated discussions of *Vertigo* in Robin Wood's *Hitchcock's Films Revisited*; William Rothman's *The "I" of the Camera*; and my own *An Eye for Hitchcock*.

2. I am grateful to William Rothman for reminding me of this connection.

3. Here, as earlier in *The 39 Steps* and later in *Psycho*, people who look like police agents threaten not only the safety or forward motion of a protagonist with whom we identify but, because of this, the onward flow of the narrative itself. The policeman is usually a "false alley" in the Hitchcockian story.

4. In *The Man Who Knew Too Much* (1956), Hitchcock will repeat this camera gesture, in the upstairs room of an embassy as a little boy climbs out of a chair in which he has been told to sit. Our sense of presence with this boy is augmented in the same subtle way. In his *Blow-Up* (1966), Michelangelo Antonioni uses the technique in homage, as his photographer protagonist rises out of a chair in the apartment of his artist neighbor.

5. According to Daniel Bubbeo, who was not present during the production of *Saboteur*, one of Priscilla Lane's favorites and "arguably her best screen performance," Hitchcock had wanted Gary Cooper and Barbara Stanwyck in place of Cummings and her. (Bill Krohn makes the same assertion [41].) "As such, Pat remembered him as being stern and gruff throughout the entire filming. By contrast, Pat found Cummings friendly and amusing" (Bubbeo 137).

6. Smith was writing in the late 1940s.

7. Hargrave had been one of the principals in the Broadway production of James Warwick's *Blind Alley*, staged at the Booth Theatre from 24 September 1935. A 1939 film version, by Charles Vidor, did not have Hargrave in the cast.

8. Made in another time of political and emotional turmoil in America, George Stevens's *Shane* (1953) presents through Joe Starrett's hospitality and loyalty a similar moral exemplar.

CHAPTER 4. REBECCA'S SHADOW

1. A film that moved the *New York Times* to flamboyant admiration: "We must say a word about the old empire spirit. Hitch has it—Alfred Hitchcock that is, the English master of movie melodramas, rounder than John Bull, twice as fond of beef, just now ... accounting for his first six months on movie-colonial work in Hollywood" (Nugent).

2. Two filmic reprises come to mind. In his *Titanic* (1997) James Cameron famously echoes the idea of a considerably aged narrator recollecting with vividness a time of her youth; but in this film his opening passage signals the identity of this rememberer. More stunning is Joseph Losey's *The Go-Between* (1971), in which we follow the story through teenaged Dominic Guard without suspecting, as we watch, who it is recounting all this; the stunning mystery is revealed only at the end.

3. Selznick wrote irritably to Hitchcock 12 June 1939 after an impressive treatment was shown him: "We bought *Rebecca*, and we intend to make *Rebecca*. The few million people who have read the book and who worship it would very properly attack us violently for the desecrations which are indicated by the treatment; but quite apart from the feelings of these few

million, I have never been able to understand why motion-picture people insist upon throwing away something of proven appeal to substitute things of their own creation. It is a form of ego which has very properly drawn upon Hollywood the wrath of the world for many years, and, candidly, I am surprised to discover that the disease has apparently also spread to England" (Behlmer 284).

4. Easy enough, as in James Ivory's *The Remains of the Day* (1993), to suggest an active life in a grand space and then show a time much later, when that life has been evacuated, so that the space calls out in its emptiness. Hitchcock's stunning achievement in *Rebecca* is to produce the effect of this emptiness in the complete absence of a portrait of a fulfilling, active social life at Manderley in the days before Rebecca died.

5. The power of Danvers's touch upon the peignoir suggests a haptic effect, but the hapticity involved here differs from what is discussed by Martine Beugnet when she points to the denial of perspective "perturbing" the "visual hierarchy that tends to designate the human figure as a self-standing, autonomous entity at the centre of the representation" (63). Hitchcock's haptic moment clarifies instead of perturbing the visual organization of the picture.

6. Too much blabbiness, perhaps, according to some of the more than two hundred folk who previewed the film on 26 December 1939 (Preview Reports).

CHAPTER 5. CATCHING *TO CATCH A THIEF*

1. I am grateful to Bill Krohn for suggesting to me that as early as 1951, in issue 1 of the *Cahiers,* Jacques Doniol-Valcroze had already lifted Hitchcock and his work to a high point of philosophical esteem; thus the impact of Bazin's meeting may have been less stunning than Spoto thinks.

2. For considerably more on VistaVision and *White Christmas* see Pomerance, "Curtiz."

3. A "transparency" or "plate" was the technical term in use for the footage used in rear projection, which was often called "process" work.

4. I am grateful to Nellie Perret for offering this insight about returning fighting men and the culture they wanted to share with their wives by way

of the "trip to Europe" that became a staple of much middle-class routine in the 1950s.

5. "The more primitive the technology, the less attuned the parts of the machine to each other, the greater the degree of play. The more perfected the technology, the less play the individual parts have in regard to each other. 'I am convinced,' wrote Reuleaux in 1875, 'that the cogwheel working entirely without play will be the rule within a few years'" (Schivelbusch, *Journey* 169).

CHAPTER 6. FAMILY PLOT

1. I am much indebted to Michael Chazan for discussing Egyptian burial practice with me.

2. That pipe is lively in the film, but was even livelier in planned action that didn't make the final cut: Lumley is in the cathedral when Fran and Adamson kidnap the bishop, pipe in mouth; "For some reason," Ernest Lehman wrote to Hitchcock, "I found myself, just for a moment, thrown by Fran's referring to Lumley [driving away, in the car with Adamson] . . . as 'the man with the pipe'":

> It's a good line, and I think it should remain as is. But then, I wondered, why was I thrown? And then I realized it was because you had MADE A POINT—and a good bit of business, it is—of having the verger cause Lumley to PUT HIS PIPE AWAY in the Cathedral. It is true that, if one thinks about it in retrospect, one realizes that Lumley might have been seen by Fran BEFORE he put the pipe away. But that retrospect came to me AFTER I was momentarily thrown. If this is in any way, shape or form a valid point, I have several suggestions to shore it up a bit. If it isn't valid, please ignore it.
>
> The first suggestion, which would be my preference, is that after Lumley puts the pipe in his pocket, and after the verger's attention is no longer on him, Lumley absent-mindedly, and out of habit, takes the pipe out of his pocket and slips it BACK into his mouth again. (Even if that might be amusing, I don't know whether you have the time to fit that into the action).

Hitchcock may have appreciated Lehman's idea but he didn't use it. Lumley stows the pipe, but in a notable manner, a signal that we may take our eyes and mind off him entirely, until later.

3. A few years later, Steven Spielberg would borrow this Hitchcockian idea for the closet scene of *E.T.* (1982), but with a development: he had a creature from beyond rationality hiding among things.

REFERENCES

Albee, Edward. *The American Dream, The Sandbox, The Death of Bessie Smith, Fam and Yam*. New York: Dramatists Play Service, 2009.

Allen, Richard. "Voyeurism Revisited." In *Hitchcock's Moral Gaze*, ed. R. Barton Palmer, Homer B. Pettey, and Steven M. Sanders, 151–70. Albany: State University of New York Press, 2017.

Bakhtin, Mikhail. *Rabelais and His World*. Trans. Hélène Iswolsky. Bloomington: Indiana University Press, 2008.

Baldwin, James. "Theater: The Negro In and Out." In *The Cross of Redemption: Uncollected Writings*, ed. Randall Kenan, 19–28. New York: Vintage International 2011.

Baudrot, Sylvette. "Hitch, au jour le jour." *Cahiers du cinéma* 39 (October 1954): 14–17.

Bazin, André. "Hitchcock contre Hitchcock." *Cahiers du cinéma* 39 (October 1954): 25–32.

———. "The Ontology of the Photographic Image." In *What Is Cinema?*, vol. 1, trans. Hugh Gray, 9–16. Berkeley: University of California Press, 1967.

Beach, Christopher. *A Hidden History of Film Style: Cinematographers, Directors, and the Collaborative Process*. Berkeley: University of California Press, 2015.

Behlmer, Rudy. *Memo from David O. Selznick*. New York: Modern Library, 2000.

Benjamin, Walter. *The Arcades Project*. Trans. Howard Eiland and Kevin McLaughlin. Cambridge, MA: Harvard University Press, 1999.

———. *Charles Baudelaire: A Lyric Poet in the Era of High Capitalism*. London: Verso, 1997.

———. "The Newspaper." In *Selected Writings, Vol. 2 1927–1934*, trans. Rodney Livingstone et al., ed. Michael W. Jennings, Howard Eiland,

and Gary Smith, 741–42. Cambridge, MA: Harvard University Press, 1999.
Bernheim, Hippolyte. *De la suggestion et de ses applications à la thérapeutique*. 2nd ed. Paris: Octave Doin, 1888.
Beugnet, Martine. *Cinema and Sensation: French Film and the Art of Transgression*. Edinburgh: Edinburgh University Press, 2007.
Boswell, James. *Life of Johnson*. Unabridged. 1904. Reprint, Oxford: Oxford University Press, 2008.
Boulding, Kenneth. *The Image: Knowledge in Life and Society*. Ann Arbor: University of Michigan Press, 1961.
Bourne, John C. *London and Birmingham Railway*. London: J. C. Bourne, Lamb's Conduit, 1839.
Brackett, Oliver. "The Interior of the House." In *Johnson's England: An Account of the Life & Manners of His Age*, ed. A. S. Turberville, 125–59. Oxford: Clarendon Press, 1933.
Brand, Dana. "Rear-View Mirror: Hitchcock, Poe, and the Flaneur in America." In *Hitchcock's America*, ed. Jonathan Freedman and Richard Millington, 123–34. New York: Oxford University Press, 1999.
Brisset, Tifenn. "La question de l'engagement dans les films de guerre d'Hitchcock." *Influxus*, 28 June 2016, online at influxus.eu/article1033.html.
Bubbeo, Daniel. *The Women of Warner Brothers: The Lives and Careers of 15 Leading Ladies*. Jefferson, NC: McFarland, 2002.
Burke, Kenneth. *Permanence and Change: An Anatomy of Purpose*. 3rd ed. Berkeley: University of California Press, 1984.
Carey, John. "Temporal and Spatial Transitions in American Fiction Film." *Studies in the Anthropology of Visual Communication* 1, no. 1 (1974): 45–50.
Cavell, Stanley. *Conditions Handsome and Unhandsome: The Constitution of Emersonian Perfectionism*. Chicago: University of Chicago Press, 1990.
———. *Pursuits of Happiness: The Hollywood Comedy of Remarriage*. Cambridge, MA: Harvard University Press, 1981.
Chion, Michel. *The Voice in Cinema*. Trans. Claudia Gorbman. New York: Columbia University Press, 1999.
Cohen, Paula Marantz. *Alfred Hitchcock: The Legacy of Victorianism*. Lexington: University Press of Kentucky, 1995.

Coleman, Herbert. *The Hollywood I Knew: A Memoir: 1916–1988*. Lanham, MD: Scarecrow Press, 2003.
Corber, Robert J. "Hitchcock's Washington: Spectatorship, Ideology, and the 'Homosexual Menace' in *Strangers on a Train*." In *Hitchcock's America*, ed. Jonathan Freedman and Richard Millington, 99–121. New York: Oxford University Press, 1999.
Cortázar, Julio. *End of the Game and Other Stories*. Trans. Paul Blackburn. New York: Pantheon, 1966.
Crary, Jonathan. *Techniques of the Observer: On Vision and Modernity in the Nineteenth Century*. Cambridge, MA: MIT Press, 1992.
Crookes, William. *Researches in the Phenomena of Spiritualism*. London: J. Burns, 1874.
Curtis, Scott. "The Making of *Rear Window*." In *Alfred Hitchcock's Rear Window*, ed. John Belton, 21–56. New York: Cambridge University Press, 2000.
Davenport, Guy. *Cities on Hills: A Study of I–XXX of Ezra Pound's Cantos*. Ann Arbor: UMI Research Press, 1983.
Davis, Mike. *City of Quartz*. New York: Vintage, 1992.
———. *Ecology of Fear: Los Angeles and the Imagination of Disaster*. New York: Vintage, 1998.
De Beauvoir, Simone. *The Second Sex*. Trans. Constance Borde and Sheila Malovany-Chevallier. 1949. Reprint, New York: Alfred A. Knopf, 2009.
De Crèvecoeur, J. Hector St. John. *Letters from an American Farmer*. 1783. Reprint, Mineola, NY: Dover, 2005.
Deleuze, Gilles. *Difference and Repetition*. Trans. Paul Patton. London: Continuum, 2009.
de Montaigne, Michel. "That It Is Madness to Judge the True and the False from Our Own Capacities." In *The Essays: A Selection*, trans. M. A. Screech, 74–78. London: Penguin, 2004.
de Tocqueville, Alexis. *Democracy in America*. Vol. 2. New York: Schocken, 1961.
Didion, Joan. *Where I Was From*. New York: Vintage, 2003.
Dixon, Wheeler Winston. "The Endless Embrace of Hell: Hopelessness and Betrayal in Film Noir." In *Cinema and Modernity*, ed. Murray Pomerance, 38–56. New Brunswick, NJ: Rutgers University Press, 2006.

Doty, Alexander. "Queer Hitchcock." In *A Companion to Alfred Hitchcock*, ed. Thomas Leitch and Leland Poague, 473–89. Malden, MA: Wiley-Blackwell, 2011.

Du Maurier, Daphne. *Rebecca*. 1938. Reprint, London: Arrow, 1992.

Durrell, Lawrence. *Balthazar*. New York: Penguin, 1991.

———. *Mountolive*. New York: Penguin, 1991.

Eksteins, Modris. *Solar Dance: Genius, Forgery, and the Crisis of Truth in the Modern Age*. Toronto: Knopf Canada, 2012.

Eliade, Mircea. *The Myth of the Eternal Return*. Trans. Willard R. Trask. New York: Pantheon, 1954.

Emerson, Ralph Waldo. *The Essential Writings of Ralph Waldo Emerson*. New York: Modern Library, 2000.

Foucault, Michel. *The Birth of the Clinic: An Archaeology of Medical Perception*. New York: Vintage, 1994.

———. "Lecture of 7 February 1973." In *The Punitive Society: Lectures at the Collège de France 1972–1973*, trans. Graham Burchell, 99–121. London: Palgrave Macmillan, 2015.

Freud, Sigmund. *The Interpretation of Dreams*. Trans. A. A. Brill. 1913. Reprint, Mineola, NY: Dover, 2015.

Friedan, Betty. *The Feminine Mystique*. New York: W. W. Norton, 1963.

Goffman, Erving. *Frame Analysis: An Essay on the Organization of Experience*. Cambridge, MA: Harvard University Press, 1974.

———. *The Presentation of Self in Everyday Life*. Garden City, NY: Doubleday Anchor, 1959.

Gomery, Douglas. *Shared Pleasures: A History of Movie Presentation in the United States*. Madison: University of Wisconsin Press, 1992.

Gottlieb, Sidney, ed. *Hitchcock on Hitchcock: Selected Writings and Interviews*. Berkeley: University of California Press, 1997.

Gould, Stephen Jay. "Art Meets Science in *The Heart of the Andes*: Church Paints, Humboldt Dies, Darwin Writes, and Nature Blinks in the Fateful Year of 1859." In *I Have Landed: The End of a Beginning in Natural History*, 90–109. New York: Three Rivers, 2003.

———. "Homage to Mickey Mouse." In *The Panda's Thumb: More Reflections in Natural History*, 95–107. New York: Norton, 1980.

Gross, Kenneth. *Puppet: An Essay on Uncanny Life*. Chicago: University of Chicago Press, 2011.

Gunning, Tom. "The Exterior as Intérieur: Benjamin's Optical Detective." *boundary 2* 30, no. 1 (2003): 105–30.

———. "Tracing the Individual Body: Photography, Detectives, and Early Cinema." In *Cinema and the Invention of Modern Life*, ed. Leo Charney and Vanessa R. Schwartz, 15–45. Berkeley: University of California Press, 1995.

Halberstam, David. *The Fifties.* New York: Fawcett, 1993.

Hall, Barbara. *Oral History with Peggy Robertson.* Beverly Hills: Academy of Motion Picture Arts and Sciences, 2002.

Hall, Edward T. *The Hidden Dimension.* Garden City, NY: Doubleday Anchor, 1990.

Hammond, J. L., and B. Hammond. "Poverty, Crime, Philanthrophy." In *Johnson's England: An Account of the Life & Manners of His Age*, vol. 1, ed. A. S. Turberville, 300–335. Oxford: Clarendon Press, 1933.

Herman, Daniel. "Whose Knocking? Spiritualism as Entertainment and Therapy in Nineteenth-Century San Francisco." *American Nineteenth Century History* 7, no. 3 (September 2006): 417–42.

Highsmith, Patricia. *Strangers on a Train.* 1950. Harmondsworth: Penguin, 1974.

James, Henry. *The Portrait of a Lady.* 1881. Reprint, New York: Oxford University Press, 2009.

Jay, Martin. *Downcast Eyes: The Denigration of Vision in Twentieth-Century French Thought.* Berkeley: University of California Press, 1994.

Kasson, John. *Amusing the Million: Coney Island at the Turn of the Century.* New York: Hill and Wang, 1978.

Kierkegaard, Søren. *Repetition and Philosophical Crumbs.* Trans. Edward F. Mooney. Oxford: Oxford University Press, 2009.

Krohn, Bill. *Hitchcock at Work.* London: Phaidon, 2003.

Kucich, John J. "The Politics of Heaven." In *Spectral America: Phantoms and the National Imagination*, ed. Jeffrey Andrew Weinstock, 101–23. Madison: University of Wisconsin Press, 2004.

Kynaston, David. *Family Britain: 1951–57.* London: Bloomsbury, 2010.

Lawrence, D. H. *Studies in Classic American Literature.* Cambridge: Cambridge University Press, 1990.

Lemire, Elisa. "Voyeurism and the Postwar Crisis of Masculinity in *Rear Window*." In *Alfred Hitchcock's Rear Window*, ed. John Belton, 57–90. New York: Cambridge University Press, 2000.

Lerner, Max. *America as a Civilization: Life and Thought in the United States Today*. New York: Simon and Schuster, 1957.

Lethbridge, Lucy. *Servants: A Downstairs View of Twentieth-century Britain*. London: Bloomsbury, 2013.

Lifton, Robert Jay. *Death in Life: Survivors of Hiroshima*. New York: Random House, 1968.

Locke, John L. *Duels and Duets: Why Men and Women Talk So Differently*. New York: Cambridge University Press, 2011.

May, Elaine Tyler. *Homeward Bound: American Families in the Cold War Era*. New York: Basic Books, 2008.

McFarland, Douglas. "Bruno's Game, or the Case of the Sardonic Psychopath." In *Hitchcock at the Source: The Auteur as Adaptor*, ed. R. Barton Palmer and David Boyd, 189–99. Albany: State University of New York Press, 2011.

———. "The Philosophy of Space and Memory in *Solaris*." In *The Philosophy of Steven Soderbergh*, ed. R. Barton Palmer and Steven M. Sanders, 267–79. Lexington: University Press of Kentucky, 2011.

McGilligan, Patrick. *Alfred Hitchcock: A Life in Darkness and Light*. New York: HarperCollins, 2003.

McIntosh, Mary. "Changes in the Organization of Thieving." In *Images of Deviance*, ed. Stanley Cohen, 98–133. Harmondsworth: Penguin, 1971.

McWilliams, Carey. *Southern California Country: An Island on the Land*. New York: Duell, Sloan and Pearce, 1946.

Meillassoux, Quentin. *After Finitude: An Essay on the Necessity of Contingency*. Trans. Ray Brassier. London: Continuum, 2009.

Merleau-Ponty, Maurice. *Phenomenology of Perception*. Trans. Donald A. Landes. New York: Routledge, 2012.

Miller, Arthur. *Death of a Salesman*. New York: Dramatists Play Service, 1948.

Modleski, Tania. *The Women Who Knew Too Much: Hitchcock and Feminist Theory*. New York: Routledge, 1989.

Musil, Robert. *The Man without Qualities*. Vol. 1. New York: Vintage, 1996.

Nugent, Frank S. "Splendid Film of du Maurier's 'Rebecca.'" *New York Times*, 29 March 1940, 28.

Nye, David E. *Electrifying America: Social Meanings of a New Technology.* Cambridge, MA: MIT Press, 1992.

Ohler, Norman. *Blitzed: Drugs in the Third Reich.* Trans. Shaun Whiteside. New York: Houghton Mifflin Harcourt, 2017.

Ortega y Gasset, José. *The Dehumanization of Art and Other Essays on Art, Literature and Culture.* Rev. ed. Princeton, NJ: Princeton University Press, 1968.

Perkins, V. F. *Film as Film: Understanding and Judging Movies.* New York: DaCapo Press, 1993.

Pomerance, Murray. *Alfred Hitchcock's America.* Cambridge: Polity Press, 2013.

———. "A Bromide for Ballantine: *Spellbound*, Psychoanalysis, Light." In *An Eye for Hitchcock*, 58–91. New Brunswick, NJ: Rutgers University Press, 2004.

———. "The Dramaturgy of Action and Involvement in Sports Film." *Quarterly Review of Film and Video* 23, no. 4 (2006): 311–29.

———. "Empty Words: Houdini and *Houdini*." In *Invented Lives, Imagined Communities: The Biopic an American National Identity*, ed. William H. Epstein and R. Barton Palmer, 25–48. Albany: State University of New York Press, 2016.

———. *An Eye for Hitchcock.* New Brunswick, NJ: Rutgers University Press, 2004.

———. "Michael Curtiz's Gamble for *White Christmas*." In *The Many Cinemas of Michael Curtiz*, ed. R. Barton Palmer and Murray Pomerance. Austin: University of Texas Press, 2018.

———. *Michelangelo Red Antonioni Blue: Eight Reflections on Cinema.* Berkeley: University of California Press, 2011.

———. "Recuperation and *Rear Window*." *Senses of Cinema* 29 (November–December 2003). Online at sensesofcinema.com.

———. "Some Hitchcockian Shots." In *A Companion to Alfred Hitchcock*, ed. Thomas Leitch and Leland Poague, 237–52. Malden, MA: Wiley-Blackwell, 2011.

———. "Two Bits for Hitch: Small Performance and Gross Structure in *The Man Who Knew Too Much* (1956)." *Hitchcock Annual* (2000): 127–45.

Proust, Marcel. *Remembrance of Things Past.* Vol. 1. Trans. C. K. Scott Moncrieff and Terence Kilmartin. 1922. Reprint, Harmondsworth: Penguin, 1983.
Raab, Jennifer. *Frederick Church: The Art and Science of Detail.* New Haven, CT: Yale University Press, 2015.
Rohmer, Eric, and Claude Chabrol. *Hitchcock: The First Forty-four Films.* Trans. Stanley Hochman. New York: Ungar 1979.
Rothman, William. *The "I" of the Camera: Essays in Film Criticism, History, and Aesthetics.* 2nd ed. New York: Cambridge University Press, 2004.
———. *Must We Kill the Thing We Love?* New York: Columbia University Press, 2015.
Sanders, Steven M. "Hitchcock's Immoralists." In *Hitchcock's Moral Gaze,* ed. R. Barton Palmer and Steven M. Sanders, 117–32. Albany: State University New York Press, 2017.
Schefer, Jean-Louis. *The Enigmatic Body: Essays on the Arts.* Ed. and trans. Paul Smith. New York: Cambridge University Press, 1995.
Schivelbusch, Wolfgang. *Disenchanted Night: The Industrialization of Light in the Nineteenth Century.* Trans. Angela Davies. Berkeley: University of California Press, 1995.
———. *The Railway Journey: The Industrialization of Time and Space in the Nineteenth Century.* Berkeley: University of California Press, 1986.
Schlör, Joachim. *Nights in the Big City: Paris – Berlin – London 1840–1930.* Trans. Pierre Gottfried Imhof and Dafydd Rees Roberts. London: Reaktion Books, 2013.
Sebestyen, Victor. *1946: The Making of the Modern World.* New York: Pantheon, 2014.
Simmel, Georg. *The Sociology of Georg Simmel.* Trans. Kurt H. Wolff. New York: Free Press, 1950.
———. "Sociology of the Senses: Visual Interaction." In *Introduction to the Science of Sociology,* ed. Robert E. Park and Ernest W. Burgess, 356–61. Chicago: University of Chicago Press, 1921.
Smith, Henry Nash. *Virgin Land: The American West as Symbol and Myth.* Cambridge, MA: Harvard University Press, 1950.
Solomon, Matthew. *Disappearing Tricks: Silent Film, Houdini, and the New Magic of the Twentieth Century.* Urbana: University of Illinois Press, 2010.

Sontag, Susan. *On Photography*. New York: Picador, 2001.

Spengler, Oswald. "The Soul of the City." In *Classic Essays on the Culture of Cities*, ed. Richard Sennett, 61–88. New York: Appleton-Century-Crofts, 1969.

Spoto, Donald. *The Dark Side of Genius: The Life of Alfred Hitchcock*. New York: DaCapo Press, 1999.

Steedman, Carolyn Kay. *Landscape for a Good Woman: A Story of Two Lives*. New Brunswick, NJ: Rutgers University Press, 2010.

Thoreau, Henry David. *Civil Disobedience*. 1849. Raleigh, NC: Hayes Barton Press, n.d.

———. "A Week on the Concord and Merrimack Rivers." In *Walden and Other Writings*, ed. Joseph Wood Krutch, 25–88. New York: Bantam, 2004.

Tinniswood, Adrian. *The Long Weekend: Life in the English Country House between the Wars*. London: Jonathan Cape, 2016.

Toles, George. "The Forgotten Lighter and Other Moral Accidents in *Strangers on a Train*." *Raritan* 28, no. 4 (Spring 2009): 111–37, 161.

Truffaut, François. *Hitchcock*. New York: Simon and Schuster, 1984.

Tynan, Kenneth. *The Sound of Two Hands Clapping*. New York: Holt, Rinehart and Winston, 1975.

von Humboldt, Wilhelm and H. Alexander, with Aimé Bonpland. *Personal Narrative of Travels to the Equinoctial Regions of the New Continent, During the Years 1799–1804*. Vol. 1. Trans. Helen Maria Williams. London: Longman, Hurst, Rees, Orme, and Brown, 1814.

Waller, Gregory A. *Main Street Amusements: Movies and Commercial Entertainment in a Southern City, 1896–1930*. Washington, DC: Smithsonian Institution Press, 1995.

Weinstein, Sheri. "Technologies of Vision: Spiritualism and Science in Nineteenth-Century America." In *Spectral America: Phantoms and the National Imagination*, ed. Jeffrey Andrew Weinstock, 124–40. Madison: University of Wisconsin Press, 2004.

Welsford, Enid. *The Court Masque: A Study of the Relationship between Poetry & the Revels*. 1927. Reprint, Cambridge: Cambridge University Press, 2015.

———. *The Fool: His Social and Literary History*. 1935. London: Faber and Faber, 1968.

White, Susan. "A Surface Collaboration: Hitchcock and Performance." In *A Companion to Alfred Hitchcock*, ed. Thomas Leitch and Leland Poague, 181–97. Malden, MA: Wiley-Blackwell, 2011.

Willeford, William. *The Fool and His Scepter: A Study in Clowns and Jesters and Their Audience*. Evanston, IL: Northwestern University Press, 1979.

Williams, William Carlos. "The American Background: America and Alfred Stieglitz (1934)." In *Selected Essays*, 134–61. New York: Random House, 1954.

Wood, Robin. *Hitchcock's Films Revisited*. Rev. ed. New York: Columbia University Press, 2002.

Woolf, Virginia. "A Sketch of the Past." In *Moments of Being*, ed. Jeanne Schulkind, 64–137. Brighton: Sussex University Press, 1976.

Worden, Helen. *The Real New York*. Indianapolis: Bobbs-Merrill, 1932.

ARCHIVAL SOURCES

HER = Margaret Herrick Library, The Academy of Motion Picture Arts and Sciences, Beverly Hills.

WB = Warner Bros. Archives, University of Southern California, Los Angeles.

Caffey, Frank. Letter to Jacob Karp. 8 October 1953. Re Eastmancolor. Paramount Pictures Production Records for *Rear Window*, file 14, HER.

Erickson, C. O. ("Doc.") Letter to Frank Caffey. 16 May 1954. Paramount Picture Production Records for *To Catch a Thief*, file 19, HER.

———. Letter to Frank Caffey. 13 June 1954. Paramount Picture Production Records for *To Catch a Thief*, file 21, HER.

———. Letter to Frank Caffey. 22 June 1954. Paramount Picture Production Records for *To Catch a Thief*, file 21, HER.

Family Plot. First Draft Screenplay with Notes. 15 April 1974. Scrapbook file 1626, Alfred Hitchcock Collection, HER.

Finestone, Al. Typed letter. n.d. Re Grace Sprague. Paramount Pictures Production Records for *Rear Window*, file 12, HER.

Hitchcock, Alfred. Memorandum re Statue of Liberty Exteriors Shots Required. 17 November 1941. Production file 637, Alfred Hitchcock Collection, HER.

Johnson, "Mac" [Joseph Macmillan]. Letter to C. O. ("Doc") Erickson. 5 October 1953. Re set production. Paramount Pictures Production Records for *Rear Window*, file 14, HER.

Lehman, Ernest. Letter to Alfred Hitchcock. 24 April 1975. File 167, Alfred Hitchcock Collection, HER.

Lloyd, Norman. Personal Interview. 15 October 2016.

Rear Window. Untitled, undated memorandum about costume fitting. Paramount Pictures Production Records for *Rear Window*, file 6, HER.

Rebecca Preview Reports. Compiled 4 January 1940. *Rebecca* Miscellaneous file 627, Alfred Hitchcock Collection, HER.

Research report on the Star of Sierra Leone diamond. 23 May 1975. *Family Plot* file 220, Alfred Hitchcock Collection, HER.

Selznick, David O. Dictated Notes on *Saboteur* from Santa Barbara Story Conference. 1 August 1941. *Saboteur* Production file 637, Alfred Hitchcock Collection, HER.

Strangers on a Train production notes. *Strangers on a Train* research file, WB.

Thinnes, Roy. Letter to Alfred Hitchcock. 25 May 1975. Re Adamson shaving. *Family Plot* file 190, Alfred Hitchcock Collection, HER.

Varden, Norma. Note to Alfred Hitchcock. 2 January 1964. *Marnie* Casting file 440, Alfred Hitchcock Collection, HER.

Wehmeyer, Ed. Letter to Mr. William Lord. 19 March 1975. Re Lexington Avenue location. *Family Plot* file 204, Alfred Hitchcock Collection, HER.

INDEX

Academy Award, 168
Adorno, Theodor (Ludwig Wiesengrund) (1903–1969), 61
Adventures of Pinocchio, The (Carlo Collodi), 189–190
Allen, Richard, 67, 93
"All in the Game" (Carl Sigman and Charles Gates Dawes), 14
Alper, Murray, 53, 104
America: "absence of class" in America, 141, 203; the American Dream, 116; American appetite for seeing Europe, 169; aviation of, 96; carnival of vision, 196; characteristic heart, 107; Civil War, 211; colonies, 203; democratic ideas in, development of, 116; Donner Pass (California), 117; dream fantasies of American audience, 138; duties of citizenship in, 114; Eastern aristocracy in, 118; as garden, 120; as generalization, 123; Godly image of, when undeveloped, 115; as hypothesis, 127; interstate highways in, after 1950, 115; isolationist cadre in, early in World War II, 101; journey across, 97; kidnapping, 203; landscape in, 105; mid-nineteenth-century myth of, 116; "New America," 122; as New World, 203; Pilgrims, 141; postwar, 169; pro-Nazi force in, 101; republican spirit of, 120; as the road, 123; rural space, 106; servitude in, 203; Southern Pacific Railroad, 118; Spiritualism in, 196, 197 (*see also* California); stage in, as busy, 109; symbolized, 96; view of class-centered Europe, 118; at war against Nazism, 96; war posture of, 96; wilderness of, 115; yeoman spirit in, 109
American Dream, The (Edward Albee; October 2, 1968), 116, 117
American Legion, The, 103
Amos 'n Andy Show, The (CBS 1951–1953), 61
Andersen's Pea Soup. *See* Pea Soup Andersen's
Anderson, Judith, 138, 140, 149, 150; Australian origin, 150
Angel City (Sam Shepard), 201
"Angling *To Catch a Thief*" (Murray Pomerance), 232
Antonioni, Michelangelo, 230n4
April in Paris (David Butler, 1952), 169
Arcades Project, The (Walter Benjamin), 58
"Archaic Torso of Apollo" (Rainer Maria Rilke), 53
Arnaz, Desi, 62
Arnold, Jack (1916–1992), 228n5
Arsenic and Old Lace (Frank Capra, 1944), 170
Asian Legacy and American Life, The (William York Tindall), 201

Attlee, Clement (Richard) (1883–1967), 58. *See also* United Kingdom
Atwater, Edith, 218
Auber, Brigitte, 168
Aubusson tapestries, 128
Australia, 150. *See also* Anderson, Judith

Bakhtin, Mikhail (Mikhailovich) (1895–1975), 181
Baldwin, James (Arthur) (1924–1987), 70, 109
Ball, Lucille, 62
Barcelona, 134
Barnes, George (1892–1953), 150
Barrie, (Sir) James M(atthew) (1860–1937), 6
Barrymore, Lionel, 83
Baskin-Robbins, 119
Bataille des fleurs (Nice), 169, 183
Bates, Florence, 139
Baudelaire, Charles (Pierre) (1821–1867): *flâneur*, 92
Baudrot, Sylvette, 166–167
Bazin, André (1918–1958), 91, 166, 167, 194–195, 202, 203, 232n1; mummification and imagery, 194–195; publishes about Hitchcock in *Cahiers du cinéma*, 167
Beach Boys, The, 193
Beach, Christopher, 66
Bel Geddes, Barbara, 9–10, 94
Bell, Douglas, 89
Benjamin, Richard, 229n8
Benjamin, Walter (1892–1940), 2, 17, 28–29, 58, 60, 61, 62, 63, 64, 65
Bennett, Tony [Anthony Dominick Benedetto] (b. 1926), 71
Berner, Sara, 73
Bernheim, Hippolyte (1840–1919), 149; somnambulism, 149

Bethune Street (New York), 70
Beugnet, Martine, 232n5
Bierstadt, Albert (1830–1902), 127; sees Yosemite, 1863, 127
Birds, The (Alfred Hitchcock, 1953). *See* Hitchcock, Alfred
Black, Karen, 193
Black, Shirley Temple (1928–2014), 177
Blackmail (Alfred Hitchcock, 1929). *See* Hitchcock, Alfred
Blind Alley (James Warwick; September 24, 1935), 121, 231n7
Blind Alley (Charles Vidor, 1939), 231n7
Blow-Up (Michelangelo Antonioni, 1966), 68, 230n4
Bohemian Club (of San Francisco), 199; Bohemian Grove, 199; Bosqui, Edward, 199. *See also* California
Bonwit Teller (New York), 228n1
Bosqui, Edward. See Bohemian Club
Boswell, James, 6
Boulding, Kenneth, 229n13
Bourne's London and Birmingham Railway (John Cooke Bourne), 227n4; "Locomotive Energy House," 227n4
Boyle, Robert, 88, 104, 121
Brand, Dana, 74
Bride of Frankenstein (James Whale, 1935), 115
Bringing Up Baby (Howard Hawks, 1938), 170
Brisset, Tifenn, 103
Bristol. *See* Grant, Cary
Brown, John, 56
Brown, Norman O., 2
Bruce, Nigel, 138, 139
Bruges-la-morte (Georges Rodenbach), 149
Bubbeo, Daniel, 231n5

INDEX   249

Buchwald, Art(hur) (1925–2007), 175
Bullock's (Wilshire Blvd., Los Angeles), 213, 216
Burger King, 119
Burke, Kenneth, 56
Burks, Robert, 52, 66, 91, 168
Burr, Raymond, *58–59*, 72, 89–90

Cabinet of Dr. Caligari, The (Robert Wiene, 1920), 92
Cady, Frank, 73
Caffey, Frank (Paramount Production Manager), 229n12
Cage Jr., John (Milton) (1912–1992), 70
Cahiers du cinéma, 232n1. *See also* Bazin, André
California, 94, 95, 96, 103: aircraft industry in, 94–96, 102, 118–119; all the way west, 117; as bright future, 118; Burbank, 95, 96, 102; Canoga Park, 95; citizens of, allergic to thinking about class, 118–119; Culver City, 102; decline of aircraft industry in, late 1980s, 119; (Joan) Didion's, 130; Downey, 95, 102; dreamer, 131; El Segundo, 102; European cultural constraints and, 106; fictional, 214; Hawthorne, 102; Highland Park, 103; history, 130; Inglewood, 102; Hollywood, *see* Hollywood film; LAX, 102; Long Beach, 95, 102; Los Angeles, 90, 95, 96, 102, 103, 104, 199, 200, 201; as "Looks-Within place," 201; majesty of, 105, 106; Marin County, 199; Northern California, 199; Orange County, 119; Owens Valley, waters "stolen" from, 199; Palos Verdes, 103; Pasadena, 201–202 (*see also* Hitchcock, Alfred); Pomona, 95, 96; population increase, after 1940, 119; pride in, 118; program of watchfulness in, 102; religious edifices described by Yeats, 201; San Diego Freeway (405), 119; San Fernando Valley, 94, 96, 118; San Francisco, 201: Bohemian Club of, 199; as Spiritualist hub, 197 (*see also* Hitchcock), Alfred; San Gabriel Mountains, 104; San Joaquin Valley, 119; Santa Monica, 102; South Pasadena, 201; Southern California, 95, 118, 193, 199; Californian spirit, 198–202; and Spiritualism, 198, 200; Tehachapi Mountains, 198; as utopian garden, 128; visit of William Butler Yeats, 96
Calthrop, Donald, 109
Camera Lucida (Roland Barthes), 229n6
"Canto LXXVI" (Ezra Pound), 140
Carey, Leonard, 139
Carl's Jr. Restaurants, 119
Carnival. *See* Welsford, Enid *and* Durrell, Lawrence
Carroll, Leo G., 17, 19, 153
Casablanca (Michael Curtiz, 1942), 48
Cavell, Stanley (Louis) (1926–2018), 2, 33, 45, 160; "comedies of remarriage," 33, 160; and Emerson, 123; "eventual human city," 123
Chabrol, Claude (Henri Jean) (1930–2010), 97, 167
Chazan, Michael, 233n1
Chien andalou, Un (Luis Buñuel and Salvador Dalí, 1929), 223
Chion, Michel, *acousmêtre,* 137
Churchill, Sir Winston (Leonard) Spencer- (1874–1965), 58, 59. *See also* United Kingdom

250 INDEX

Cinema 6, 119
CinemaScope, 176
Civil War. *See* America
Clock, The (Vincente Minnelli, 1945), 30
Cohen, Paula Marantz, 80
Colasanto, Nicholas, 209
Colbert, Claudette, 107
Cold War, The, 119
Coleman, Herbert, 73, 88, 89
Comte de Buffon. *See* Leclerc
Coney Island, Reginald Marsh paintings of, 40
Connecticut, probable setting of "Metcalf," 227n5
Cooper, Gary, 231n5
Cooper, Gladys, 138, 140
Copland, Aaron (1900–1990), at La Guardia airport, 228n8
Corber, Robert J., 23
Corey, Wendell, 64
Cornwall, 137
Cortázar, Julio (Florencio) (1914–1984), 83
Côte d'Azur. *See* Hitchcock, Alfred
Cotten, Joseph, 44
Coventry, 59, 61. *See also* United Kingdom
Crary, Jonathan, 82
Crookes, William (1832–1919), 226
Crowder, Farnsworth, 94
Cummings, Robert, 96, 100, 112, 231n5
Cunningham, [Mercier Philip] "Merce" (1919–2009), 70
Curtis, Billy, 131

Daisy Miller (Henry James), 145
Dall, John, 228n7
Damone, Vic [Vito Rocco Farinola] (1928–2018), 71
Daphnis et Chloé (Maurice Ravel), 195
Darcy, Virginia, 73

Darwin, Charles Robert (1809–1882), 11
Davenport, Guy (Mattison) (1927–2005), 140
Davis, Mike, 95, 96
Death in Life: Survivors of Hiroshima (Robert Jay Lifton), 147
Death of a Salesman (Arthur Miller; February 10, 1949), 72
De Beauvoir, Simone, 45
De Cordoba, Pedro, 131
De Crèvecoeur, J. Hector St. John (1735–1813), 120
De Cuir, John, 88
Deighton, Len, 221
Deleuze, Gilles (1925–1995), 13
Delius, Frederick (Theodore Albert) (1862–1934), 110
De' Medici, Lorenzo (1449–1492), 184
De Montaigne, Michel (Eyquem) (1533–1592), 2, 223, 225
Denny, Reginald, 138
Denny's, 119
D'entre les morts (Pierre Boileau and Thomas Narcejac), 157
Dern, Bruce, *192–193*, 193, 205–206
Descartes, René (1596–1650), 188
De Tocqueville, Alexis (Charles Henri Clérel) (1805–1859), 129
Deuxième sexe, La (The Second Sex) (Simone de Beauvoir), 45
Devane, William, 193, 212, 213; entry into the production, 213
Devonshire, 137
Dial M for Murder (Alfred Hitchcock, 1954). *See* Hitchcock, Alfred
Diary of a Mad Housewife (Frank Perry, 1970), 229n8
Didion, Joan (b. 1934), 117, 118, 119, 128, 130, 199
Disney, Walt, early animation of, 107; enterprise, 100

Dixon, Wheeler Winston, 42
Doctor Doolittle (Richard Fleischer, 1967), 48
Doniol-Valcroze, Jacques, 232n1
Donner Pass. *See* America
Dor, Karin, 5
Douglas Aircraft Company, 102, 118
Dover sole. *See* United Kingdom
Dr. Jekyll and Mr. Hyde (John S. Robertson, 1920), 63
Dr. Jekyll and Mr. Hyde (Rouben Mamoulian, 1931), 63
Dufy, Raoul (1877–1953), 172
Du Maurier, Daphne (1907–1989), 139, 150
Du Maurier, Gerald (Hubert Edward Busson) (1873–1934), 139
Du rififi chez les hommes (Jules Dassin, 1955), 206
Durkheim, (David) Émile (1858–1917), 11
Durrell, Lawrence (George) (1912–1990), 180

East of Shanghai (Alfred Hitchcock, 1931). See *Rich and Strange*
Eastmancolor negative, used instead of Technicolor film for *Rear Window,* 229n12; processed at Technicolor lab, 229n12
Edgerton, Harold (Eugene "Doc") (1903–1990), 228n5
Edward VII, King of England (1841–1910), 117
Egyptians, body practices among ancient, 194; Egyptologists' knowledge of statuary and sarcophagi, 195, Underworld, 195; *ushabtis*, 195, 202, 204
Einstein, Albert (1879–1955), 207
Eksteins, Modris, 92, 93
Eliade, Mircea (1907–1986), "myth of the eternal return," 137

Elizabeth II, Queen of England (b. 1926): coronation, 59. *See also* United Kingdom
Elliott, Laura, 19, 38, 41
Emerson, Ralph Waldo (1803–1882), 123; and "moral perfectionism," 123, 124, 133
Erickson, C(larence) O(scar) "Doc" (1923–2017), 89, 91, 169, 230n14
E.T. the Extra-Terrestrial (1982), 234n3
"Eternal Vérities" (William Rothman), 88
Evelyn, Judith, 73
Eye for Hitchcock, An (Murray Pomerance), 1, 124

Family Plot (Alfred Hitchcock, 1976). *See* Hitchcock, Alfred
Faulkner, Charles J(ames) (1847–1929), 129
Fax, Jesslyn, 74
F-18 aircraft, 131
Feminine Mystique, The (Betty Friedan), 45
Ferrara (Italy). *See* Welsford, Enid
Fiedler, Leslie A(aron) (1917–2003), 21, 131
Fielding, Edward, 138
Finch, Christopher, 100
Fly, The (Kurt Neumann, 1958), 63
Fonda, Henry, 8
Fontaine, Joan, 5, *134–135*, 149, 150, 159
Food 4 Less, 119
Forrest, Steve, 74
Fortnum and Mason (Madison Avenue, New York, c. 1942), 128
Foucault, Michel, "acceptability," 185–186; surveilling gaze, 101
Frawley, William, 62
Freaks: Myths and Images of the Secret Self (Leslie A. Fiedler), 131

French Connection II, The (John Frankenheimer, 1975), 193
French Résistance, 175, 176, 186
Frenzy (Alfred Hitchcock, 1972). See Hitchcock, Alfred
Freud, Sigmund [Sigismund] (1856–1939), 11, 27, 69, 147–148, 189, 198, 215; and Viennese thought, 189
Friedan, Betty, 45
Frost, Robert (Lee) (1874–1963), 61, 108

Gable, Clark, 107
Garland, Judy, 83
Garson, Greer, 83
Gaslight (George Cukor, 1944), 63
Genovese, Kitty, slaying of 13 March 1964 in Queens, 229n9
Gentlemen Prefer Blondes (Howard Hawks, 1953), 48
George, Henry (1839–1897), 118
Georgia, 131
Girouard, Mark, 59
Glazer, Vaughan, *94–95*, 106
Go-Between, The (Joseph Losey, 1971), 231n2
Goffman, Erving (1922–1982), 75–76
Goldbergs, The (CBS 1949–1957), 61
Gomery, Douglas, 36
Goodman, Paul, 127
Gothic architecture, 137. See also Hitchcock, Alfred
Gould, Stephen Jay, 10, 12, 99
Gourdon (France), 182
Granger, Farley, 19, 31, 228n7
Grant, Cary, *166–167*, 166, 168, 169, 170, 171, 177, 178, 179, 183, 186; collaboration with Alfred Hitchcock, 172, 187; and "Cary Grant" persona, 171, 186; early career as acrobat, 168; in lap dissolves, 171; Leach, Archibald, 186; origins in Bristol, 170; *Philadelphia Story* vehicle for, 184; sailing to New York, 166
Granville-Paris Express, collision at Gare Montparnasse 22 October 1895, 227n1
Great Expectations (Charles Dickens), 72
Grey Shadow (German shepherd), 109
Guard, Dominic, 231n2
Gunning, Tom, 17, 60, 61, 198; and detection, 198

Halberstam, David, 44, 46
Hale, Jonathan, 19
Hall, Barbara, 213
Hall, Edward T(witchell), Jr. (1914–2009), 49
Hamlet (William Shakespeare), 110, 178
Harding, Emma, 201
Hargrave, Roy (1896–1966), 121, 231n7
Harper, Rand, 74
Harris, Barbara, 5, *192–193*, 193, 222
Hayes, John Michael, 58, 71, 75, 79
Head, Edith, 90, 168–169, 218
Heart of the Andes, The (Frederic Edwin Church, 1859), 10, 11, 12
Helmond, Katharine, 200
Herman, Daniel, 195, 197, 198
Hibakusha. See Lifton, Robert Jay
Highland Park (California) Organization for Co-operation in Civilian Defense, 103. See also California
Highsmith, Patricia, 31, 32, 35, 38, 39, 40, 42
High Society (Charles Walters, 1956), 184
Hines, Harry, 54
"Hiroshima" (John Hersey), 152

INDEX 253

Hiroshima (John Hersey), 152; banned in Japan until 1948, 152; US edition read secretly in Tokyo, 152
Hiroshima. *See* Lifton, Robert Jay
His Girl Friday (Howard Hawks, 1940), 170
Hitchcock (François Truffaut), 4
Hitchcock, Alfred (1899–1872), and ambiguity, 33ff; and American citizenship, 44, 203; and architecture of films, 9–10, 43, 28, 187, 188, 192; arriving in America with reputation to uphold, 159; blonde women in films of, 5; and Bull, John, 231n1; cameos, 71, 187; camera movement, 205; casting at St. Regis Hotel, 121; and Catholic concerns, 97; and character actors, 48; cinematic fascination with California, 198; as cinematic kidnapper, 209; cinematological technique, 113; collaboration with artists, 88; collaboration with Cary Grant, 172, 187; collaboration with Herbert "Herbie" Coleman, 89; collaboration with writers, 79; debate over status as serious artist, 167; and decoration, 9; dream topographies of, 227n5; early work, 92; ecological critique by, 115; and effect of emptiness in *Rebecca,* 232n4; emblematic police in work of, 104, 230n3; *Encyclopedia Britannica* and, 1; English heritage, 96; enjoying *Rear Window* set, 89; enjoying food at 21, 90; experience of, analogous to central character in *Rebecca,* 159; first experience working in American studio, 141, 159, 161; first experience working with American crew, 141; first visits to the United States, 90; German influences on, 92; and haptic moment in *Rebecca,* 232n5; knowledge of British upper-class life, 141; and lap dissolves, 171; and life for British women in wartime, 156; loves automatic garage opener, 207–208; love of trains, 227n4; as "Master of Suspense," 5; films and misleading impressions, 183; as movie watcher, 170; and music, 1; ornamentalism of, 9–10; and Peeping Tomism, 7, 61, 86; perspectival trick used by, 133; and philosophy, 6; pictorial technique of, 7–8, 11; planning projects, 58; and police, 183, 186, 187; presence of, felt, 29; recipient of letter from Lehman, 233–4n2; recipient of letter from Selznick, 231–2n3; recounting stories of his pictures, 121; and research, 214; Santa Cruz house, 208; set pieces in works of, 200; setting as important in films of, 98; sex and death in films of, 4; social class reference in, 16, 24, 34, 43, 141, 156, 161, 197, 208; and social space, 8; sociological observation in work of, 141; technique studied by André Bazin, 166; treatment of star type, 170; use of zoom, 150; using set for production business on *Rear Window,* 89–90; Victorian love story and *Rebecca,* 161; Washington society, shown in, 42ff; and Weimar Germany, 92; "wronged man" theme in, 97

films: *Birds, The* (1963), 4, 124, 217; *Blackmail* (1929), 109; *Dial M for Murder* (1954), 217; *Family Plot* (1976), 2, 4, 5, 6, 8, 10, 11, *192–193*, 192–226; *Frenzy* (1972), 4; *I Confess* (1953), 1, 124, 217; *Lady Vanishes, The* (1938), 124; *Lodger, The* (1927), 31, 124; *Man Who Knew Too Much, The* (1956), 8, 30, 44, 47, 216, 227n3, 230n4; *Marnie* (1964), 1, 2, 216; *Mary Rose* (planned but not filmed), 205; *Mr. and Mrs. Smith* (1941), 9, 33; *North by Northwest* (1959), 1, 4, 10, 54, 170, 200; *Notorious* (1946), 170; *Psycho* (1960), 4, 30, 62, 217, 230n3; *Rear Window* (1954), 2, 6, 7, 8, 10, 11, 30, *58–59*, 58–93; *Rebecca* (1940), 2, 5, 6, 7, 8, 10, 11, 96, *134–135*, 134–165, 231–2n3; *Rich and Strange (East of Shanghai)* (1931), 4; *Rope* (1948), 66, 228n8; *Saboteur* (1942), 2, 6, 8, 10, *94–95*, 94–133, 231n5; *Shadow of a Doubt* (1943), 5, 44, 100, 217; *Spellbound* (1945), 1, 4, 41, 189, 197, 229n10; *Strangers on a Train* (1951), 2, 5, 6, 7–8, 10, *14–15*, 14–57; *Suspicion* (1941), 5, 96, 139, 170; *39 Steps, The* (1935), 10, 187, 230n3; *To Catch a Thief* (1955), 2, 6, 8, 10, 65, *166–167*, 166–191, 217; *Topaz* (1969), 5; *Torn Curtain* (1966), 1, 4; *Trouble with Harry, The* (1955), 5; *Vertigo* (1958), 1, 9–10, 87, 94, 124, 197, 205, 211, 216, 230n1; *Wrong Man, The* (1956), 8, 124

locations: Adamson residence exterior (San Francisco), 199; Adamson garage exterior (San Francisco), 199; Adamson jewelry store exterior images (San Francisco), 199; Associated Life of New York (insurance company), 8; Baie des Anges (Nice), 174; Blanche Tyler's bungalow (Lexington Avenue, Silver Lake), 200, 213; Bodega Bay (California), 217; Brooklyn, 127; Cannes beach, 183; Carlton Hotel (Cannes), 166, 168, 171, 172; Corniche (near Nice), 172; Côte d'Azur (France), 10, 137, 145, 168, 172, 176, 186; Deep Springs Ranch (California), 105; Eiffel Tower, model of, 172; Fifth Avenue (New York), 10, 128; flower market (Cours Saleya, Nice), 166, 183; Forest Hills Stadium (Queens, New York), 8, 20, 49, 52, 57; France, 173; Grace Cathedral (Taylor Street, San Francisco), 8, 199, 233–4n2; Greenwich Village (New York), 65, 70, 88, 91, 230n14; Hoover Dam (Arizona-Nevada border, near Lake Mead), 125; London, 153, 161; London Palladium, The (Argyll Street, London), 10; Los Angeles, 200; marché au fleurs (flower market) (Cours Saleya, Nice), 8; Monte Carlo, 139, 141, 142, 145, 146, 151, 152, 153; Mt. Wilson (near Los Angeles), 200; National Gallery of Art (Madison Drive NW, Washington DC), 25–6; New York City, 60, 70, 74, 91, 92, 111, 121, 125, 131; Nice, 168, 175, 182; Paris, 175; Pasadena (California), 10, 193, 197, 200; Quai des États-Unis (Nice), 172, 174; Riviera, 175, 190, 217; Royal Albert Hall (Kensington, London), 8; San Francisco, 199; Sierra Madre Cemetery, 200;

INDEX 255

Soda City, 105, 128; Statue of Liberty, The (New York), 8, 119, 120–124, 126; Telegraph Hill (San Francisco), 94; Twentieth Century Limited, The, 10; 2230 Sacramento Street (San Francisco), 193; Union Station (Columbus Circle, Washington DC), 15–16, 18

props: chandelier, 215; Courvoisier brandy (*Rear Window*), 85; Cupid statuette (*Rebecca*), 141, 154; diamonds, 215; floral bouquet (*Rebecca*), 142, 144; four-poster bed at Manderley (*Rebecca*), 143, 144; fur coat (*Rebecca*) 143; Graflex camera (*Rear* Window), 85; Hermès bag (*Dial M for Murder*), 217; Jasper the Spaniel (*Rebecca*), 138, 139, 142, 153; jewelry box (*To Catch a Thief*), 174; maillot (*To Catch a Thief*), 170, 183, 191; Mark Cross overnight case (*Rear* Window), 85; panties (*Rebecca*); 143, 144; peignoir (*Rebecca*), 143, 144; Pentax SLR (*Rear Window*), 68; pipe (*Family Plot*), 219; portrait of Lady Caroline de Winter (*Rebecca*), 151; purse (*Family Plot*), 220; silk-lined jewelry box (*To Catch a Thief*), 176; silver hair brushes (*Rebecca*), 142–143, 144;

settings, fictional: Abe and Mabel's Diner (Mt. Wilson), 217; Adamson residence (San Francisco), 199; Adamson garage (San Francisco), 199, 220; Adamson jewelry store (San Francisco), 199, 217, 218; aircraft plant (California), 94–97, 126; Antony mansion (Maryland), 10, 19, 20, 52; ballroom (Fifth Avenue, New York), 125; Barlow Creek, 211; Barlow Creek Cemetery, 210; Bates home in *Psycho*, 197; Bates Street (Los Angeles), 217; Bellini's (Nice), 171, 183; courtyard set for *Rear Window*, 88–90; golf course (Los Angeles), 220; Harley Street (London) consultation room, 153, 161; high windows at Manderley, 153; Manderley, 11, 135, 137, 138, 139, 140, 141, 142, 143, 146, 147, 148, 149, 151, 152, 153, 154, 155, 156, 161, 162, 163, 164, 165, 232n4; Metcalf, 19, 20, 35, 36, 41, 42, 52; McKittrick Hotel (San Francisco), 197; Metcalf amusement park, 20, 36ff, 39–41, 51, 52–55, 57; Rainbird house (Pasadena), 220; Robie's House (Saint Jeannet), 174; skyscraper (New York), 127; Tunnel of Love. *See* Metcalf amusement park; West 10th Street (Manhattan), 89, 91; West Wing bedroom at Manderley, 142

Hitchcock at Work (Bill Krohn), 6, 232n1
"Hitchcock contre Hitchcock" (André Bazin), 167
Hitchcock, Patricia, 19
Hitler, Adolf, 98, 101, 127
Holiday (George Cukor, 1938), 170
Holiday Inn, 119
Hollywood, 169, 171, 179, 231–2n3
Homespun of Oatmeal Gray (Paul Goodman), 127
Honeymooners, The (Paramount Television, 1955–1956), 61
Houdini, Harry [Erik Weisz] (1874–1926), 223
Houseman, John [Jacques Haussmann] (1902–1988), 120

Howard, John, 206
Howards of Virginia, The (Frank Lloyd, 1940), 133
Howell, William, 60
Hughes Aircraft, 95, 102, 118; Missile Division, 96
Hugo (Martin Scorsese, 2011), 227n1

I Confess (Alfred Hitchcock, 1953). *See* Hitchcock, Alfred
I Love Lucy (CBS 1951–1957), 62
Impressionism. *See* Ortega y Gasset, José
Incredible Shrinking Man, The (Jack Arnold, 1957), 228–229n5
Innis, Harold Adams (1894–1952), 28
Invasion of the Body Snatchers (Don Siegel, 1956), 44
I Remember Mama (CBS 1948–1957), 61
Iron Curtain, The, 152
"Isle of the Dead" (Arnold Böcklin, 1886), 39
Isle of the Dead (Sergei Rachmaninoff), 39
Italy. *See* Renaissance
It Happened One Night (Frank Capra, 1934), 107

James, Henry, 2, 46, 102
Jay, Martin, 101
Jeanneret, Charles-Édouard (Le Corbusier) (1887–1965), 59
Johnson, Joseph MacMillan "Mac," 88, 91, 230n14
"Joyland" (Lexington KY), 40
Jungle Book, The (Rudyard Kipling), 52
Justine (Lawrence Durrell), 180–181

Kant, Immanuel (1724–1804), 123: "Realm of Ends," 123

Karp, Jacob (Paramount Assistant Secretary), 229n12
Kasson, John, 40
Keats, John, 44
Kelly, Grace, 65, 78, 90, *166–167*, 168, 169, 217; and *High Society*, 84; and Rainier of Monaco, 169
Keynes, John Maynard (1883–1946), 95
Kipling, (Joseph) Rudyard (1865–1936), 52
Kierkegaard, Søren (Aabye) (1813–1855), 101, 136, 137
Kings Row (Sam Wood, 1942), 150
Koenekamp, Hans, 52
Kracauer, Siegfried (1889–1966), 92, 93
Krohn, Bill (b. 1945), 2, 6, 132, 231n5
Kruger, Alma, 126–127
Kruger, Otto, 105
Kubrick, Stanley, 149
Kucich, John, 196, 211
Kynaston, David, 59, 60

La Belle et la bête (Jean Cocteau, 1946), 205
Lady Vanishes, The (Alfred Hitchcock, 1938). *See* Hitchcock, Alfred
Land Was Everything, The (Victor Davis Hanson), 119
Landis, Jessie Royce, 168
Lane, Priscilla, 111, 231n5
Lang, Fritz, 92
Lassie, 83
Lauter, Ed, 200
Lawrence, D(avid) H(erbert) (1885–1930), 140, 200
Leach, Archibald. *See* Grant, Cary
Leclerc, Georges-Louis (Comte de Buffon) (1707–1788), 10
Le Corbusier. *See* Jeanneret, Charles-Édouard

LeDeaux, Marie, 131
Lehman, Ernest, 194, 207–208, 233–4n2
Lemire, Elisa, 77
Lethbridge, Lucy (b. 1963), 164
Lewis, Jerry [Joseph Levitch] (1926–2017), 183
Life magazine, 65
Le Figaro, 14
Lerner, Max, 45
Lethe, Island of, 39
Levittown, 44
Lifton, Robert Jay (b. 1926), 147, 151; forbidding of photography in post-bomb Japan, 152; *hibakusha*, 147, 148, 151; Hiroshima, 148, 151, 152; Japan, 1946 events in, 152; Nagasaki, 148, 152
"Little Old Lady from Pasadena" (The Beach Boys), 193
Lloyd, Frank, 133
Lloyd, Norman, 99, 100, 115, 120, 125; desiring part of "Fry," 120
Lloyd's of London, 179
Locke, John, 19
Lockheed Corporation, 95, 96, 118; Burbank shutdown, 96; P-38 Lightning, 102
Lodger, The (Alfred Hitchcock, 1927). *See* Hitchcock, Alfred
Lorne, Marion, 19
Louis XIV (1638–1715), 195
"Louis XIV" (Charles Le Brun, 1668), 195
Louis XV (1710–1774), 178
Louisiana, 131
Lubitsch, Ernst, 92

MacLaine, Shirley, 5
Magritte, René (François Ghislain) (1898–1967), 71
Major and the Minor, The (Billy Wilder, 1942), 48

Man from Beyond, The (Harry Houdini), 223
Manichaeism, 180
"Man of the Crowd, The" (Edgar Allan Poe), 86
Man Who Knew Too Much, The (1956). *See* Hitchock, Alfred
Marlborough. *See* Spencer-Churchill
Marnie (Alfred Hitchcock, 1964). *See* Hitchcock, Alfred
Marsh, Reginald, 40
Marx, Arthur "Harpo" (1888–1964), 177
Marx, Karl (1818–1883), 11, 118
Mary Rose (James M. Barrie), 6
Mary Rose (Alfred Hitchcock, planned but not filmed), 205
Masquerade, 185. *See also* Welsford, Enid *and* Durrell, Lawrence
May, Elaine Tyler, 45
McDonald's, 119
McDonnell Aircraft, 95, 118
McFarland, Douglas, 24
McGilligan, Patrick, 92
McIntosh, Mary, 185
McLuhan, (Herbert) Marshall (1911–1980), 28
McWilliams, Carey, 95–96, 201
Measure for Measure (William Shakespeare), 140
Mediterranean Sea, 182; Hitchcock's Mediterranean romance, 185
"Mending Wall" (Robert Frost), 61
Mercury Theater (1937), 120
Merleau-Ponty, Maurice (1908–1961), 75, 192, 226
Merrill, Bob [Henry Robert Merrill Levan] (1921–1998), 61
Methot, Mayo, 201
MGM (Metro Goldwyn Mayer), *High Society*, 184; 1943 star photograph, 83
Michelet, Jules (1798–1874), 65

Michelson, Harold, 88
Mickey Mouse: and neoteny, 99; discussed by Gould, 99–100
Minnelli, Vincente, 30
Miss Lonelyhearts (Nathanael West), 73
Modena (Italy). *See* Welsford, Enid
Modleski, Tania, 73
Moffitt, Jack, 171
Montgomery, Robert, 25
Mr. and Mrs. Smith (Alfred Hitchcock, 1941). *See* Hitchcock, Alfred
Murnau, F(riedrich) W(ilhelm), 92
Musil, Robert (1880–1942), 98
Mystery of the 13th Guest, The (William Beaudine, 1943), 62

Nagasaki. *See* Lifton, Robert Jay
National Health Service (NHS), 58. *See also* United Kingdom
National Velvet (Clarence Brown, 1944), 48
Nazism, 96, 101, 118, 119, 122, 124, 125; Aryan purity, 129; National Socialism, 230n15
Nesbitt, Cathleen, 193, 203
Nevada, 197
New Brutalism, 59
"New Colossus, The" (Emma Lazarus), 107, 122
New World. *See* America
New York City, 60; apartment dwellers in, 63; Cary Grant sailing to, 166; paintings of downtown area 63; Statue of Liberty, 119, 120–124; St. Regis Hotel (E. 55th Street, Manhattan), 121; West Village artistic type in, 74. *See also* Hitchcock, Alfred
New York Times, 17, 169, 231n1
New Yorker, The. *See* "Hiroshima"
Nile river, 202

Nin, Anaïs, 67
North American Aviation, 102
North by Northwest (Alfred Hitchcock, 1959). *See* Hitchcock, Alfred
Northrop Corporation, 102, 118
Notorious (Alfred Hitchcock, 1946). *See* Hitchcock, Alfred
Nutty Professor, The (Jerry Lewis, 1963), 183
Nye, David, 125; technological sublime, 125

Ohler, Norman, 230n15
Olivier, Laurence (Kerr) (1907–1989), 138, 146, 154, 178
On Photography (Susan Sontag), 26
On the Town (Leonard Bernstein, with Betty Comden and Adolph Green; Dec. 28, 1944), 82
"Ontology of the Photographic Image, The" (André Bazin), 194–195
"Ordinary Man of Cinema, The" (Jean-Louis Schefer), 99
Orphée (Jean Cocteau, 1950), 205
Ortega y Gasset, José (1883–1955): on Impressionism, 173; on the Quattrocento, 215; on "the real," 215;
Oscar. *See* Academy Award
Overland Monthly, 118

Panic Room (David Fincher, 2002), 63
Paramount Pictures: care devoted to production at, 230n14; Edith Head at, 90; Stage 18, 88–90; VistaVision, 169
Parker, Dorothy (née Rothschild) (1893–1967), 115
Passenger, The [Professione: Reporter] (Michelangelo Antonioni, 1975), 134

INDEX 259

Payless, 119
Pea Soup Andersen's, 119
Pearl Harbor (Honolulu), 102
Peeping Tomism, 61. *See also* Hitchcock, Alfred
"People" (Jule Styne and Bob Merrill), 61
Perkins, V[ictor] F., 2, 12
Perret, Nellie, 232–3n4
Peter and Wendy [Peter Pan; or, The Boy Who Wouldn't Grow Up] (James M. Barrie; December 27, 1904), 139
Peterson, Dorothy, 103
Philadelphia Story, The (George Cukor, 1940), 170, 184
Pickup on South Street (Samuel Fuller, 1953), 174
Pilgrims. *See* America
Plan séquence (Sequence shot), 66
Plato, 39
Poe, Edgar Allan (1809–1849), 86, 92. *See also* "Man of the Crowd, The"
Pomerance, Michael Harold (1906–1967), 17
Pope Leo X (1475–1521), 184
Prince, William, 209
Production Code Office, 169
Proust, (Valentin Louis Georges Eugène) Marcel (1871–1922), 138
Psycho (Alfred Hitchcock, 1960). *See* Hitchcock, Alfred
Pygmalion (Anthony Asquith, Leslie Howard, 1938), 193

Quattrocento. *See* Ortega y Gasset, José

Raab, Jennifer, 10, 11
Railway Journey, The (Wolfgang Schivelbusch), 17
Rainier III of Monaco [Louis Henri Maxence Bertrand Grimaldi, of Monaco (1923–2005), 169

Random Harvest (Mervyn LeRoy, 1942), 48
Rathbone, (Philip St. John) Basil (1892–1967), 219
Rattner, Abraham (1895–1978), 29; abstract expressionism, 29
Rear Window (Alfred Hitchcock, 1954). *See* Hitchcock, Alfred
"Rear Window" (Cornell Woolrich), 75
Rebecca (Daphne du Maurier), 139, 150, 161–162, 163
Rebecca (Alfred Hitchcock, 1940). *See* Hitchcock, Alfred
Redmond, Marge, 212
Remains of the Day, The (James Ivory, 1993), 232n4
Renaissance, 184
Reuleaux, Franz (1829–1905), 233n5
Reynolds, (Sir) Joshua, 9
Rich and Strange (Alfred Hitchcock, 1931). *See* Hitchcock, Alfred
Rilke, Rainer Maria (1875–1926), 53
Ritter, Thelma, 61
Riviera. *See* Hitchcock, Alfred
"Road Not Taken, The" (Robert Frost), 106
Robertson, Peggy, 213
Rockwell (International), 118
Rohmer, Eric [Jean Marie Maurice Schérer] (1920–2010), 97, 167
Roman, Ruth, 5, 19
Romeo and Juliet (William Shakespeare), 185
Romer, Jeanne, 131
Romer, Lynn, 131
Rope (Alfred Hitchcock, 1948). *See* Hitchcock, Alfred
Rosenberg, Ron, 44
Rothman, William (b. 1944), 2, 29, 88, 230n2; and "moral perfectionism," 123
Rousseau, Jean-Jacques (1712–1778), 103

Russo, Vito, 23
Ryder, Loren, and VistaVision, 169

Saboteur (Alfred Hitchcock, 1942). *See* Hitchcock, Alfred
Sam Spade, 221
Sanders, George, 139
Sanders, Steven, 38
Sartre, Jean-Paul (Charles Aymard) (1905–1980), 101
Schantz, Lieutenant Paul (U.S. Army, Fourth Interceptor command), 103
Schefer, Jean-Louis (b. 1938), 99
Schivelbusch, Wolfgang, 14, 24, 178; amateur sport, 178; nightfall, 185; "panoramic perception," 24
Scotland, east coast of, 146
Secret Garden, The (Fred M. Wilcox, 1949), 48
Seduction of the Minotaur (Anaïs Nin), 67
Self-Portrait with Straw Hat (Elisabeth Louise Vigée le Brun, 1782), 157
Selznick, David O. (1902–1965), 96, 97, 103, 120, 139, 141, 159, 161; employing Hitchcock, 161; irritated at Hitchcock regarding *Rebecca*, 231–2n3; scrutinizing gaze, 159
Selznick International Pictures, 141, 159
Shakespeare, William, 139, 216
Shane (George Stevens, 1953), 231n8
Sharp-Bolster, Anita, 131
Sherlock Holmes, 219
Simmel, Georg (1858–1918), 18, 28, 64
Simpson, Wallis (later Duchess of Windsor) (1896–1986), 141
Skirball, Jack, 96, 133
Sloan, John (French) (1871–1951), 63

Smith, Henry Nash (1906–1986), 116, 123, 129; virgin land, 123. *See also* yeoman
Smithson, Alison, 59, 63. *See also* "Urban Reidentification"
Smithson, Peter, 59, 63. *See also* "Urban Reidentification"
Snodgrass, Carrie, 229n8
Sombart, Werner (1863–1941), 11
Sontag, Susan, 26
Sorcerer's Apprentice, The (James Algar, 1940; part of *Fantasia*), 99
Sound of Music, The (Robert Wise, 1965), 48
Southern Pacific Railroad. *See* America
Spellbound (Alfred Hitchcock, 1945). *See* Hitchcock, Alfred
Spencer-Churchill, John (10th Duke of Marlborough) (1897–1972), 162
Spengler, Oswald (Arnold Gottfried) (1880–1936), 90
Spielberg, Steven, 234n3
Spoto, Donald, 167, 227n4, 232n1
Sprague, Grace, 90
S. S. Mauritania, 166
Stanwyck, Barbara, 231n5
Star of Sierra Leone (diamond), 214
Statue of Liberty (New York): filming matte and composite shots of, 121; numerous rear projection plates of, required, 121. *See also* Hitchcock, Alfred
Steamboat Willie (Ub Iwerks, Walt Disney, 1928), 100
Steedman, Carolyn (b. 1947), 163; literary framework for escape, 164
Steele, Mrs. Frank (San Pedro), 102
Steinway and Co. (W. 57th Street, New York), 71
St. John, Howard, 53
Stranger on the Third Floor (Boris Ingster, 1940), 62

Strangers on a Train (Patricia Highsmith), 31, 35, 38, 39, 40, 42. See also Highsmith, Patricia

Strangers on a Train (Alfred Hitchcock, 1951). See Hitchcock, Alfred; British release of, 57

Stewart, James, 62, 75, 78, 83, 87, 89, 90

St. Regis Hotel (New York). See New York

Summer Night on the River (Frederick Delius, 1913), 110, 114, 117

Summers, Virgil, 97

Supreme Commander for the Allied Powers [in Japan] (SCAP), 152

"'Surrender' and 'Catch'" (Kurt Wolff), 166

Taco Bell, 119

Technicolor: camera, 169; imported to France for *To Catch a Thief*, 169; lab, 178, 229n12; and VistaVision, 169

Tempest, The (William Shakespeare), 123, 135–136, 140

Temple, Shirley. See Black, Shirley Temple

Tennant, David, 178

They Were Expendable (John Ford, 1945), 25

Thief of Bagdad, The (Michael Powell and Emeric Pressburger, 1940), 228n3

Thinnes, Roy, 213

39 Steps, The (Alfred Hitchcock, 1935). See Hitchcock, Alfred

Thomas, Dylan (Marlais) (1914–1953), 70

Thoreau, Henry David (1817–1862), 108, 130, 131

Three Coins in the Fountain (Jean Negulesco, 1954), 48, 169, 193

Threepenny Opera The [*Die Dreigroschenoper*] (Bertolt Brecht), 213

Tindall, William York (1903–1981), 201

Titanic (James Cameron, 1997), 231n2

To Catch a Thief (Alfred Hitchcock, 1955). See Hitchcock, Alfred

Tokyo. See *Hiroshima*

Toles, George (b. 1948), 37

Topper (CBS, 1953), 227n3

Torn Curtain (Alfred Hitchcock, 1966). See Hitchcock, Alfred

Transparency plates (plates), 232n3

Truffaut, François, 4, 5, 54

TRW, Inc., 118

21 (21 W. 52nd Street, New York), 10, 77, 90

2001: A Space Odyssey (Stanley Kubrick, 1968), 149

Tynan, Kenneth (Peacock) (1927–1980), 181

Tyner, Charles, 204

United Kingdom: attainment of class in England, 141, 203; bombing of Coventry, 59; Britain on film, 145; British class system, 161ff, 203; British mansion, 138; Conservative Government (1940–1945), 58; Conservative Government (1951–1957), 59; coronation of Elizabeth II (2 June 1953), 59; English children stolen and transported, 203; flight from, 203; food shipped to Hitchcock from London, 58; Great Fire of London (1666), 163; Hitchcock's ties to, 58; Labour Government (1945–1951) in, 58, 59; marriages in higher class, 162; National Health Service, founding (1949), 58; persistent rationing in, 58

Universal Studios, 96, 199; Stage 12, 207; Stage 27 (blue-screen), 207; Stage 24, 207
University of Durham, 59
University of Michigan, The, 21
"Urban Reidentification" (Alison and Peter Smithson), 59–60
U.S. Civil Defense, 102
U.S. Navy: Long Beach station and shipyard, 118; San Pedro Section Base, 102
U.S. Senate Appropriations Committee (investigation into same-sex behavior, c. 1950), 23

Vance, Vivian, 62
Varden, Norma, 48
Variety, 168, 169
Vence (France), 182
Versailles, Palace of, 178
Vertigo (Alfred Hitchcock, 1958). *See* Hitchcock, Alfred
Victorian age, 3
VistaVision, 168, 169, 175, 232n2
Von Humboldt, Alexander (1769–1859), 10, 11
Vultee Aircraft Corporation, 102

Walker, Robert, 19, 23, 24, 27, 30, 41
Waller, Gregory, 40
Wal-Mart, 119
Harry Winston, Inc. (New York), 214
"Wasteland, The" (T. E. Eliot), 151
Waxman, Franz (1906–1967), 71, 93, 161
Wayne, John, 25
Week on the Concord and Merrimack Rivers, A (Henry David Thoreau), 116
Welles, (George) Orson (1915–1985), 120
Welsford, Enid, 171, 184; and Carnival, 184–185; and Harlequin, 171; and Trickster, 171
Wendy's, 119
West, Nathanael, 73
Westbeth (West and Bethune Streets, New York), 70
Where I Was From (Joan Didion), 117ff
White Christmas (Michael Curtiz, 1954), 169, 232n2
White Horse Tavern (Hudson and 11th Streets, New York), 70
Whitman, Walter "Walt" (1819–1892), 108
Willeford, William, description of Harpo Marx, 177
Williams, John (actor), 168, 221
Williams, John (composer), 195, 218, 226
Williams, William Carlos (1883–1963), 203
Wimbledon, 8
Winston, Irene, 72
Witness for the Prosecution (Billy Wilder, 1957), 48
Wolff, Kurt (Heinrich) (1912–2003), 166
Wood, Robin, 24
Woolf, (Adeline) Virginia (née Stephen) (1882–1941), 81
Woolrich, Cornell (George Hopley-) [William Irish] (1903–1968), 75
World War I, 92
World War II, 94–98, 101, 168
WPA (Work Projects Administration), 125
Wright, Teresa, 5
Wrong Man, The (Alfred Hitchcock, 1956). *See* Hitchcock, Alfred
Wuthering Heights (William Wyler, 1939), 146, 161

Yale University, 115

Yeats, William Butler (1865–1939), 96; occult experiences of wife, 201
Yeoman: American, 116; English, 116; yeoman farmer, 120, 122, 123, 128, 129; labor, 116; yeoman nation, 127; Western, 116, 130.

See also America

Yosemite National Park, 127. *See also* Bierstadt, Albert

Zanuck, Darryl F(rancis) (1902–1979), 176

www.ingramcontent.com/pod-product-compliance
Lightning Source LLC
Chambersburg PA
CBHW060946230426
43665CB00015B/2087